SOMEWHERE
NEAR TO
HISTORY

SOMEWHERE NEAR TO HISTORY

The Wartime Diaries of Reginald Hibbert,
SOE Officer in Albania, 1943-1944

EDITED BY JANE NICOLOV

Signal

Signal Books
Oxford

First published in 2020 by
Signal Books Limited
36 Minster Road
Oxford OX4 1LY
www.signalbooks.co.uk

A catalogue record for this book is available from the British Library

ISBN 978-1-909930-80-3 Cloth

Cover Design: Tora Kelly
Typesetting: Tora Kelly
Cover Images: 3Dhun/freepik; corgarashu/shutterstock; collection of Reginald Hibbert
Printed in India by Imprint Press

For Reg's granddaughters

I remember wondering if I could get a job in those parts. It struck me that Albania was the sort of place that might keep a man from yawning.

John Buchan, *The Thirty-Nine Steps*

CONTENTS

FOREWORD

Reginald Hibbert ended his career as a prominent diplomat and British Ambassador to Paris, and a widely respected figure in many walks of life. Yet as a young man his international experience began in the isolated and dangerous world of the Albanian mountains under Nazi occupation in the Second World War. This early wartime period was to return to preoccupy him in his retirement as the ex-Yugoslav conflicts broke out after 1991. His experience as an underground soldier in Albania was in the Second World War struggle to free the Balkans. The Special Operations Executive (SOE) had been formed in London after Prime Minister Churchill's invocation 'to set Europe ablaze', and the occupied Balkans were an early target for its operations in secret warfare.[i] The directorate of SOE rightly saw the complex and often remote mountainous Balkan landscapes as ideal for guerrilla warfare, and intelligence was reaching London as early as 1941 on the formation of groups of armed Partisans in the different Balkan countries. The SOE Mediterranean headquarters was in Cairo. It was from an airfield there that Hibbert was parachuted into Albania in 1943, after a period of training and indoctrination under the formidable Margaret 'Fanny' Hasluck (1885-1948), wife of a leading scholar on the Bektashi religion, F. W. Hasluck.

The background to the formation of the Albanian SOE Mission, as in Greece and Yugoslavia, was to make contact with the nascent groups of Partisan guerrilla fighters which were forming in the mountains and remote areas of these countries, and then to assist them in harrying and disrupting the Nazi occupation.[ii] In this respect, the *modus operandi* of the British SOE

---

i   For a general introduction, see M. R. D. Foot, *SOE: The Special Operations Executive 1940-46* (London: Greenwood Press, 1984).

ii See M. R. D Foot, *History of the Second World War: SOE in France* (London: HMSO, 1966) for the first full account of the basis for SOE recruitment, training and operations. An early popular account was E. H. Cookridge, *Inside SOE* (London: Arthur Baker, 1966). Also Bickham Sweet-Escott, *Baker Street Irregular* (London: Methuen, 1965).

forces drew on several recent antecedents. In the mind of Prime Minister Churchill memories remained of his own early military and journalistic experience in the Boer War and the exploits of his much admired Lawrence of Arabia in the First World War using guerrilla tactics and methods against the disintegrating Ottoman forces in Palestine and Syria. The British Army had a fund of Balkan experience in its background gained on the Macedonian Front in that conflict, where prominent military intelligence officers like academic classicist Stanley Casson learned a great deal about irregular and regular warfare in the region.[iii]

The Albanian society they found when the SOE parachutists arrived was still in essence an ultra-conservative pre-modern world, based on intensely patriarchal extended families, the *fis*, each under the authority of an older man who was seen as, in essence, a tribal chieftain by the British soldiers like Hibbert. A legal code, the *Kanun of Lek Dukagjini*, which had its origins in early medieval Albania as a written document, although embodying much earlier archaic conventions, dominated life and legal conduct, particularly in the central and northern mountain regions of the country. The briefings received in Cairo before departure from Hasluck were very directly derived from her own pre-1939 anthropological and ethnographic research, which following very strongly in the pioneering intellectual footsteps of her Edwardian predecessor Mary Edith Durham (1863-1944).[iv] The young soldiers were thus in some senses ill-prepared for the realities of the society they encountered, where the active resistance movement in the south was communist-dominated.[v] In the north it was still under the power of local *fis* leaders who saw

---

iii For background, see his autobiography *Steady Drummer* (London: G. Bell and Sons, 1935). Casson was in charge of training Patrick Leigh Fermor and other later prominent SOE operatives as British military intelligence officers for the 1940-41 Greek campaign at the beginning of the Second World War after he returned to the army from academic life.

iv Author of several books such as *The Struggle for Scutari, High Albania* and *Through the Land of the Serb*. For a general introduction to the history, see Miranda Vickers, *The Albanians: A Modern History* (London: I. B. Tauris, 1996). There is a voluminous secondary literature on Durham's Balkan activities.

v Various conversations between Reginald Hibbert and James Pettifer, from 1993 to the end of Hibbert's life in 2002.

themselves as anti-communist nationalists and in some cases had collaborated passively or more actively with the occupation forces.[vi] Although the SOE role was to stimulate the anti-Axis resistance and to report back to Cairo and London on its progress, in fact the officers soon became participants in a nascent civil war over the post-war future of Albania that was developing, as it was also in Yugoslavia between Tito's communist Partisans and the Royalist Chetnik forces.

The Balkan SOE officers have contributed a large number of written memoirs on these events, published in the post-war period, which have perhaps obscured the fact that SOE was a world-wide organisation, with important activity in Africa, South East Asia and elsewhere. In the main there is a limited source literature for historians from SOE operations outside Europe.

The young Hibbert was a man with acute historical sense, who had been plucked from his undergraduate studies in history at Worcester College Oxford to service in the British Army. In Cairo he encountered an army with many highly political aspects, undergoing modernisation under Montgomery and others and with a specifically radical ethos among many young officers.[vii] He was encountering a world as different from the tranquillity of his lower middle-class Anglo-Catholic home in London and subsequent short period in Oxford as it was possible to imagine, and it did not take him long to realise that he was to be a witness to the most seminal events in the short history of Albania since it became an independent country in 1913. His reaction was to start to keep a diary, if in contravention of Queen's regulations, to record what he saw.

Hibbert joined the British military mission in 1943 when he was parachuted into northern Albania to join one of the SOE teams under the overall command of Brigadier 'Trotsky' Davies, who had dropped into central Albania two months earlier to lead Britain's missions in the country.[viii] By something of a series of

---

vi A view based on discussions with those involved in the post-Cold War controversies over Albania in the post-Cold War period.

vii See Richard Kisch, *Days of the Good Soldiers: Communists in the Armed Forces, WW II* (London: Pluto, 1987).

viii For Davies' own account of its mixed fortunes, see Brigadier 'Trotsky' Davies, *Illyrian Venture* (London: The Bodley Head, 1952).

lucky chances and his own care of the growing manuscript, his diary survived the physically very difficult world of his Albanian posting, his time with his regiment at the end of the war and subsequent return to civilian life.

For many years after the war ended, when Hibbert was following an orthodox diplomatic career, it naturally remained in his closed archive, but as the end of the Cold War approached and personal retirement after a distinguished last few years when he was Political Director of the Foreign and Commonwealth Office and then Ambassador to Paris, the future of Albania began to preoccupy his thinking. He exemplified the proverb that it is possible to take a man out of Albania but not to take Albania out of anyone who has been involved there. His book *Albania's National Liberation: The Bitter Victory* was published in 1991 just after the Cold War ended and when the one-party state in Albania was in terminal decline.[ix] In the Introduction he referred to the diaries as something that 'might have been published successfully as a wartime adventure story', and now considered that what had happened as the Axis occupation collapsed and the Albanian communists took power as 'needing deeper analysis'.[x]

The text will form a valuable addition to the literature from Albania during the Second World War and for historians of Special Forces activity and guerrilla warfare, and to the growing study of Albanian communism and the origins of the Cold War in the Balkans.

---

ix Published by Pinter in London in that year, and in Albanian as *Fitorja e hidhur: lufta nacional clirimtare e Shqiperise*, translated by Xhervat Lloshi (Tirana: A. Z. Cajupi, 1993).

x Hibbert was aware of the quite numerous volumes of memoirs by ex-SOE Albanian section participants. The most important, in terms of influencing Hibbert's view of the literature, are David Smiley's *Albanian Assignment*, Julian Amery's *Sons of the Eagle* and 'Trotsky' Davies' *Illyrian Venture*. On the ideological basis of this literature and its role in the often intense and bitter controversies about the Second World War's history after the Cold War, see paper by Miranda Vickers, 'A Tale of Two Societies', in James Pettifer (ed.), *Albania and the Balkans: Essays in Honour of Sir Reginald Hibbert* (Port Isaac & Pristina: Elbow Publishing, 2013). In general, the Albanian SOE memoirs were published based on the parameters of what could be said set out by C. M. (Monty) Woodhouse and others on SOE Greece.

In his 1984 study of SOE, M. R. D. Foot commented on the difficulty of establishing what had really happened in SOE's Albania section, given the complexities of the war, the complexities of the politics and the numerous strong personalities involved. This issue has been clarified in later historical writing, exemplified by Roderick Bailey's book *The Wildest Province*.[xi] SOE files are now in the main open in the Public Record Office in Kew, London, and it is likely they will be augmented by further FCO material from the large archives held in a Home Counties store and in process of declassification. The clouds that obscured the wartime landscape for so many years are lifting, and Hibbert's diary is likely to add to knowledge in the important sectors where he was active as a junior officer in 1944, particularly in connection with the Battle of Dibra. It is also a moving tribute to the extraordinary bravery of the British secret soldiers in the most difficult and demanding material conditions in the mountains, exemplified by the deaths of senior officers such as Brigadier Arthur Nicholls. Some gave everything they had in the difficult struggle to free Albania from fascist occupation.

James Pettifer

---

xi Roderick Bailey, *The Wildest Province: SOE in the Land of the Eagle* (London & New York: Vintage, 2011).

INTRODUCTION

This diary is not only an eye-witness daily account of the events sweeping away centuries of tradition and changing the course of Albanian history but also a coming of age story of a young British officer plunged into guerrilla warfare in the Balkan mountains. In many regards, it is also a manual for how life is lived, both physically and psychologically, embedded with a foreign resistance movement in the field. Those that have lived such intense experiences carry them for the rest of their lives.

When he was recruited by Special Operations Executive (SOE) in the summer of 1943 to be parachuted into Albania, Reginald Hibbert, known to family and friends as Reg or Reggie, was a twenty-one-year-old North London grammar school boy and Oxford graduate, with six months' tank officer training at Sandhurst. Born in Barnet on 21 February 1922, he won an exhibition at the age of eighteen from his grammar school, Queen Elizabeth's School, to read history at Worcester College, Oxford, but wartime circumstances had meant cutting his three-year course to only two. Even that short time at university meant spending many hours with the Senior Training Corps and involved 'plenty of motor cycling and truck and scout-car driving round the country side and villages of Oxfordshire'. His history course barely featured the Balkans and politics was not of particular interest to him but Albania was soon to provide a crash course in both.

In the immediate post-war years there was a huge appetite for tales of daring and heroism in the fight against the Germans. Several former SOE officers published memoirs of their Albanian experiences soon after 1945. Few if any personal diaries from SOE's Albanian campaign have been made available to the general reader, however, although several held in archives have been important sources for historians of this period of the war. Foremost among these is the diary of John Hibberdine who was parachuted into Albania on the same night as Hibbert in December 1943.[1] The

---

1   Hibberdine's diary is now held in the Imperial War Museum archives.

post-war memoirs of David Smiley, Peter Kemp, Brigadier 'Trotsky' Davies and others are key accounts of British attempts to coordinate Albanian resistance to German occupation.[2] Many are lively texts, full of detailed descriptions of the landscape, customs, costumes, houses and individuals and the adventures and bravery of the British Liaison Officers (BLOs). Conversations are reproduced or reimagined in detail, events are presented dramatically in hindsight. Of all of them, Hibbert himself considered that Peter Kemp's memoir, *No Colours or Crest*, most closely conveyed events and the BLO Albanian experience. During the war itself the activities of SOE officers had to be kept secret but in peacetime they could be made public and the often extraordinary, daring, courageous and sometimes tragic actions could be revealed. Officers in other SOE Balkan missions also published memoirs, in particular C. M. Woodhouse and Fitzroy Maclean, who had served in Greece and Yugoslavia respectively.[3] Albanians too published memoirs, most notably Enver Hoxha the Albanian communist Partisan leader and later dictator, who published his own in French for a Western audience.[4] The suppression of wartime protagonists and the rewriting of history and memory under Hoxha's dictatorship, however, left fewer contemporary accounts. Events experienced by Albanians, many recorded in SOE memoirs and diaries, have had to be reimagined in novels, notably those of Ismail Kadare.[5] Furthermore, those memoirs that exist, some written in exile, are mostly in the Albanian language and, untranslated, inaccessible to a wide readership.

---

2   Peter Kemp, *No Colours or Crest* (London: Cassell & Co., 1958); Brigadier 'Trotsky' Davies, *Illyrian Venture* (London: The Bodley Head, 1952); David Smiley, *Albanian Assignment* (London: Chatto & Windus, 1984); Julian Amery, *Sons of the Eagle* (London: Macmillan and Co., 1948).

3   C. M. Woodhouse, *The Struggle for Greece* (London: Hart Davis, McGibbon Ltd, 1976); Fitzroy Maclean, *Eastern Approaches* (London: Jonathan Cape, 1949).

4   Enver Hoxha, *Mémoires* (Paris: Editions Nagel, 1984).

5   Ismail Kadare, *Chronicle in Stone* (an imagined account of a boy's experience of wartime Albania) and *The Successor* (a re-imagination of the life of the communist Partisan leader Mehmet Shehu).

Some modern historians have claimed that 'memory has become... one of the central preoccupations of historical scholarship' and many studies of SOE's role in wartime Albania have relied on memoirs and oral history. As historical source material, memoirs are problematic, however, as they raise issues of memory and recall, selectivity, interpretation, exaggeration and accuracy. While memory can be understood to preserve 'residues, traces, impressions or relics of earlier experience' it can also be an exercise in reconstruction where in present time there is an attempt to rebuild an image of past reality, 'guided and motivated less by aspects of the past that is being reconstructed than by the present's need for meaning'. In retrospect, the author can perceive patterns to events not clear to the protagonists at the time.[6] Later life experience can influence the selection of events. In addition, particularly in a situation such as the dilemma facing SOE as to which faction to support with advisers, materiel and funds, different BLOs felt more committed to one side or another. Post-war recollections consciously or unconsciously promoted particular narratives which themselves took on an almost mythical quality, particularly in the post-communist era. To that extent, they can be seen as having a political character. Furthermore, most did not have access to the decision-making of the higher command which is now the province of historians as material is released from the archives.

Unlike a memoir, this diary consists of a daily entry for every single day that Hibbert spent in the field over the course of ten months with few exceptions. At the same time it can be said that the diary entries are also subject to a certain level of selectivity in retrospect. What did he choose to record on any given day? Why does he not record more of the sights and sounds of this extraordinary environment, unlike his colleague Hibberdine in his diary? Hibbert's entries are more concerned not only with the day-to-day physical and mental effort to master his situation but also with his attempt to understand and interpret the events in which he was playing a part. While reflecting on his daily experiences,

---

6 Geoffrey Cubitt, *History and Memory* (Manchester: Manchester University Press, 2007).

including the physical hardship and alienation of living embedded in Albanian Partisan life in the mountains, the diary also reveals how he witnessed and took part in the unfolding of historical events, which were 'momentous for Albania' and its neighbours as they happened. Hibbert himself has remarked that 'The BLOs were small figures in a very large scene.' We follow how that experience transformed a green if intelligent young man into a mature and reflective adult in the space of ten months. As he says in his entry on 10 September 1944, 'Most of us volunteered for our jobs to find out more about ourselves.' This diary records that inner journey.

In the summer of 1943, bored after a few idle months in a military holding camp, Hibbert volunteered for intriguing 'parachute duties' which turned out to be the adventure of his life in the Balkans with SOE. Until then his family's idea of abroad had been a genteel tour of the Swiss lakes. By December he had enjoyed the nightlife of Cairo, been rushed through parachute training in the desert and hastily coached in radio communications. At his last school speech day he had declaimed Mallarmé's 'Le Lac' and received the school Classics prize. His language skills therefore consisted of Latin, French and also schoolboy German. The only preparations for the language and culture of his destination, Albania, were to be haphazard lessons delivered by the unusual Mrs Margaret Hasluck, Balkan enthusiast, linguist, ethnographer and collector of Albanian customs and folklore.[7] As Hibbert remarked, 'There was no instruction in Albania's short and troubled history

---

7   Margaret Masson Hardie Hasluck (1885-1948) was a classicist and graduate of Newnham College, Cambridge. She studied at the British School in Athens, eventually marrying her former Cambridge friend, the School's director and librarian, Frederick Hasluck. Both had a great interest in archaeology and together they spent several years travelling the Balkans, still at that time part of the Ottoman Empire. She developed a passionate attachment to the region, particularly to Albania. After her husband's death, she settled in Elbasan and dedicated herself to the collection of folklore, gypsy lore, magic, superstition and tribal custom. She was a well-known figure in the country. After the Italian invasion in 1939 she moved to Athens and then to Cairo where she was adviser to SOE on all matters Albanian.

and none in wider Balkan history.'[8] The bitter problems of relations between Albanians and Slavs (Serbs) in Kosovo, western Macedonia and southern Montenegro, or with Greeks in southern Albania (northern Epirus), were not mentioned. The officers were told to 'keep clear of politics and concentrate on promoting resistance'.[9] By Christmas he found himself in the snow-bound mountains of what is now the Albanian-Kosovan-Macedonian borderland, much of it spent on the Korab massif which straddles that area.

To begin with, as the youngest and least experienced officer, he was used as his group's errand boy. He was sent almost constantly on marches, up and down mountainsides, day and night and in all weathers, on foot, with or without mules, often alone with only the radio operator (for whom he was responsible) and an interpreter, carrying messages to and from local clan leaders. This twenty-two-year-old middle-class London boy was never sure whether his reception in villages and hamlets would be friendly or hostile, where he would be sleeping or what he would eat, the latter being of great importance to most young soldiers expending huge amounts of physical energy and dependent on others to feed them. To begin with, his enthusiastic naiveté is obvious to the reader but as the weeks and months pass we see him drawn into negotiations and complex relationships with the people he encounters, many of whom are now recognised as key figures in one of the most important periods in Albanian history. The diary witnesses how, 'At close hand and within a very short space of time, we saw the fate of a nation turn on chance encounters, narrow margins, narrowly missed opportunities and extraordinary turns of luck,' as he commented much later.[10] His initial bafflement at the mindset of the Albanian peasants and resistance fighters is gradually replaced by insight and empathy. The small size of the BLO missions in the field gave him responsibilities far beyond his

---

8 Reginald Hibbert, 'Albania, Macedonia and the British Military Missions, 1943 and 1944', in James Pettifer (ed.), *The New Macedonian Question* (London: Palgrave Macmillan, 1999) p184-198.

9 *Ibid.*

10 Nicholas Bethell, Robert Elsie and Bejtullah Destani (eds.), *The Albanian Operation of the CIA and MI6 1949-1953: Conversations with Participants in a Venture Betrayed* (Jefferson: McFarland & Company Inc., 2016) p. 92.

young age, developing his innate ability for strategy and tactics through discussion with local personalities, both Partisan and nationalist, and working with other BLOs often with conflicting views on the best way forward. His natural curiosity about how people think and react led him to gather a quick understanding of the political implications of any given situation and insight into human motivation. As he himself says, life was lived intensely, both physically and mentally. His experience of Albania was transformative; it was his true university.

Those who have taken part in more recent conflicts where they may have been required to spend time embedded in the local life and culture may well recognise some of the difficulties faced by the BLOs in the field in Albania. Conditions were particularly dangerous in winter high up in the mountains in freezing temperatures and heavy snow, when the officers and their radio operators needed to be constantly on the move, reliant on the cooperation and goodwill of the people who were deeply fearful of German reprisals. In the mountain villages there was, of course, no electricity, running water, sewerage or heating other than open fires. The almost daily treks the young men undertook through snow, rain and high summer temperatures up and down the steep gradients of Albania's fearsome mountain ranges meant they were almost continually hungry. The next meal was a huge concern and there was no guarantee that what the local people could provide would be adequate, they themselves being poor. The BLOs were constantly moved, often at night, from safe house to safe house where they frequently had to endure boredom cooped up in cellars or attics as well as being tormented by fleas and other parasites from bedding. Body lice were their constant companions. Albanian hosts received strangers and visitors in special guest rooms, well away from the other living quarters, and sleeping arrangements were often communal. Baths were a rare luxury, and summer was welcomed when they could swim in mountain streams. There was an almost complete lack of medical help so infected wounds could lead to gangrene as in the case of Brigadier Arthur Nicholls. He was eventually killed by this and the deadly effects of frostbite and exposure after weeks on the run from the Germans in the mountains. There was no medication for viral and bacterial infections and many almost died. The men had to doctor themselves. All suffered constantly from stomach complaints.

The BLOs' supplies, equipment and money were, understandably, coveted by their hosts and companions. Being outside the clan and social structure, the British were owed no particular loyalty so building confidence and trust was one of the hardest tasks. Learning the courtesies and social expectations of their hosts was vital. The BLOs were ill-prepared for the language barrier and relied on interpreters. Here Hibbert's knack with languages gave him an advantage with some of the more educated French-speaking clan leaders and in the space of ten months he had learned Albanian from his companions as well as Italian from the Italian Alpini prisoners-of-war who had joined the British as cooks, farriers, barbers and muleteers. Nevertheless a major challenge was mastering the formalities of social etiquette and the dangers of a misjudged joke. The BLOs found themselves in an entirely masculine environment. The only females visible to the foreigners in this Muslim society were children and old women past marriageable age or, later, female Partisan comrades. Many service personnel may identify with the drinking, parties, picnics and girls back at base in Italy once the grip of discipline lifted after extraction from the field.

One powerful presence on almost every page of the diary, however, helps to explain the lifelong hold that this Balkan country had on so many of the British liaison officers. The magnificent but forbidding landscape ruled and shaped every moment of their lives which fell, in Kadare's words, under the 'heavy shadow of the Albanian mountains'.[11] The mighty Korab range, located on the border between Albania, Kosova and Macedonia, has some of the highest peaks in the Balkan Peninsula. It dominated their movements, as they scrambled up steep hillsides, accompanying their mule trains along rocky and precipitous trails used for generations by muleteers and shepherds moving from hamlet to

11 Ismail Kadare, *The Siege* (Edinburgh: Canongate, 2008) p. 10.

hamlet or to upland summer pastures and down to the winter byres in the valleys. In summer they camped in the high meadows, bathed in the mountain streams and rode their horses through the great forests, while in winter they plunged through feet-high snowdrifts. In autumn they trudged through drenching rain and in spring rode through swathes of wild flowers. They crossed the powerful Drin and Mat rivers, fording with the Partisan troops and their mule trains. When a new radio receiver is brought to their summer camp, 'it seems strangely flat and unconvincing among these resonant and powerful mountains. Civilisation speaks through it with an unconvincing and undistinguished voice,' Hibbert notes.

With their Albanian guides and helpers they entered into a way of life in many ways unchanged for centuries. As in Ottoman times the mountains limited the ability of the invaders, in this case the Germans, to physically control the whole of Albania. The British officers rallying resistance to the German occupation of Greece at the same time had a similar experience. C. M. Woodhouse, head of the British Military Mission in Greece from 1943 to 1944, was convinced that the Greek mountains played a critical role in preventing an all-out German takeover and that without them 'no guerrilla movement would have been born'. The BLOs cursed the snow and the mountain tracks but the Germans would have been able to occupy the whole of Albania if the mountains 'were not rendered impassable by snow in winter; if they were traversed by motor roads rather than goat tracks,' as Woodhouse commented, pointing out that 'Thanks to the nature of these mountains, we could travel at will.' Similarly, because the BLOs kept largely to the Albanian high country, direct encounters with Germans are surprisingly few in the diaries.[12] They frequently witnessed the shocking aftermath, however, of German reprisals on villages and hamlets in response to local resistance.

Over the months, Hibbert developed a taste for this austerity:

---

12 C. M. Woodhouse, *Apple of Discord* (London: Hutchinson, 1948). Christopher Montague Woodhouse (1917-2001) was parachuted into Greece in 1942 and then commanded the British Military Mission there from 1943.

'I find myself unwilling to return to England to meet the inevitable discord between myself and the world, unwilling to lose the simplicity of this life.' Perhaps his choice of Mallarmé's translation of Edgar Allan Poe's poem 'The Lake' on his last school speech day revealed a natural penchant for the romance of wilderness:

> In spring of youth it was my lot
> To haunt of the wide world a spot
> The which I could not love the less
> So lovely was the loneliness
> Of a wild lake, with black rock bound,
> And the tall pines that towered around

On his return he experienced an inner conflict between a desire for life after the war to reproduce the heightened sense of personal significance in the greater order of things that he had experienced in the Albanian wartime microcosm and a reluctance to leave the simple life and be challenged or 'tested' as a man. On the one hand, he had experienced the complexity of human behaviour and the lack of control any one individual has over events, but on the other he had understood the sense in which an individual can make a contribution to the course of those events. He fears the 'failure to create and control something in the world, failure to understand and manoeuvre amongst the complications of human change' once he returns to the outside world from which he has been cut off. By the end of his leave in Italy in the winter of 1944, however, his disillusion is complete once he realises that 'No one in the office is very interested in what we have to say' and that his lengthy debriefing report will simply be shelved. The waters close over his head. As a result he joins his regiment to fight in Italy rather than return to England.

In the late autumn of 1944 when the final entries were written, Hibbert, still aged only twenty-two, had just returned from ten months of transformative experiences and a daily life of physical hardship, discipline and austerity. In Albania he had come into close daily contact with people who were attempting either to preserve the world they knew in the face of German occupation or to make long-lasting and radical changes to their country and the lives of their fellow-Albanians. He had witnessed the incompatible ideological conflict between the nationalists and monarchists and the communist Partisans which was reflected in the contrasting strategies and policy advice being offered to SOE's headquarters in Bari by different groups of BLOs. Throughout his diary he refers to the long political discussions held with fellow liaison officers and with both nationalist and Partisan Albanians in the long hours spent waiting to move on to the next safe house or in their mountain camps. The fact that Hibbert felt it worth commenting that on leave he and other officers who had worked with the Partisans lived 'on the best of terms with the other BLOs even with those who have been on the other side of the political fence in Albania' (those who had supported Abas Kupi and the Balli Kombëtar nationalists rather than the Partisan communists) suggests how deeply divided the SOE personnel on the ground were over the merits of supporting one or other group in the dispute over Albania's future. At the same time, in spite of those differences, the intense nature of their experience bound them together. This is clearly illustrated by the case of Julian Amery, a BLO fiercely committed to the nationalist cause and a life-long advocate of the view that Britain had offered the nationalists up to their fate at the hands of the post-war communist regime.[13] While Hibbert did not see eye to eye with him politically, Julian Amery's

---

13 Julian Amery (1919-96) was a lifelong member of the Conservative Party and a leading MP for thirty-nine years, holding various ministerial posts. He was the son of Leo Amery, a prominent politician who was Secretary of State for India during the war years. He was also son-in-law to Prime Minister Harold Macmillan. Before the Second World War he was a war correspondent in Spain during the Civil War. Later he was an attaché at the British Embassy in Belgrade. He joined the RAF as a sergeant in 1940 and transferred to the British Army in 1941, reaching the rank of captain. The first part of his war career took him to the Middle East, Malta and Yugoslavia. He served as a BLO in Albania for about four months from1943 to April 1944 during which time he kept a diary. He was attached to Colonel Neil 'Billy' McLean's mission, primarily working with the supporters of King Zog under their local leader, Abas Kupi. He referred to himself, David Smiley and 'Billy' McLean as the Three Musketeers. Later Amery became a close friend of the exiled King Zog whom he much admired.

summary of what they did have in common, cannot be bettered:

> Yet in those violent circumstances, where only the normal
> seemed strange, we found freedom; for though our tasks
> were hard we were our own task masters, answerable only
> to ourselves; outlaws in the land where we worked, strangers
> among the guerillas and cut off from our own kind.[14]

Amery also reflects that this freedom and the slow pace of life
enabled a contemplative and philosophical state of mind. It
convincingly explains the hold the Albanian experience had on
BLOs of all persuasions.

A Political Education

As well as offering images of life in the 1930s and 1940s familiar
to readers from modern films and TV series - dining and dancing
in London hotels, recruitment of agents in country houses, visits
to military tailors, the charms of Oxford undergraduate life - the
diaries also recall another feature of those times. Not a few young
people recruited into SOE held left-wing ideas and Hibbert was
clearly one of them. It is known that in his undergraduate days
he held an interest in the work of the Fabian Society.[15] Hibbert
rewrote many of the diary entries for October to November
1944 in his first typed transcript in the early 1990s in order to
play down the frank expression of his wartime left-wing political
beliefs and criticism of some of his erstwhile companions. These,
the last entries, mainly reflected on his previous ten months in
Albania from the distance of Italy where he was resting and
reporting back on his tour of duty. This transcript restores the
original text.

Hibbert's intellectual landscape was formed not only by
the classical education he received at his grammar school and

---

14 Julian Amery, *Sons of the Eagle: a Study in Guerilla War* (London: Macmillan
   & Co. Ltd, 1948) p. viii.
15 The Fabian Society was founded in 1884 with the aim of promoting
   social justice and a gradualist approach to social democracy as opposed to
   revolutionary overthrow.

at Oxford but also by his family background of the aspiring lower middle class. His father, a fervent Anglo-Catholic, was a government ministry clerk and autodidact from Dalston in North London and his mother was a former primary school teacher and daughter of a railway clerk from Hackney. Oxford, his Sandhurst experience and the war itself threw Hibbert into contact with a class of people he had hardly ever encountered before: public school boys, sons of traditional army families of the officer class and even members of the nobility. One prominent writer on the history of SOE points out that the England of the time was run by an 'educated governing class' still being produced by the country's elite private schools to administer the Empire.[16] At least two if not more of his fellow BLOs in Albania had been school friends at Eton. Many of them no doubt saw him as a pretentious upstart while he found it difficult to understand their sense of entitlement and, in some cases, lack of intellectual energy.

Hibbert identified himself as an intellectual and, like many others of his generation, was drawn to the ideas of cultural Marxism attracting young intellectuals in the 1930s and 1940s. SOE recruited quite a few young men with similar or even more radical ideas. Among them was Frank Thompson, for instance, brother of the Marxist writer and theorist E. P. Thompson, who had developed communist sympathies while at Oxford. Thompson was originally sent to Macedonia but was executed by Bulgarian gendarmes near Sofia while working with Bulgarian partisans in June 1944, aged twenty-three, having been carried away by his political support for them.[17] Cairo itself had a busy socialist or communist sub-culture among the young expatriates stationed there.

In Bari, Hibbert became friends with John Naar and John Eyre in SOE's Albanian Department whom he describes as 'committed left-wingers'. According to Roderick Bailey's *The Wildest Province*, Eyre, whom Hibbert admired, was a Political and Intelligence Officer who later admitted that he had become

16 M. R. D. Foot, *SOE 1940-1946* (London: British Broadcasting Corporation, 1984).
17 Peter J. Conradi, *A Very English Hero: the Making of Frank Thompson* (London: Bloomsbury, 2012).

convinced of the class basis of society during his experience with SOE. Furthermore, the recent Spanish Civil War and the attraction of the International Brigade for young socialists and sympathisers was an undeniable factor. Indeed, the Spanish Civil War played an important role in the military and political formation of several BLOs and Albanian Partisans. Major Peter Kemp, for instance, had fought on the monarchist side in Spain and had fostered a powerful dislike of communists. Mehmet Shehu, Commander of the Partisan First Assault Brigade, had also gained his military expertise in Spain, as commander of the Republican XII Garibaldi Brigade.[18] The looming pre-Cold War presence of what was still termed Russia and its communist experiment also stimulated intense questions about the Europe that might emerge from the defeat of fascism. Hibbert assuredly felt he was fighting for Europe's future, rather than a narrow British cause. These preoccupations are reflected throughout the diary. By the end of his tour of duty he is questioning how the war can produce solutions to social and political problems in the Europe being forged out of the conflict. At one point he reflects that if he had been born Albanian he would probably have joined the Partisan side.

After ten months in Albania, shuttling between the different factions, Hibbert had come to the conclusion that only the communist Partisans could resist the Germans effectively. While some BLOs posted to Albania wanted to see the British maintain or restore the pre-war social and political status quo in that country, others, in Eyre's words, were helping to stir up a 'hurricane' of social and political change. Reg Hibbert was swept up in this ongoing debate after the war largely due to the time he had spent in the British camp at Bizë with fellow SOE officer Lt. Winn in September 1944, shortly before Hibbert's departure. Hibbert tended Winn who had broken his leg parachuting into

---

18 Former SOE officer Capt. Donald MacDonald, who had served in Macedonia and knew Kemp personally, recalled in a 1997 letter to his family that Kemp 'had fought for Franco in the Spanish Civil War and had Franco decorations. He would flaunt these to the Partisans many of whom had fought in the International Brigade and this would infuriate them.'

Albania on 19 September. He and Winn had heated arguments about Albania's political future during the time they were thrown together. After ten months in the field Hibbert felt he had a certain level of authority for his views. Winn's thinking was probably influenced by the reports sent back to SOE headquarters by liaison officers such as David Smiley and Julian Amery who considered SOE's abandonment of the pro-Zog elements and Balli Kombëtar nationalists a betrayal.

Lt. Winn was the Hon. Rowland Winn, later the 4th Baron St Oswald (1916-84). After the war, St Oswald recalled these camp fire conversations in Albania and caused Hibbert considerable trouble in his Foreign Office career by accusing him of being a communist. St Oswald argued that the BLOs' task had been to support the nationalist cause and halt the imposition of a communist regime rather than, as he saw it, to foster it. His allegations were investigated in 1951 and dismissed. St Oswald went further in 1980, however, during Hibbert's tenure as British Ambassador to France, and repeated these accusations to the French government. Furthermore, in an interview recorded in July 1984 but only published in 2016 after Hibbert's death in 2002, he went so far as to accuse Hibbert, quite extraordinarily, of having suggested in these wartime conversations that he, Hibbert, was plotting with the Partisans the assassination of BLOs David Smiley, Billy McLean and Julian Amery.[19] Hibbert's own response was sanguine, commenting in 1984 that 'Those who took part in the events still feel strongly about them and those that believed in conspiracy theories then still believe in them today. Most would not push their passion or their fanaticism to the extreme.' But, 'Such was the vividness of that experience and such its long lasting effect on those who endured it', adding in the same interview, 'Everybody's personal emotions were terribly tied up with the people you had been working with there. It can't be otherwise when you are living so close to people in such circumstances.'[20] Furthermore, after the war there were few ways in which former

---

19 Bethell *et al.*, *op. cit.*, p. 140. Hibbert died on 6 October 2002.
20 *Ibid*, p. 102.

SOE personnel who had served in Albania could find outlets for those feelings such as existed for others who had worked with resistance movements elsewhere, thanks to Albania's relatively low political significance and its self-imposed diplomatic isolation from the rest of Europe during the communist era.

It is clear that in the 1990s, as a recently-retired Foreign Office civil servant and one who had been accused of having espoused communism, Hibbert's youthful enthusiasm for socialism, if not communism, could have been embarrassing, particularly if he was considering transcription of his wartime diaries as a first step to publication. Many of those he mentions in his diary would have still been alive and he would not have been keen to reawaken old arguments and accusations. Furthermore, and perhaps more importantly, there had been recent regime change in Albania, with the end of communist rule in 1990, five years after Enver Hoxha's death in April 1985, and Hibbert was beginning to hope that a previously unthinkable visit might become possible. The interim was presided over by Ramiz Alia who was replaced by the reforming former communist Sali Berisha in 1992. Berisha was to lose power in 1997 amid civil unrest as a result of authoritarian suppression of dissent and the financial and economic scandal of a disastrous pyramid scheme during his presidency.

The end of the one-party state in Albania in 1990 had led to the revival of elements of social and national identity prevalent in Albanian society before the Second World War and suppressed for fifty years: religion (Islam, Catholicism and Christian Orthodoxy), clan membership, dialect, regional Balkan affiliations and sympathies, including the issue of Kosova. As elsewhere in Eastern Europe, particularly in the Balkans, former communists frequently re-invented themselves. It was no longer acceptable to be associated overtly with having been instrumental in any obvious way in having brought about the installation of the former communist regime in 1945. After 1991 it became possible, although still difficult, to travel to Albania. When Hibbert did eventually make that journey in the mid-1990s he encountered a certain degree of wariness among the political class because of his association with the Partisans, a wariness or even hostility that continues to this day towards those considered not to have endorsed the Ballist/Zogist wartime cause. Nevertheless, he revisited sites of his service in Albania and was able to meet with some former Partisan associates. As Miranda Vickers records, 'Besides meeting Albanian political leaders, he searched out his old wartime comrades. On one occasion, he returned to the northern Albanian village into which he had been parachuted in December 1943. After an arduous, extremely uncomfortable journey along a mountainous dirt track, two elderly men, who remembered his arrival in their village 55 years earlier, embraced him.'[21]

Throughout his life Hibbert held Albania in a very special place in his affections.

Finally, this is a short chronicle of great poignancy recording as it does the last months of a world that was about to disappear forever, peopled with an older generation who had lived through the last years of the Ottoman Empire and were the bearers of centuries-old tradition.

The Diaries

The question arises why Hibbert kept these diaries at all. Wartime letters were censored and Albania was a covert destination. Throughout his life Hibbert was a prolific and entertaining commentator on his own life and experiences although he mainly expressed himself through letters. One explanation is that he never overcame the sense of particularism that his leap from lower middle-class expectations, albeit aspirational, his place at Oxford and the transformational opportunities of war all gave him. He was his modest family's golden boy, leapfrogging his older brother in achievement. He was always ambitious to make a mark. His life was deeply interesting to him so he recorded it because he believed it would be interesting to others.

Hibbert did not start his diaries until he went to a holding camp at Welbeck in the Midlands. Before that he had kept up a

---

21 Miranda Vickers, 'Reginald Hibbert Obituary', *The Guardian*, 15 October 2002.

running commentary on his life in the often daily letters to his girlfriend and former fellow Oxford undergraduate, Ann Pugh, whom he eventually married in 1949 after 'many adventures'. In order to provide a context for the diaries kept in the field, Part 1 is a combination of his own notes, letters to Ann Pugh, which she had carefully kept until they were unearthed in the 1980s, and his own diaries. The diaries themselves were completely clandestine. Military personnel were strictly forbidden to keep diaries while on active service although many did, fortunately. The Welbeck diary is a substantial 6.5 by 4 inch notebook starting with the Sandhurst passing out parade on 7 May 1943 and ending after a final drunken weekend in Oxford on 14 July with the words 'We are glad to leave'. The Albanian ones were three small pocket or note books, each page densely covered in tiny handwriting so as to make the most of the paper. The first of the two diaries written in the field is a refill pad for a Field Message Book 153. It is written in pencil from his first night in the field 19 December 1943 up to 10 February 1944 and then continues in ink after his propelling pencil is stolen. When he reached the end of the pad in March he turned it and wrote on the reverse of the pages. The second diary is a 2.5 by 4 inch black notebook with tiny writing crammed into every line. This starts on 23 June and ends on 8 September 1944. Some is written in ink and some in pencil. The third is another Field Message Book 153. The evenness and more relaxed appearance of the writing here, however, suggests that he copied out the last month of his field diary after arrival back in Italy on 8 October 1944 and then added a lengthy reflection on his experience.

*

Although the text has been edited, this has been to make it more understandable to the reader. Firstly, consistency in the spelling of place names has been introduced. In 1943 the Albanian language had not been entirely standardised. The standardisation of the written language has been an important task in all Balkan states

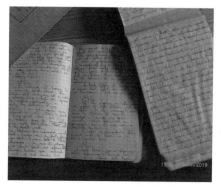

since finally gaining independence from the Ottoman Empire, in Albania's case in 1912. Regional dialects or usage and the lack of a single accepted orthography at the time that Hibbert wrote his entries meant that some spellings of place names varied considerably from modern Albanian. Standard modern Albanian is based on one of the two main Albanian dialects, the Tosk. The Gheg, spoken in northern and central Albania predominantly, is not a separate official language although some authors write and publish in Gheg. The dividing line is the Shkumbin river, and Gheg is the variant of Albanian spoken in the area where Hibbert spent his time.[22] Where Hibbert has used one particular spelling throughout, it has been kept even if it is old-fashioned. For instance, he refers throughout to Dibra, which has other variants: Dibër or Dibra e Madhe in Albanian, Debar in Macedonian. Where he has guessed the spelling or has used different spellings the modern equivalent has been used as far as possible. In the case of the capital city, the internationally used variant of Tirana is used throughout the edited text. In many places he introduced Albanian words and phrases. Usually they were phonetically spelt or even just guessed at and often needed considerable editorial research. They have been rendered in modern Albanian as far as possible. The same applies to the Italian dishes that the camp

---

22 According to Robert Elsie, Gheg is spoken 'in most of Albania north of the Shkumbin river, as well as in Kosovo, Montenegro, Serbia, most of the western part of the Republic of Macedonia'. There is a Northern Gheg subdialect spoken north of the Mat river, including the Shkodra region, Lezha, Malësia e Madhe, Dukagjin, Puka, Mirditë, Malësia e Gjakovës, Luma, Has, Kosovo. Readers of this diary will recognise many of these place names. Internet Archive Wayback Machine http://www.albanianlanguage.net/dialects.

cooks produced for the British contingent.

Conclusion

Editing the diaries has been a strange experience for me. As a child I was well acquainted with these little books which my father kept wrapped up in oil cloth. They were precious to him and from time to time he would bring them out and show them to us so I have always been aware of their existence. A small child cannot have a sense of the passing of adult time. My father's tales of his life in Albania seemed to be outside any specific chronology, simply a long time ago, in the same time frame as a folk tale or a story in a book. Yet for him, ten or fifteen years after the events he carefully reported, they must have seemed fresh in his mind. Extraordinarily, I had not read them until I edited them as they seemed personal to him and in his gift to offer them to me to read, which he did not. His typed transcription, however, clearly suggests that he intended to publish them himself. After he appointed me as his literary executor in 2002 shortly before his death and expressed his hope that they could be published, I took possession of them but did not read them.

At Professor James Pettifer's invitation in 2018, however, publication became a possibility. Transcribing them for this purpose was my first reading and I am very grateful that I came to them fresh. Transcription involved a very close reading a few hours a day. Each daily session was an encounter with the past as it unfolded in present time and an interaction with the powerful presence of the Albanian landscape. Moving through the months day by day I also became closely acquainted with someone I knew well in a different, child-parent relationship. I got to know and like this young man in a way that I never knew the older man during his lifetime although he showed many characteristics I recognised: his humour, his impatience with people who were less able to take the spartan life, his enjoyment of rather highbrow music and literature, his love of and skill with languages, his ability to party and have fun. Going for a walk with him on holiday in Scotland as children meant a five-hour hike across moorland and bog and up and down hill, a mere stroll after Albania.

Of course, it was a matter of regret that I did not undertake this project during his lifetime so that I could question him more about the events and feelings he describes. Nevertheless this is a remarkable journey into adulthood. As he wrote to Ann Pugh, my mother, on the eve of rejoining his regiment for the next stage of his war in the Italian Campaign, 'I imagine the life to be so much more simple and straightforward than anything which I have known in the past year. As you say, I have grown older but I hate to admit it.'

Reg Hibbert (second left) and Richard Riddell (far right shaking hands) in Tirana in June 1992, reunited with their former Partisan comrade Haxhi Lleshi and former President of Albania (1953-82) during the communist era.

Albania 1941-1943

N

Y U G O S L A V I A

MONTENEGRO
(Italian protectorate)

SERBIA
(under German
occupation)

KOSOVA

Prishtina

Gjakova

Degë

Drin

Prizren

Shkodër

Kukës

Black Drin

Mt.Korab

Peshkopi

MACEDONIA
(under Bulgarian occupation
Oct 1941 - Sept 1944)

Mat

Dibra

TIRANA

Durrës

Elbasan

Ohrid

Lake
Prespa

Shkumbin

Lake Ohrid

Gramsh

Berat

Tomorricë

Korçë

GREECE
(German
occupation zone)

Vlorë

Tepelenë

Këlcyrë

Gjirokastër

GREECE
(Italian occupation zone)

Adriatic
Sea

Sarandë

Corfu

© S.Ballard (2019)

Albanian territory
& borders 1941-43

22

ALBANIA IN 1943

A singular characteristic of the way the SOE officers and men were prepared for field work, as Hibbert pointed out later, was the almost complete lack of briefing on the history and politics of the Albania they were about to be dropped into. The complex ethnic and historical issues preoccupying the varied populations of these southern Balkan areas, be they Albanians, Slavs (both Serbian and Montenegrin) or Greeks, were ignored. Yet the SOE personnel were to be dropped into the border areas where these tensions were at their strongest: Kosova, Western Macedonia, Southern Montenegro and northern Epirus. Their task was to organise resistance to the Germans and to ignore politics.[23] Yet their work required them to intermingle, work with and rely on people whose history and recent politics provided the very reasons why they might or might not be motivated to fight the common enemy, first the Italians then the Germans. The work of the BLOs in north-eastern Albania, including Hibbert, was complicated further by territorial ambiguities created by boundaries laid down after the end of Ottoman rule and two internecine Balkan wars early in the twentieth century which particularly concerned Kosova and Macedonia.

Within a few entries in the diary it becomes clear to the reader that the Albanian resistance to the German occupation was not a united force. Incompatibility of aims and antagonism between guerrilla groups, which consisted of both nationalist and communist elements, bedevilled the British liaison missions in their attempts to encourage all groups to provide consistent resistance to the German forces rather than vie with each other for control of the different regions and territories and eventually for the control of post-war Albania. In September 1942 the communists proposed a conference at Pezë near Tirana with the intention of bringing these elements together under one

---

23 Reginald Hibbert, 'Albania, Macedonia and the British Military Missions, 1943 and 1944', *op. cit.*, p. 184.

centralised National Liberation Front, the Lëvizja Nacional-Çlirimtare (LNÇ), in order to form a united anti-German front. The Pezë project started with both prominent nationalists and a preponderance of communist members, including their leader Enver Hoxha. These two elements, however, were irreconcilable in their allegiances, aims and politics. In the face of communist hostility, the nationalists formed their own movements, the Balli Kombëtar (National Front), the Legaliteti and the organisation of the independent Muharrem Bajraktar. While the Ballists principally sought a non-communist republican future for the country, the Legaliteti supported the exiled King Zog and the restoration of the monarchy.

The Legaliteti emerged after the failure of a short-lived initiative by the British to bring the two groups together once more in the summer of 1943. This was the Mukje Conference, which took place on 1-3 August near Krujë in central Albania. Here the Balli Kombëtar and the LNÇ signed a treaty with the idea of forming a Committee for the Salvation of Albania. The nationalists' call for the post-war creation of a Greater Albania, however, which would have included Kosova was rejected by the communists who were closely linked to the Yugoslav communists for whom such territorial claims were unacceptable. The treaty failed. The idea of a Greater Albania continued to be a key aspiration for the Legaliteti. As a result the Ballists reinforced their separate identity and the rivalry between the groups intensified to the point of 'virtual civil war'.[24] Ultimately, the British command in Cairo took the decision to throw in its lot with the communist LNÇ as being the better organised militarily and the more effective in fighting the Germans. It should be noted that the nationalist resistance was faced with invidious choices. The clan leaders were well aware that acts of resistance would provoke brutal German reprisals of destruction and burning on the villages and people within their territories. Any clan leader who brought destruction to his people and villages by blatantly taking up arms against the Italians or

---

24 R. J. Crampton, *The Balkans Since the Second World War* (Abingdon: Routledge, 2013) p. 40.

Germans would lose his leadership status both morally and literally. The role of the British Missions was to strengthen their hand by setting their activities in the greater scenario of the war and providing the wherewithal for successful insurgency. Albania was finally liberated from German occupation on 17 November 1944 by which time the LNÇ had set up an Anti-Fascist Committee for National Liberation and was politically structured to take control and completely eliminate opposition. As a result, the remnants of nationalist opposition, many of whose leaders and members fled the country, were subject to the harshest persecution.

*

The failure of these attempts both at Pezë and at Mukje reflect key aspects of Albania's complex history since its declaration of independence from Ottoman rule thirty years earlier in 1912. The Ottoman state finally withdrew from the Balkans, renouncing all rights over Albanian lands, after the peace accords marking the end of the Second Balkan War in May 1913. Albania was the last independent country to be forged out of former Ottoman territory, its national boundaries disputed by both Serbia and Greece from the outset. Within the Ottoman Empire, whose rule over the Balkan Peninsula had started in the fourteenth century, there were no internal borders. Areas were identified by tradition and by greater and smaller settlements of people, whether Albanians, Serbs, Greeks or Bulgarians. This demographic patchwork presented a serious dilemma to politicians, ethnographers and historians trying to establish the physical boundaries of the newly emerging states. Should language, tradition and custom or religion be the determining features? All these factors opened up endless possibilities for dispute. The peace accords left no Balkan state satisfied and the boundaries of the new Albanian state did not represent all the regions where Albanians were to be found. In particular, Kosova with its large Albanian population was allocated to Serbia. At the same time Serbia and Bulgaria had aspirations to possess Macedonian lands, landlocked Serbia for reasons of access to northern Greek ports and Bulgaria for historical and ethnic reasons.

For a brief period in 1913, both Serbia and Greece attempted to seize additional land from Albania, the Serbs in the east and the Greeks in the south. The Great Powers - France, Britain and Austria - allocated Pejë, Prizren, Gjakova and Dibër to Serbia, in spite of local protest, in exchange for withdrawal. Historians have remarked that it was in Serbia's interest to maintain unrest in Northern Albania in order to frustrate the viability of the new state.[25] From that time on, Serbian (later, Yugoslav) interest and interference in Albanian affairs was a constant concern for successive Albanian governments. The First World War provided yet another opportunity for neighbours to partition Albania. By 1918, the Kingdom of Serbs, Croats and Slovenes had come into existence (later to become Yugoslavia in 1929) and had inherited Serbian ambition for possession of northern Albanian lands. One common thread running through all this territorial chopping and changing, however, was that Albanian demands were repeatedly ignored in favour of the Great Powers' preferences, particularly with regard to Serbia. There was general Great Power support for Serbia's claims that Kosova had been essential to Serbian national identity since the end of the fourteenth century. By 1920 the whole of Kosova was back in Serbian hands as the result of the Great Powers' juggling of different national interests. This time the Serbs embarked on a programme of colonisation and suppression of Albanian identity and language, including name-changing, putting the now marginalised Albanian population under severe pressure.

The fledgling Albanian state, even in its unsatisfactory territorial conformation, was nevertheless still independent. This was in spite of another threat beginning to emerge. At the end of the First World War, Italian involvement in pushing back Greek control of southern Albanian territory had laid the foundation for Italian efforts to treat Albania as its protectorate. While Kosova was undergoing a Serbian assimilation programme to the east, Italy was exerting creeping pressure over the south.

---

25 Miranda Vickers, *The Albanians: A Modern History* (London: I. B. Tauris, 1995) p. 81.

The withdrawal of Ottoman rule had left behind powerful landowners in the north, usually clan leaders, both Muslim and Catholic. The Mirditë, for instance, located in north-western Albania, was the largest Catholic clan or *fis* with powerful regional influence. A key feature, therefore, of Albania's historical character that affected the BLOs' experience in these border areas, and for which they were not properly prepared, was the domination of the mountainous north of the country by these powerful clans who valued their independence from any central control, be it Ottoman or home-grown. It was out of this northern *fis* system that an indigenous Albanian leadership emerged in the person of Ahmet Zogu. Successor in 1911 to the chieftain of the Muslim Mati tribe, one of the largest tribes in the country based on the River Mat, he came from rugged highlands that had never been fully controlled by the Ottomans.

Zogu had fought on the side of Austro-Hungary during the war and then spent time in Vienna and Rome. On his return to Albania, between 1919 and 1924 he took on a number of government posts, gradually gathering control over the state. He changed to the better-known name of Zog in 1922. Internal unrest after the assassination of one of his opponents in 1922 sent him into exile. Backed by the Yugoslavs and reinforced by a war band of Mati tribesmen he returned in 1924. In January 1925 he was appointed President of the Albanian Republic with Tirana as its capital. To consolidate power he took steps to crush Kosovan opposition, pursuing and sometimes killing its leaders. The long-term viability of an Albanian state depended on the establishment of law and order. Over time, however, he became increasingly dependent on Italian support and signed a friendship pact with Italy in 1926. By 1928 Zog had accumulated 'unrestricted legislative, judicial and executive powers'.[26] On 1 December 1928 he declared himself King Zog the First.

Through the 1930s, Zog manoeuvred to remain in power although he was compelled to make some concessions to liberalisation and modernisation including secularisation and the

---

26 *Ibid*, p. 123.

Kap. FIQRI DINEA   PRENK PERVIZI MUHAREM BAJRAKTARI   HYSNI DEMA

The four military leaders appointed by King Zog in 1926 and prominent figures during Albania's wartime occupation: Muharrem Bajraktari of Lumë controlled the north-east Kruma region, Fiqri Dinë the north-west (Shkodra), Prenk Pervizi the centre (Tirana) and Hysni Dema the south (Vlorë).

unveiling of women. Nevertheless, the time-honoured system of customary law, the *Kanun of Lek*, continued to regulate lives in remoter regions together with the influence of local Muslim, Catholic or Orthodox Christian clerics. While the Ottoman administration had applied a common code of law throughout the Empire, it had permitted different traditional systems of social regulation or *kanun* to be recognised and applied locally.

In 1937, Mussolini's son-in-law called for the total annexation of Albania by Italy, which already controlled the greater part of the Albanian economy. In 1939 Italy invaded and occupied Albania and then set about installing a fascist state along Italian lines. Zog and his family fled to Greece and from there into permanent exile in Britain. Keen to persuade the Albanians to accept their regime and to appease irredentist elements, the Italians had entered into an agreement with Germany to return the Kosovan region to Albania. This did indeed take place at the beginning of the war after the invasion of Yugoslavia by the Germans in 1941. Many welcomed the return of Kosova, first under military and then under civil administration from Tirana. Italian troops and Carabinieri, however, continued to occupy parts of Kosova including the area where Hibbert's mission was stationed, Dibër and Kukës. After the capitulation of Italy in September 1943 and the German invasion of Albania, some Italian soldiers preferred to hand themselves over to the Albanian Partisans rather than to the Germans. A few of these found employment with the British field missions as orderlies, while others formed a unit within the Partisan fighting force, hence references to Italian officers with the Partisans in the diary. Italian rule in Albania was resented on the whole, particularly among the some of the northern clans. The Mirditë and the Mati, for instance, had already started to organise resistance to the occupiers resulting in armed uprisings and civil disobedience.

While this convoluted history provides the backdrop to the nationalist element of the resistance to the Italian and German occupations, the history of the other group, the communist Partisans, was more recent. By 1920, Albania was the only Balkan state without a Communist Party although individuals had created committees in Paris and Vienna affiliated to the Balkan Federation of Communist Parties, which in turn came under Comintern control. In 1928 an Albanian Communist Party was set up in the Soviet Union but members had difficulties forming a single unified party back in Albania itself. Until 1941, efforts resulted in ever increasing factions preoccupied with in-fighting which were largely confined to intellectual and student circles.

In 1940 the Yugoslav Communist Party (CPY) set up a regional communist sub-group known as the Kosmet Regional Committee in the Kosova Metohija (southern Kosova) area. The Committee provided the seed corn for the creation of the Albanian Communist Party. In June 1941, the CPY leader Josef Broz Tito, under the direction of the Comintern, sent the leader of the Kosmet Regional Committee, Miladin Popović, together with Dušan Mugoša, to Albania. The pair were highly effective in recruiting members and setting up new cells until an Albanian Communist Party with a united leadership and a coherent political programme officially came into being on 8 November 1941. Enver Xoxha, originally from Gjirokastër in southern Albania, was appointed leader. This close relationship with the Yugoslav Communist Party continued throughout the war. In southern Kosova and Macedonia, one of Tito's closest associates, Svetozar Vukmanović-Tempo, coordinated Albanian resistance with the Yugoslavs. Party membership spread among young people and poorer peasants, attracted by ideas of national self-determination, land reform and economic and social reform. Two guerrilla brigades were created and propaganda campaigns were aimed at encouraging people to resist the Italian occupation.

By 1943, therefore, the formation of a communist structure prepared to resist the occupying Germans coincided with the emergence in north-eastern Albania of a parallel guerrilla movement led by powerful leaders such as Myslim Pezë, the monarchist Abas Kupi and the nationalist chieftain Muharrem Bajraktar. The two groups came together briefly at Pezë in 1942 and at Mukje in 1943 but to no avail. The very area into which Hibbert was to be parachuted in December 1943 was thus at the centre of some of Albania's strongest irredentist aspirations and in the heart of some of its most traditional and independent highland regions.

ALBANIAN PRONUNCIATION

Albanian has been a literate language since the medieval period and over time has been expressed in a number of different alphabets including Greek, Latin and Ottoman Arabic. Furthermore, the Albanian language exists in two predominant versions, the Gheg spoken in northern Albania and the Tosk spoken south of the Shkumbin river. The variety of alphabets reflected the cultural and religious influences in the two different dialect regions as well as the centuries of Ottoman administration. The foundation of the modern Albanian alphabet was devised in the late nineteenth century during the revival of Albanian cultural and national identity and, after a number of revisions, additions and disputes, the current Bashkimi alphabet based on the Tosk dialect became the standard. There are thirty-six letters, some consisting of compound letters. Albanian is a phonetic language. English speakers should note the pronunciation of the following letters:

C, c	ts as in tsunami
Ç, ç	ch as in much
Dh, dh	th as in then
Ë, ë	e as in fern*
Gj, gj	'dj as in adjoin
J, j	y as in yard
Nj, nj	ny as in lanyard
Q, q	ch as in child
X, x	dz as in adze
Xh, xh	j as in just
Zh, zh	as the s in measure

The letter 'ë' is sometimes transliterated as 'a' in non-Albanian texts e.g. Tiranë/Tirana.

THE DIARIES

TRAINING

ENGLAND

March 1942-August 1943

NOTE BY REG HIBBERT

I was sworn in as a Territorial Army recruit on 27 March 1941, immediately after my nineteenth birthday, at a recruiting office in Edgware but my actual call-up was deferred.

I went up to Oxford in the autumn of 1940 at the age of eighteen and, having been awarded an exhibition in history at Worcester College, read modern history there with military history as my special subject. Expecting to be called up for the army in a year or so, I joined the Senior Training Corps (STC) as did most of my contemporaries. I gained war certificates A (infantry) and B (armour) and so was qualified for direct entry to officer training on call-up. Instead of being called up at the end of the academic year as I expected, I was invited to become a Cadet Instructor in the STC and was told that if I accepted this I could complete a second year and obtain an honours degree. I had joined the armoured wing of the STC where the moving spirit was regimental Sergeant Major Picton, who gave the unusual impression of being a thinking and even a sensitive man. He also attracted a certain amount of interest among some of us young men for having been at Bovington in the Royal Tank Corps with T. E. Lawrence when the latter was there as an RTC trooper, from 1922 to 1925, between his two spells in the ranks of the RAF. The armoured wing took up a big share of my time in 1941/42, my second year, but I was able to obtain my degree.

After the end of the Trinity [Summer] term in 1942, there was an intensive STC course in which I had to take a full-time part as a cadet instructor. Then my deferred call-up occurred and I joined the army at Blackdown Camp as a pre-Cadet in the Officer Cadet Training Unit (OCTU), before joining the main Armoured Corps OCTU at Sandhurst as a full Officer Cadet.

LETTERS TO ANN PUGH

16th August 1942, Blackdown, Hants

This third paragraph is the third attempt to write this letter... even now a lively altercation on the cooks is deafening me on one side, whilst on the other someone tries to polish the floor under my feet. There are some amusing characters here. One young soldier from Manchester excels in buffoonery and draws on a limitless store of suggestive stories, rhymes and witticisms. He enlivens our routine enormously. Then we have some hardened old soldiers who know life so well that it can no longer have a capital L for them. A clean, straight Englishman from St Alban's School, against whom I used to play rugger, completes the picture gallery. His amorous adventures with the scullionesses make him popular with the boys. He and the veterans have shaken the Oxford boys a little – they have taken to ostentatious oaths and heroic self-exaggeration. That has reacted on me to cure me of swearing pro tem.

It has been fun to see how the arduous work affects different people. Some have started to whine, some to creep to the officers, some to indulge in various forms of escapism and the rest to laugh. The latter are the best company.

16th October, RAC, OCTU, Sandhurst, Camberley

Three of us sleep in one room, share a servant with six other men and take it in turns to breathe in and out for lack of space... Every night we dine in a red-tiled Valhalla with trophies of armour and pistols and swords round the walls. The officers join us three days a week and on Mondays the orchestra (the RMC Band) plays in the musicians' alcove. It seems like a cross between the Cadena Cafe in peace-time, a garrison theatre and an officers' mess. Some of the cadets preen themselves in their mufti and act as though they were already in the officer class. When we have dined we can retire to the ante-rooms for coffee. The chief characteristic of these rooms is a series of pictorial variations on the haggard soldier theme: haggard soldier less entrails, h.s. gasping for water, h.s. saying farewell to wife and child, h.s. dropping glad eye to

19th century A.T., h.s. shouting 'Floreat Etona' and so on until h.s. becomes the unknown warrior.[27]

Cadets are treated as all-but officers – very gratifying. We have the most gracious set of officer instructors – exquisite Guards officers, a dashing young Captain in cherry-red trousers from the 11th Hussars, a Commandant who talks sense, carries himself superbly and turns out at 6.45 a.m. to join us in P.T. and a charmingly foul-mouthed young campaigner from the RTC. They are all slimly tailored to make you swoon.

24th October 1942

I am confined by a strange affliction known as 'assault heel'. The last compels me to move on permanent tiptoe and has taught me to cool my ardour to resemble dashing young subalterns in prints of the Zulu War. It felt grand to leap off a fifteen-foot log-pile, rifle in hand and all that but army boots were not built to act as cushions.

…We have spent a comical morning at the army school of hygiene studying the sanitary applications of old tin cans, bits of string and almost any odds and ends of salvage. It should convince you of our efficiency to know that we study soldiering from the backside as well as from the right, left and front.

November 1942 from the Wildernesses of Wales

Life has been full of minor tribulations (e.g. yawning on parade when the RSM was speaking) and major trials such as moving on foot in full battle order for 6 miles in 50 minutes. And then to cap everything, they send us to Pembroke by night train and make us begin a firing course as soon as we arrive in the morning. So three cheers for the indomitable spirit of English cadets!

28th January 1943, Sandhurst

At present you would find me a somewhat distraught companion. Some battering rugger and torturing P.T. have altered my body from something human to something mechanical. And fierce

---

27 A.T. refers to a member of the ATS, the Auxiliary Territorial Service which was the women's branch of the British Army. Ann Pugh herself joined the ATS and served as an army driver.

attempts to read Morse at 12 words per minute threaten to reduce my brain to a quivering nervous pulp – it has even led me to renounce tobacco for a week. Just to cheer us in this troublesome life we must slow march tomorrow at the military funeral of a cadet who was caught in the track of his tank – bags of military bearing and smartness with a minimum of mournfulness.

3rd February

Our last week has been great fun. We have toured the Thames Valley from Marlow to Oxford and have explored Ruritania from Princes Risborough to Basingstoke. I say Ruritania because our maps were entirely overprinted with foreign names and we could never ask our way because we did not know the equivalent English names. John Briggs and I had a very charming ATS driver called Suzanne who added plenty to the entertainment of the trip. She was only too willing to streak across Oxfordshire from café to café and pub to pub. By Friday morning I was over 10 shillings in debt. Alfresco living is as good or bad as one cares to make it and as our truck was bursting with humour we made it very good.

Ann Pugh, Reg Hibbert's fellow student at Oxford and future wife.

18th February

If you hear that I am in the army for life, don't be surprised. I have signed for a Cruiser tank of which I am appointed commander and have therefore pledged my penniless estate for £15,000 of H.M.'s property. If I lose it or set it on fire or run it over a cliff etc., I shall have to pay for it in weekly pay stoppages... As matters stand, or hustle at present, odd weekends will be unobtainable. Sunday seems destined to become a day of labour on tank log-books, record sheets and report forms.

27th February Cambridge Military Hospital, Aldershot

As you can see from the address, I have retired from the turmoils of the world for a few days of boredom and rest. I am really quite fit but as my jaw is fractured and lacerated I have to undergo all the torments reserved for the worst invalids. My mouth is now wired tight shut so that I can neither talk nor eat and I am confined to bed for lack of food and loss of blood.

It all happened this way. I was commanding my precious tank across country at a fairly fast speed when it hit some hidden obstacle and bounced. Several tons of steel hit me under the chin and the turret flap added to the party by breaking loose on top of me.

Since then I have been having the hell of a time. All the x-ray enthusiasts and specialists and dental surgeons thought I was fair meat and had me touring the hospital on their little tumbrils looking grimy and bloody enough to be Robespierre on his way to the guillotine. However I had my own back by trying to break everyone else's jaw in the theatre. One RAMC sergeant has grown a fine black eye as a result.

Now that this has happened, I have not the least idea when I shall be able to see you again. I shall probably be 'retarded' at Sandhurst.

4th March

The rest of the ward tends to regard me as an unusual sort of patient. They suspect me of unconventionality in such things as being visited, taking tea with the Sisters, staying in bed when there is work to do and conversing in halting languages with wounded Italians.

We are very busy this morning as all those of us who are out of bed have to help the nurses with a glut of candidates for the theatre. Nothing to beat it for officer training – man-management of the unconscious, blood by the pint and even a little unarmed combat with a shaggy Pioneer.[28][29]

6th March

I have been watching the smart uniforms of a few enemy airmen most of the afternoon. They all look disconcertingly upright and clean. It is useful to have read history to guard against being too easily impressed by a good German military bearing.

7th March

It is a great pity that I should have christened my majority in blood and ether [he had turned 21 on 21 February]. I shall not now be commissioned until May.

14th March

Ward 26 has been darkened by the advent of another of our cadets, the Hon… potential Grenadier. The other ranks cannot stand him. He was 20 two days ago and is intolerably coltish. He picks on me as a target for his one-man conversations and the other ranks pick on me as a target for their impolite opinions on officers and gentlemen who are not fit to be cadets. And the Sisters and Nurses ask me with astonishment whether we keep any more like the Hon. at Sandhurst. Diplomacy has thrust itself to the fore and I am more than usually busy being all things to all men.

I hope to be discharged from hospital before the end of next fortnight. The surgeon cuts my wires next Friday.

---

28 The Royal Pioneer Corps was a combat corps used for logistical and technical tasks ranging from stretcher bearing, laying tracks on beaches, moving and handling stores and equipment to building airfields and temporary bridges.

29 All these activities turned out to be useful training for life in the field in Albania.

17th March

I have acquired a new hobby, a Free French airman who sleeps next to me and speaks not a word of English. There is no one else who can talk to him so that I have had to assume ambassadorial functions on behalf of the C.O., the M.O., Matron, Sisters, Nurses and Orderlies. My accent through my teeth has a Jean Gabin nuance – but no one appreciates that. Some of the hospital staff ask the most word-bound and untranslatable sentences but Pierre and I get our own back by indulging in mountainous conversations which bring forth no more than a mousy 'yes' or 'no' for the doctors.

4th April Normandy Avenue, Barnet

I was discharged yesterday morning, granted 36 hours leave by my Squadron Commander and will start work with 26 Troop, D Sqn. tomorrow.

11th April Sandhurst

I shall be paying a flying visit to London on Wednesday in order to be interviewed by a Major of the 4th Hussars at the Cavalry Club, Piccadilly at 5.30 p.m. I may then go hunting for a regimental tailor.

26 Troop is none too pleasant compared with the departed 15 Troop heroes. Of course things are not what they were.

22nd April

Rogers have shown much assiduity in their tailoring. I hope to be in London for a final fitting on Wednesday. After Wednesday we shall disappear to camp with our tanks, not to return until the eve of our passing-out parade on Friday 7 May.

The officer atmosphere is beginning to grow in our troop. There is talk of regiments and mess procedure, applications for commissioned pay are being filled out, a signature with 2nd Lieut. appended has been encouraged. Yet one more victim was 'retarded' from our troop today and the threat still lingers.

Thursday

Passing-out parade is now timed for 11.30 a.m. ... have you found my chin-strap in your handbag? Could you post it to me as soon as possible? Despite dust and oil and sweat.

DIARY

17th May 1943

Into harness once more. Nine days of leave have been enough to make Sandhurst very distant. Once more we glow with newness and publish it for all the world to see by our studied pose of independent dignity. But the regiment herds us into a 15cwt truck – life will not be very different after all. [At Welbeck] no one takes any notice of us: the mess is open to us, nothing more. Thus the new prefects find that the first day of term is not an occasion but threadbare routine. Only in our communal tent are we once again grown to our newly-won Atlas stature.

18th May

Welbeck is explored – a beautiful ducal park lying trimly and hospitably behind woodlands which screen, tactfully, the ducal mining villages. A regiment could ask for no better summer station nor a more delightfully sylvan tank station... The Lancashire Fusiliers greet us cheerfully but even the promises of their pep-talks cannot find us work. The War Office says we are to be trained but the colonel says we are to be amused pro-tem. We are offered panem et circenses. As men we don't object but as officers we need something more.

26th May

Jim Phillips departs on draft to join the 4th Hussars. We had hoped to leave England together but the army always breaks up friends, making regiments into business corporations rather than the 'families' which haunt the dreams of Cols. Rtd.

28th June

A regimental scheme and road march begins. Providence and the C.O. agree to let the attached officers play too – in nice harmless positions as front-guards, Sqn. Guides etc.. I am lucky as I am given command of the regimental recce troop – 4 carriers, 8 men and three other subalterns – my first command! With great self-importance I attend the C.O.'s order group with the

Majors, Adjutants and other such dignitaries. Lt.Col. Ponsonby is a charming man … but he should chase us more and insist on first-class, super-soldiering. Instead he is content with an officer who does his work quietly, efficiently and responsibly with no flap and no questions. So I say 'Yes, Sir', salute smartly, rouse the Recce Troop and get cracking. The C.O.'s method is good if his subordinates are good and hard-working. But it does nothing to protect troops from lazy, ignorant, stupid and 'creeping' officers. But perhaps these men can never be eliminated. Perhaps the C.O. is right.

However, the Recce Troop starts off keenly, racing along and enjoying all the cheap thrills of traffic control in a carrier. A regiment of Shermans looks most awe-inspiring as it erupts around a corner at speed, leaving the road looking like a ribbon of lava and deafening the astounded bystanders. We have good carrier crews and my driver is first class. We harbour very comfortably near Leicester, the Carrier Troop having fortified its morale all day at convenient cafés etc. Such is the benefit of an independent mission!

23rd July

Off to Midhope for some firing. Lovely weather in the foothills of the Pennines as a good start! I am in charge of a 75mm gun – a cushy job but range-work is fairly tiring. In the evening we visit Stocksbridge under Major Royds' guidance… Stocksbridge gives a shock to Southerners with its huge foundry, palls of smoke, drab streets and neglected children. Everyone is a bit chilled but Major Royds and Sgt. Roddy warm us with some wrestling. What would the War Office say to the spectacle of a field-officer and an NCO grovelling on the ground together – both equally tight?

24th July

A day of steady uneventful firing and thirsty work. At night we spend precious petrol on a fifteen mile trip to Wakefield in search of amusement. I find a man-trap of a barmaid and a charming WAAF. Wakefield has a prudish atmosphere about it but we spend a wild enough night.

25th July

I manage to get a shoot when routine firing is finished... During the day a mysterious call is made for immediate volunteers for parachute duties. Duncan Williams and I send in our names in hope of some cheap thrills. Sgt. Flanagan gives us his blessing and tells that we should do well together. We should like to know more about the job. We return to Welbeck and en route Major Royds demonstrates again his free and easy methods of man-management by halting the column outside a pub and dismissing all ranks for a drink. He gets away with it – so three cheers for Major Royds!

27th July

Very little is happening at Welbeck but I am detailed to start at midnight for Oxford with the other ranks for an interview about the parachuting business. In the afternoon the regiment holds its sports meeting. They do all the right things – a band, a bar, plenty of tugs-of-war and brilliant sunshine. In the Mess in the morning some newcomer from the Wimbledon Arts School tries to tell us what we are fighting for – apparently in the name of art for art's sake... However, we start at midnight on what proves to be a fairly comfortable journey, at least as far as King's Cross.

28th July

Our arrival at Water Eaton Manor with several other RAC. officers and other men is shrouded in secrecy.[30] Then suddenly half a dozen officers are gathered in one of the old rooms of this lovely house and told that our parachute duties will take us into [the Balkans]

---

30 The RAC was the Royal Armoured Corps which included Hibbert's own regiment, the 4th Queen's Own Hussars. Originally a cavalry regiment formed in 1685, the 4th Hussars was mechanised in 1936 and became a tank regiment. The regiment played a significant part in the Charge of the Light Brigade during the Crimean War. It was also Winston Churchill's regiment. In the Second World War it distinguished itself in the Italian Campaign, Hibbert's next assignment after Albania. In 1958 the 4th and 8th Hussars were amalgamated.

as liaison officers to help the [guerrillas there].[31] It sounds like an excellent job and we are swiftly interviewed, examined medically and accepted. The interviewing officers are most pleasant and genial. The Manor House is a romantic spot for hatching Ruritanian plans but copies of the Official Secrets Act remind us that even Ruritania can be at war. Once accepted we were away to start embarkation leave, reaching Welbeck again shortly after midnight, busy with exotic dreams about a new future in occupied Europe.

29th July

It wastes much time to pack and draw tropical kit but I am at last free from the hearty boredom of Welbeck.[32] My going is envied by many. The other officers have some very kind things to say. My own one-pipped friends say a cheerful farewell. The sergeants are all enthusiastic to give volunteers for parachute duties a good send-off. Welbeck has a pleasant taste when I leave it and an embarkation welcome greets me when I reach home. This week will evidently be very full of handshakes.

31st July

Lunch with Ann gives the weekend an ideal start and we talk much about ourselves. We part regretfully so that I can join the family at Henley in perfect Henley weather. I travel with Father and tell him, as I have already told Ann, my secret that I am a volunteer for Airborne duties. No one else can know as yet. The self-discipline of keeping such a secret makes embarkation leave a more sober affair than I expected. No doubt it is better for it to be sober and normal and one is then less conscious of departure. But already I feel the loss of those five days of freedom which I have volunteered away for the sake of the Balkans and their suffering.

---

31 Hibbert clearly realised that while he was brazenly keeping a clandestine diary, naming his destination was a step too far, having signed the Official Secrets Act that very day, and he carefully obliterated them. The words in brackets are guessed at but are fairly obvious.

32 Tropical kit was required for the weeks of training Hibbert was to receive in Egypt before deployment in Albania.

'The Manor House is a romantic spot for hatching Ruritanian plans'. (Motacilla/Wikimedia Commons)

6th August

Ann and I exhaust ourselves in a shopping tour of London. Ann refuses all offers to shop for her and I am too weary to find anything exquisite for her. In the evening a frightful flick with a trailer of a film about Jugoslav guerrillas. This gives me some secret amusement in the circumstances.

8th August

With little stir I slip away. Mother and Father and Ann see me off at Paddington. Civilians have the harder part but they take it well and I manage to be gone before I realise it. Soon the club-life of the army whirls me away and we bed down at Water Eaton in the familiar atmosphere of unthinking, instinctive heartiness. I don't know why, but men gathered together are always like that. Some must find it very lonely. Still I do not know the significance of what is behind me or what is in front.

CAIRO

August-December 1943

Hibbert does not record the weeks spent in Egypt preparing for his Albanian assignment in his diary. What follows is composed of extracts from his letters to his parents and his account of that time in his book, Albania's National Liberation Struggle: The Bitter Victory.[33]

When a circular came round asking for volunteers for special duties couched in seductively mysterious language, I jumped at it. I was accepted in a cursory interview and in no time found myself sailing from Liverpool to Alexandria in a convoy which was one of the first to go through the Mediterranean following the invasion of Sicily.

To his parents, no date or address

I am writing this in the hope that we shall soon see some dry land with post offices. This letter will probably be delayed in the interests of security. I am at present a fish out of water, a soldier at sea. I am enjoying the trip as I belong to the minority which is not seasick. A troopship does not afford a luxury cruise. I can tell you nothing of the vivid interests of the last fortnight. We have had a glimpse of sea and air power in action.

To his parents, 5th September 1943

For the present I am waiting, like everyone else to be posted somewhere in the not-too-distant-future. I must warn you now that when this happens mail will become difficult.

I am thankful that I did not come overseas in the ranks. On the ship, private soldiers were well fed but terribly crowded, overheated, stuffed together and shut in. Our overcrowding was at least relieved by fresh air but on rough or hot days their quarters were intolerable.

Our first view of the fabulous orient included a filthy sea, some mud and sand and a choice selection of hoardings which advertised nothing but whiskies and gins. Every local who walked past was either a policeman or a hawker-cum-beggar-cum-odd-job man. On the railway, train 3 arrived before train 1 and both turned up as a surprise to destination officials on the day after

---

33 Reginald Hibbert, *Albania's National Liberation Struggle: The Bitter Victory* (London: Pinter Publishers Ltd, 1991) pp. 87-8.

they were due. At every station on the way we halted long enough outside for us all to grow hungry and thirsty and then we were hauled alongside a platform full of excited vendors who sold us anything and everything at rarity prices and called us all majors. Most of them had an engaging mastery of English as not spoken in drawing rooms. They had gathered some astonishing accents and oaths from our predecessors on the trains. We made our own contribution to their knowledge of civilised manners when we heard their prices.

At first we were quartered in a desert area with sand and bare cliffs and flies and a burning blue sky – what the armies out here have been enduring for most of the war – a life which really does consist of nothing.

Since moving from our sandy tents we have lived in palatial quarters. In a fine house with a good Mess, we are near enough to European entertainments and society. For a few days we can read and write and lounge and dine at leisure. And to do all these things without blackout at the windows adds to the pleasure. In the afternoons we generally swim and sunbathe and play games and perspire, leaving work to the mornings and evenings. Some of our party have been unwell but most of us have been and are very fit.

The material differences between the lives of a white man and a brown man in this part of the world are at first astonishing. You get the impression that everyone in the country works for white men or for European importers. Recent history seems to show that some of the leading natives have had the same impression. And so nationalism begins.

From *The Bitter Victory*

In Cairo I reported to MO4 (soon to become Force 133) at Rustum Buildings where everything was secret but you could see maps of Balkan countries if you stood outside looking in when the lights were turned on in the evenings.[34] A course in paramilitary activities, sabotage, demolition and assorted weapons followed at the SOE school on Mount Carmel at Haifa

---

34 Patrick Leigh Fermor recounted that Rustum Building was known as 'secret building' to Cairo's taxi drivers.

and after that came the parachute school at Ramat David near Nazareth. I found that Albania was to be my lot and I was given a certain amount of briefing on it by Mrs Hasluck and others but nothing illuminating.[35] Perhaps the biggest surprise of the training period was that no one seemed to bother much about the language problem, although there were a few desultory Albanian lessons. Having reasonable French and passable German, I was, in comparison with many fellow officers, well equipped though not perhaps for Albania.

Major Philip Leake was in charge of the Albanian section at Rustum Buildings and there were two or three staff officers under him.[36] They were part of the new military structure which was replacing MO4's less formal organization. In early December 1943 it was officially designated as Force 133 under G.H.Q. Middle East.[37] In the Albanian section no one except Margaret Hasluck had any Albanian background. She and her colleagues tried to pull together a coherent picture of events from the pieces of paper which passed across their desks and constituted the only available intelligence. They reeled out bewildering sets of names, attaching LNÇ, Zogist, Ballist or simply 'nationalist' as the information at their disposal dictated; and they could quote dozens of unrelated events and movements and military engagements which had been reported from all parts of the country; but it was impossible to derive from all this any clear impression of the forces at work in

---

35 Margaret Hasluck was described by one SOE officer as an elderly, grey-haired, blue-eyed lady 'full of energy and enthusiasm ... totally dedicated to her beloved Albania' (Smiley, *Albanian Assignment, op. cit.*, p. 8).

36 Major Philip Leake was parachuted into Albania in May 1944 but was killed there a month later.

37 SOE's organisation consisted of several sections, each responsible for a different country. Sections were often switched according to how events were turning out in the war. The section responsible for Albania when Hibbert was recruited was MO4 based in Cairo, a title adopted from a First World War branch of the British General Headquarters there which had supported the Arab revolt against the Ottomans and still carried the reflected glory of T. E. Lawrence (Lawrence of Arabia). In 1943, MO4 was renamed Force133. In April 1944 responsibility for Yugoslavia and Albania passed to Special Operations Mediterranean (SOM) under Force 266 in Bari, Italy.

Albania. Much more interesting were the emotional forces at work in Cairo between some of the officers, and between officers and FANYs, but we fledgling BLOs [British Liaison Officers] did not stay long enough to become well versed in this or any other study.[38] Very few facts … came to our attention, and then only in an unconnected anecdotal way. We remained simpletons as far as Albanian affairs were concerned.

When I left Cairo I carried two little pieces of paper. One was signed by Major Leake and read:

'You will proceed as arranged to SNOOD on the morning of November 8th.[39] From SNOOD you will proceed, weather permitting, by air (Operation CRUCIBLE: Sortie Stables2) on or about November 11th. to the STABLES Party Dropping Area near PESHKOPI, where you will land by parachute. Reception will be arranged by Major RIDDELL, Area Liaison Officer, DEBRA, and Officer i/c STABLES Party. On arrival you will place yourself under Major RIDDELL.'

The other was in Albanian and English and was signed M.Hasluck. It read:

'Friends of mine in Albania, Lt. Hibbert who brings you this letter is an Englishman and my friend. As you received me well when I asked you for a pretty folk-story or questioned you about the Bektashis or the Kanun of Lek the Great, please receive this Englishman also, like the hospitable people you are. Friends that I never forget, I send you my best wishes.'

---

38 The FANY is the First Aid Nursing Yeomanry. It was originally set up in 1907 to provide first aid in emergencies, recruiting women who could ride. Their wartime work started in France in 1914. In the Second World War it provided nurses, drivers, wireless operators and other support staff across the globe in different theatres of war. There were two thousand in SOE with many FANY members acting as agents in the field, particularly in France. Today it still provides emergency help to civilians and the military.

39 SNOOD was the codename for Tocra airfield, near Benghazi in Libya, the base of 334 Wing and 148 Squadron of the RAF.

ALBANIA

December 1943-October 1944

Reg Hibbert, Albania, 1944.

YUGOSLAVIA

N

Gjakova

KOSOVA

Vlad

Degë

Kepenek

White Drin

Trun

Prizren

Shkodër

Drin

Kukës

Bicaj

Ujmisht

Shkavec

Rec

Vilë

Cajë

Dardhë

Kalis

Ceren

Radomirë

Shëngjin

Fushë-Lurë

Mt.Korab

Rrëshen

Kastriot

Sllatine

Sllovë

Adriatic
Sea

Kalaj

Macukull

Limjan

Peshkopi

Gramë

Mat

Burgajet

Black Drin

Grevë

Burrel

Lis

Maqellarë

Patin

Dibra

Krujë

Klos

Mukjë

Xibër

Guribardhe

MACEDONIA

Martanesh

Okshtun

Frontier
1941-45

TIRANA

Shengjergj

Bizë

Gurakuq

Durrës

Labinot

Librazhd

Struga

Elbasan

Ohrid

Shkumbin

Pre-1941
Frontier

Lake Ohrid

Northern and Central Albania

© S.Ballard (2019)

December 19th 1943

An early take-off from Snood with the same good crew in O for Orange. Slight delays and airborne at 16.25 hours. A peaceful flight and no cloud over northern Albania. We dress and wait and I hardly realise that that tonight we shall parachute. Our sergeant dispatcher is very excited but finally shouts "Action stations!... Go!" and I find myself 2000 feet above Albania, horrified to see how distant the signal fires are. There is no moon, but I land happily one foot from a river and see my first Albanians. Then follow greetings with Neel, Hands and Kemp, Brendrick and Smith and with my fellow 'joes'.[40] Some rum, some food and plenty of sleep in a little Albanian cottage. A romantic night and a memorable one, ending in an opera-bouffe brigand scene.

December 20th-26th

All our kit has been stolen – a good introduction to this people! Any of our remaining illusions are broken as we listen to Kemp and co. and watch several political conferences with local leaders.[41] There is little hope of a lively war here. Meanwhile, we ride, sleep, eat well and drink raki. Our Christmas is excellent. With Andy's Italians and Albanians we feast luxuriously and drink our toasts in Chianti, cognac, raki and Cinzano. Even Mehmet Hoxha, the Partisan, grows indiscreet and confidential – though we cannot persuade him to speak about a Serb who was present at one of our conferences. Rem Hoxha appears fresh from a fight with the Germans – the only bright spot in the gloomy outlook for allied policy in in this land. Most Missions seem to be in hiding and out of communication with Cairo. Where is Stables? Where is the Brigadier?[42] Merrett

---

40 Squadron Leader (later Wing Commander) Tony Neel, Major Peter Kemp, Flight Lieutenant (later Squadron Leader) Arthur 'Andy' Hands.

41 Major Peter Kemp (1915-93), who served in Albania from August 1943 to February 1944, wrote his own detailed record of his time there which provides lively portraits of many of the personalities mentioned in Hibbert's diary and an engaging account of events in the field. He had fought on the nationalist side in the Spanish Civil War and was strongly opposed to communism. In 1944 he went on to serve with SOE in Poland. See Kemp, *No Colours or Crest, op. cit.*

42 Brigadier 'Trotsky' Davies had parachuted into Albania in October 1943 to take overall command of the Missions in the field.

and I set off to recce the Kepenek chrome mines, but our guide prefers the comforts of Degë and so leads us astray. Such, we are told, is the way of all military operations in this country.

December 27th

Kemp and Hibberdine set off for Kossovo and Hasan Bey and a meeting of chiefs at Tetovo.[43] Neel leaves to meet Ymer Bardoshi. The three of us who remain plan to attack the Prizren-Scutari road. Meanwhile, as the charging engine is broken, we have to sweat at the hand generator. Are rewarded by hearing from London that the Scharnhorst is sunk.

Major Richard Riddell (third from right) with Major Peter Kemp (centre) and Captain Alan Hare (left). The Albanian next to Riddell is a nationalist fighter giving the Zogist salute and wearing the traditional white cap. The cap was never worn by the communist Partisans.

---

43 Both Lt. Ian Merrett and Lt. John Hibberdine had parachuted in with Hibbert. All three were sent to assist officers in the field, Hibberdine to Major Peter Kemp, Merrett to Major Tony Neel and Hibbert to Major Richard Riddell. The operations of these individual officers had code names. Riddell's was Stables. Others included Spillway (Brigadier Davies' HQ at Bizë near Tirana), and Slender (covering the Krujë and Mat areas). Hibbert had parachuted into Sq. Ldr. Andy Hands' Spinster territory at Degë in the Kukës region. Stables did not have a fixed base at this point.

December 28th

A letter from Stables! Mehmet Ali Bajraktari of Has arrives and presents a message carefully concealed by Major Riddell in a match box, but sealed by Muharrem B. in an envelope.[44] I shall move south with Goodier, Elvidge and a radio tomorrow. After seven days of rain, snow is now falling steadily. The march will be an arduous one.

December 29th

With two mules, three Englishmen and nine Albanians, my column moves off. Orlando, Amerigo, Angelo and Luigi have made our stay at Degë most comfortable – not to mention Xhiko who has been first-class.[45] The march through snow to Berisht is hard. Andy's dog Lulë joins us – an untouchable, self-contained, independent dog. At Berisht for the first time we begin to go native.[46]

---

44 Muharrem B. refers to Muharrem Bajraktari (1896-1989), nicknamed Lord of Lumë, a leading clan chieftain from the Lumë region of northern Albania on the borders of what is now Kosova. He was an early leader of the nationalist resistance to the Axis powers in Albania. A former aide-de-camp to King Zog, he spent time in Paris in the late 1930s after the invasion of Albania by the Italians and the flight into exile of Zog. Returning in 1939, he joined the monarchist Legaliteti movement aiming to restore the throne and rallied a local war band. After the communist victory in 1944 he fled to France and then Belgium where he was active in the Albanian Committee and later, during the Cold War, in the CIA-assisted National Committee for Free Albania.

45 Orlando, Amerigo, Angelo and Luigi and others were Italian Alpini servicemen who had given themselves up to the Albanians after the Italian surrender in September 1943. They made themselves useful to the BLOs as orderlies, farriers, cooks, bakers, barbers and even cobblers. While the armistice instructed Italian combatants to cease fighting and move to Allied territory, the Italian army in the Balkan Peninsula was offered no further instructions. In order to avoid being shipped off to forced labour in Germany, 'some in Yugoslavia, Albania and Greece chose to join the Partisans rather than surrender to the Germans'. B. Moore, 'The Fate of Italian Prisoners of War during the Second World War', *War in History*, 22 (Enforced Diaspora 2), 2015, 174-190, p. 10. http://eprints.whiterose.ac.uk/90913/2.

46 By 'going native' Hibbert meant learning and observing the etiquette and rituals associated with being a guest in an Albanian house, often the home of a local chieftain.

December 30th

We move to Helshun and sleep in the house of the local *bajraktar*.[47] We are entertained well and are evidently travelling under the very best patronage. We need it, for the nationalist countryside is suspicious of English actions and German house-burnings. The mules are not very fit – one has bad harness sores, the other has cast three shoes. And our Albanians are too idle to help us improve their condition.

December 31st 1943

We march to the Kukës road and cross it by night, after crossing the Drin by ferry at Vauspas. Ymer Bardoshi escorts us here – a flashy and unpleasant man who constantly shows off with his sub-machine gun. A great comedy of silence and secrecy is played as we crossed the road, and in just revenge two lorries of German troops swing round the corner behind us as we cross the vital fifty yards of bridge and road between our two mountain paths. We leap over the edge of the bridge, which is fortunately only 8 feet high at my end. As I look up I see enemy cigarettes glowing in the lorries as they pass within a few yards. All the cards are on our side, but the Albanians are terrified. If the lorries stopped, three Englishmen would find themselves alone; and one of those, Goodier, is shaken. Mehmet Ali Bajraktari embraces me too generously, expressing his enormous relief, and we march on by night by bad paths to a mountain hovel where we eat and rest, disturbed only by a fire in the roof for twenty minutes. Thus we see the new year in.

---

47 *Bajraktar*, meaning 'standard bearer', is the title given to an Albanian clan chieftain. It originates from the seventeenth-century Ottoman word *bajrak* designating a territorial area consisting of a group of villages typically located in remoter areas of the Ottoman Empire such as Kosova and Albania and from which military irregulars would be drawn. The *bajrak* would be based on one or two clans (*fis*) in a given area who would be led by the *bajraktar*. It has much in common with the Balkan Slav *voivod* who would lead a *çeta* or band of warriors connected by kinship, obligation, tradition or advantage.

Ferry on the Drin river.

1st January 1944

Before dawn we are marching again and reach Lumë before we eat. Lumë is a most lovely spot, looking down towards Prizren and up to Peshkopijë. The young son of the household assures me that he is a captain – a sure sign of the fancy-dress war in these parts. From Ibrahim's we move to Ujmisht and are feasted on sheep and politics. We can see Muharrem's area across the Drin, but it will take a five-hour march to reach it.

2nd January

On to meet Muharrem Bajraktari. Our reception is excellent – as also is the food. Muharrem has a good business mind but is not a pleasant man. He has obviously seen more of the world than just Albania; but he would like to make Albania a world of his own. Muharrem's brother, Bairam, is very pleasant and also his sons. A luxurious night of sleep free from Albanian companions.

3rd January

Our mule is shoed and we march on to Reç to stay with Mehmet Troci. He is a pleasant and apparently honest host. For the first time women appear in the same room as ourselves – unmarriageable women (i.e. the old and the very young). Some superb apples and an exchange of pidgin Anglo-Albanian with Mehmet and a promise of our journey's end tomorrow.

4th January

We present Muharrem's letter at Ibrahim Halili's. Ibrahim is absent, but his brothers have news of British officers in Kalis, two hours distant. Some honey and *buk* (bread) and we push on for fear that the rumoured officers might vanish. Kalis is a lovely valley and we see it in snow and sunshine, full of brilliant peasant dresses and the music of the hoarse Albanian flutes. A fine pastoral introduction, against a background of poplars in steep brown-green meadows, to the Stables military mission. After contemplating this union of Paul Nash and Breughel I am greeted by Richard Riddell, Tony Simcox and Michael Lis.[48] We drink raki punch and swap news and plan to leave Halili's hospitality tomorrow.[49]

5th January

A snowstorm prevents us from moving. We have time to look about. Stables appears to be a happy company; but it has no H.Q. and an unattractive band of parasite followers. I don't understand the status of Xhelal [Ndreu], an unpaid local notable who acts as interpreter and organiser: he does not impress me.[50] The radio opens up; but the operators fail to reach Cairo every time. We wind madly at the charging engine. The radio must function soon.

---

48 In the following diary entries 'Tony' refers to Capt. Tony Simcox. Capt. Michael Lis (1908-94) was a Polish officer who had attached himself to Major Richard Riddell's mission. Born Michal Gradowski, he took on the pseudonym 'Lis' from the Polish for 'fox'. Some accounts say that he was originally sent into Albania to open an escape route from Poland, others that SOE had an interest in having him contact Polish slave labourers held by the Germans in Albania.

49 Raki was home-distilled spirits, usually made from grapes but also from other fruit. Amery reported in his diary how their Albanian helpers would set up improvised stills in camp. It played a central part in all Albanian gatherings and social occasions.

50 At this time the Stables mission was still reliant on the goodwill of the Ndreu family whose houses in Sllovë near Dibrë had been burned down by the Germans in November 1943 shortly before Hibbert's arrival. Xhelal Ndreu was the son of a prominent local chieftain or *bajraktar* in the Peshkopijë region of central northern Albania and was acting as interpreter and organiser. Some members of the extensive Ndreu family, however, were associated with the LNÇ and Enver Hoxha.

6th January

A most uncomfortable march in snow and freezing wind and moonlight to Ali Solimani's house. There a chilly and barren meal, and then a further march up the mountain through snowdrifts and ice to our dropping ground at Dardhë. A smoky and inhospitable hovel receives us; but we are happy to sleep anywhere under a roof.

7th, 8th, 9th, 10th January

Difficulties begin. Stables evidently does not recce its dropping grounds but relies on Xhelal's advice. His advice seems bad. Our followers are undisciplined and overcrowd the cottage. The radio operates with difficulty. Charging by hand is awkward. Ali Dikë is not a brilliant interpreter. We change our house with no better result. We are accepted only as a source of profit. Omens are not good for the drop.[51]

11th-14th January

Constant troubles about fires and food and sentries and men.[52] We move further into Dardhë – the people fear the Germans and reject us, so we move back a little and stay halfway with a comfortable and hospitable family. The radio is not well operated but we receive an XXX message at last. As we stand by [for a drop] the local chiefs

---

51 The Stables mission was still unaware of the destruction of Brigadier 'Trotsky' Davies' headquarters at Bizë, near Tirana, and the wounding of the Brigadier himself. At the time Davies and his team were not only supposed to be coordinating the BLO missions throughout Albania but were working closely with the LNÇ communist Partisans who were in a weakened position in northern Albania. On 8th January the Bizë HQ was attacked by a group of collaborationists and nationalists augmented by Germans. During his escape Davies was shot and wounded which led to his eventual capture and handing over to the Germans. Opposition to the Germans in northern Albania was fragmented by the weakening and dispersal of LNÇ Partisan çetas [bands of warriors], the reluctance of chieftains to become proactive and a dread of German reprisals among the population. The task of missions such as Stables to organise and coordinate resistance was made even more difficult by the harsh winter conditions in the mountains.

52 Food was a constant concern. Other BLOs' accounts also repeatedly refer to food. Julian Amery records in his diary on June 10 1943 that they had had an arduous trek 'with no food only white mulberries'.

make a colossal row about their organisation. They are Xhelal's and Cen Elezi's men yet Xhelal has left us.[53] What is in the wind? Great excitement when the planes come. Stables 5 drops perfectly from 300 feet, Stables 3 from over 2,000 feet at 160 degrees and 2 kilometres from the fires. With some trouble we gather Stables 5 together and carry it to the nearby cottage. Stealing begins, led by our own employees. I fire on one chief and he shows his true colours. We lose little but grow very tired. We reserve Stables 3 for the morning.

A group of leading Dibra *bajraktars*. Murat Kaloshi, head of the Kaloshi family and grandfather of Dan Kaloshi, is seated with Cen Elez Ndreu holding beads to the left.

---

53 Cen Elez Ndreu (1884-1949), full name Hysen Elez Ndreu, was an influential clan chieftain or *bajraktar* originating in Dibra and a powerful local personality in the Reç and Peshkopijë area. He bore the *nom de guerre* Cen, 'Zeal'. His father Elez Isuf had fought for Albanian independence in the last years of the Ottoman Empire. Ali Dikë, another interpreter and go-between who was also of the wider Ndreu family, was hostile to Cen Elezi and close to another family, the Litas. These complex family relationships were an additional complication of the BLOs' mission. After the Partisan victory Cen Elezi fled to Yugoslavia but was returned to Albania and executed by Enver Hoxha's regime. Cen Elezi has been described as 'a thin fierce-looking old man with white hair, bright blue eyes and a querulous arrogant manner; his vigorous personality was reinforced by qualities of initiative and courage'. Kemp, *No Colours or Crest, op. cit.*, p. 170.

15th-16th January

The citizens of Dardhë steal most of Stables 3. Tony and I manage to rescue some items and I take a little material to Solimani's house and find some horses, only to meet crisis on my return. The chiefs of Dardhë refuse to let the material leave their village. Xhelal has led us into a highly organised robbery centre. We decide to sit on the volcano and wait, Tony and Goodier with the material and Elvidge and I with the radio. In the morning Richard and Michael arrive with Dan [Ramadan] Kaloshi, having found Sgt Gregson and Davis.[54] They came from Maçakull and Lurës after meeting Captain Bulman with Slender and brushing with German patrols.[55] Seymour and Smythe are reported very ill and in hiding. Bulman is uncomfortably near the Germans at Burelë.[56]

Dan Kaloshi does not like our situation; nor do we. After a day of disputes and robbery we finally cut our losses and slip out with a little material by a back path while the villagers mass at the front. Dan's men are as little to be trusted as other Albanians, but Richard desires to placate them. Once at Solimani's, they do not wish to help us remove the material. Some is robbed: much causes quarrels. We sleep with our property.

17th January

I go before dawn with Dan Kaloshi and men into Reç to find horses. Dan makes no effort to help, leaving me at Ibrahim Halili's. The chaos is complete. I return at midday to find Tony at the Drin bridge hiding

---

54 Dan Kaloshi was a local leader in Dibra from another prominent family and a close associate of Major Richard Riddell at this time. After taking refuge in Yugoslavia after the war, he was returned and killed by the new communist regime in Albania. Julian Amery, who served with SOE in Albania for a few months in 1943 and again in 1944, described him in his diary as 'a dark, rather brooding young man with flashes of humour'.

55 Captain Jack Bulman. Slender was another British Mission. Under Brigadier Davies' orders, Captain Frank Smythe was moving north to meet up with Tony Neel. He was joined by Captain George Seymour who had been liaising with nationalist leaders. While Hibbert and Kemp consistently spell his name Smythe, some historians refer to him as Smyth.

56 Burelë is now known as Burrel.

BFCs on the mountainside.[57] Horses and the Major [Riddell] arrive at last but so do the Partisans. I must climb back to the dropping ground with them to collect the remnants of the mortar – a rotten night.

18th January

With our new and careful follower Ali from Dardhë – the Lot of that Sodom and Gomorrah – I walk at dawn to Mehmet Troci's house. There we find some peace at last – a safe store room and a room to ourselves. We still need eyes everywhere to guard our kit from pilferers. But Mehmet is hospitable and we experiment happily with our tins of food and sacks of dehydrated mysteries. We hear that the radio cannot operate in Kalis as Halil, another of Xhelal's followers, is turning awkward. Xhelal's game is very obscure. Lack of communication with Cairo is fatal to the work which we are trying to do here.

19th January

One month in Albania. We celebrate with some superb porridge. Muharrem Bajraktari comes for a conference. Michael translates but I think he misses the correct emphasis of our English speech – so I help him now and then. Muharrem has some grand ideas for himself, but his plans and ours hardly agree. We must wait for the report which he promises for Anthony Eden and Churchill. Here is a striking case of the fly who thought he was driving the coach. When Muharrem goes we make a curry based on a pigeon shot by the son of the house – only to find that we have left the pigeon out of the pot: *Ska gullig*! [58] We eat luxuriously and count our gold and sleep.[59] And I buy a copy of Kant's *Perpetual Peace* from Mehmet Troci, who has been struggling to read it.

---

57 BFCs were the cylindrical metal containers in which materiel such as weapons, food, flares or whatever had been requested was dropped to SOE missions in the field.
58 Swedish 'That'll be nice'.
59 The BLOs were supplied with gold sovereigns and napoleons to pay all their expenses in the field, including supplies, wages for their helpers and interpreters and to reward and recompense local resistance supporters. Julian Amery commented that 'Gold was our most powerful weapon'. He claimed that his and Col. McLean's 'war chest' consisted of four thousand sovereigns and that each BLO carried one hundred sovereigns with him at any one time for expenses. (Amery, *op. cit.*, p. 93).

20th January

An English breakfast and an easy march to Kalis where Halil is soon pulled into line. Thence a night march to Eles Bajrami's where we are welcomed with luxurious bedding and coffee. Where is Xhelal?

21st January

I am with Richard [Riddell] and hear much about his ideas and plans. A regular soldier, he seems brave and determined and competent as an officer, but as Michael says, 'Pas un homme réfléchi' and unskilled in politics and diplomacy. His mind is out of its depths in this country where society survives without law or discipline. He reacts to men emotionally not rationally and, being educated in tradition, makes too little allowance for personal and selfish motives. His whims and fancies and loyalties cause Tony much trouble. He cannot imagine his own policy.

Tony has much more grasp of men and events than Richard; but he is only a Captain and must follow the Major. He knows that only factors of relative force control our situation here. Yet even he cannot get under an Albanian's skin; fortunately no Albanian can get under his. Neither Richard nor Tony speaks a foreign language – they are good Englishmen – far too good for Albania.

Michael [Lis] is older (35) and cosmopolitan and experienced and *un homme d'esprit*. He has fine ideas but lacks the strength of character to stand firm in a practical policy. I like him as a friend but should not care to work with him. He is not very useful in this whirlpool of war and politics. Richard is very intolerant of him. One has to watch one's step with Richard; he has a strong grain of self and selfishness in him. And he seems to fear too much moral responsibility. He gives something to Dan Kaloshi or to the Partisans, then pleads away his action in front of Xhelal. And I am amazed to hear him speak of one aspect of his policy being necessary for fear of court martial after the war. As if any Albanian party could enforce the dismissal of an English soldier.

Xhelal arrives – little satisfaction is obtained for his rude letter to Richard. At least Richard obtains a new .38 pistol from him and I inherit Richard's Luger. Sherif Lita comes and he and Xhelal both hint of imminent German action against Partisans – and perhaps us. They are evidently playing a double game. Xhelal speaks too much of loyalty and devotion and too little of practical war and politics. And neither he nor Sherif Lita wants any war material. Why? Like Muharrem they want us only to hide.

Sherif brings bad news in *Bashkimi i Kombit* of 16th January.[60] It reports Brigadier Davies is badly wounded and captured at Kostenje on 8 January and two of his staff with him (rumoured to be a Major and a Captain). The affairs of our Mission are going badly with many parties without their radios and now the central command destroyed. And I am due to march with the Partisans to see the remnants of our H.Q.. Trayhorn was captured on 25th December.[61] There can be little H.Q. remaining. We hear also that the Germans have dropped pamphlets in Kalis warning people against us. They evidently intend us to be powerless when the day comes. The Germans were aided against the Brigadier and the Partisans by Aziz Biçaku.

Cen Elezi, Xhelal and Bashir Sufer fail to arrive. But Michael comes with further news of difficulties with the radio and Halil in Kalis. Halil is obviously doing Xhelal's bidding. And Dan Kaloshi's arrangements for a dropping ground are not so rosy as Richard expected. Will Dan serve us better than Cen?

This day indoors has not been very welcome as I have been feeling slightly feverish. Yet another goat for dinner – out of King George's gold.

22nd January

March at 5 a.m. through cloud and frost to Ali Dikë's house via Sllovë. Here we see how the Germans terrify this people by burning. A winter war is out of the question as a result.

---

60 *Bashkimi i Kombit* ('National Unity') was the leading newspaper. It was originally founded at the end of the nineteenth century at the height of the Albanian National Awakening when ideas of Albanian language and literacy started to flourish.

61 Lieutenant Frank Trayhorn had been Brigadier Davies' wireless officer at the Spillway mission at Bizë before it was broken up.

At Ali Dikë's we meet the Partisans under Esat Ndreu with Qasim Pristina to interpret. Richard does not like Partisans and is testy with them; but the conference passes well. We find what little truth there is in rumours of Russian officers and secret radios. More news of the Brigadier – the Partisans under Baba Faja do not seem to have guarded him well – poor Brig.[62]

Baba Faja Martaneshi in conversation with Brig. 'Trotsky' Davies in the autumn of 1943. Alan Hare is present on the far right.

---

62 Baba Faja Martaneshi (1910-47) was a founding member of the National Liberation Front (LNÇ). In this role he had dealings with British Liaison Officers such as Capt. David Smiley and Col. 'Billy' McLean. In July 1943 he joined the General Staff of the Albanian National Liberation Army (the Partisans). In May 1944 he became a member of Enver Hoxha's Anti-Fascist National Liberation Council. He was also a Muslim cleric of the Sufi Bektashi order, holding the highest rank of *baba* or spiritual guide and was associated with the *tekke* (monastery) at Martanesh. The Bektashi order is an Islamic movement known for its mysticism which was widely followed in the Ottoman Empire's European territories, particularly in Albania, Bulgaria and Macedonia. In post-communist times, however, the recent influence of Sunni Islam in the area has discouraged adherence to Bektashism which incorporates many features of Shia Islam as well as practices and rituals evolved over the centuries since its founding in the early sixteenth century. Baba Faja's prominent government position after the war gave him the power to secularise many aspects of Albanian Bektashism and he was assassinated by the traditionalist head of the sect, Abas Hilmi, in March 1947.

I buy a superb cigarette holder from Ali and some Sheraps from Maslan.[63] Ali lunches us well and produces an Italian barber. Haircut and shave are a civilised delight. Richard and I brew tea and talk and wait. Our conversation never lively. We live in different worlds.

At 15.15hrs. a sudden call to start on my march to find distressed British officers, escorted by four Partisans. Good going to Peshkopijë but bad beyond in utter darkness. Only one alarm as we walk along the Peshkopijë road – few Germans hereabouts. After eight hours we reach Trenjë in secrecy – only half an hour from Germans and road. Owner of house related to Haxhi Lleshi – very afraid of Germans. Some *buk* (bread), a tin of M and V [meat and vegetables], a cigarette in my new holder and sleep. Altogether twelve hours marching today.

23rd January

We hide in the house all day and are well received. Thita Trenë is our host – is afraid but treats us well. I am accused of being Yugoslav but manage to present my Englishry. We talk dog-Italian and Albanian, sleep fitfully and eat apples and chicken. After dark we march five hours to Reshan. To save trouble we use a long stretch of the Peshkopijë-Dibra road, seeing only two lorries, which drove us to cover. My stomach marches badly today: a short good road is even more welcome than ever. I am asked if I will travel in peasant dress as the Partisans could then smuggle me through by day. But fancy-dress is strictly forbidden.[64] We must

---

63 These were probably 'Sharri Special' cigarettes produced by the 'Kosova' factory in Prishtina. They were named after the Sharr (Malet e Sharrit in Albanian, Šar Planina in Macedonian) mountain range, east of Kukës at the conjunction of Albania, Kosova and Macedonia and were therefore likely to have been a popular local brand.

64 This stricture against disguise did not prevent the BLOs from adopting items of local clothing such as fezzes, caps, cummerbunds and jackets, usually to compensate for having few changes of clothes but also to satisfy a taste for eccentricity. Personal possessions were reduced to whatever could be carried. An extract from an earlier account by the Hungarian traveller Baron Nopsca of the traditional clothes of the Kalis area explains that 'The costumes worn by the men of Ujmisht include white *çakshir* trousers, wide at the top and narrow at the bottom, and stockings that reach up to the calves, often with a red pattern. The trouser legs are held together at the bottom by the laces of the *opankas* [sandals]. On their upper bodies they wear an *anteri* [long-sleeved jacket] and a thin *xhurdi* [black woollen jacket] with no fringes on the back. It goes down to the hips.' *Reisen in den Balkan. Die Lebenserinnerungen des Franz Baron Nopcsa*: Eingeleitet, herausgegeben und mit Anhang versehen von Robert Elsie, translated by Robert Elsie (Peja: Dukagjini Balkan Books, 2001), pp. 124-36.

keep to the stony path of night. We reach the house of Abdul Lleshi, and a bed gives me an excellent sleepy night.

24th January

Another long day of waiting, but this time with a shopping expedition to add interest. Some cigarettes, raki and toffee added to the household food are a good investment. My Partisan guides read aloud their propaganda journals most of the day. In the evening heavy rain and deep darkness. We wait for the weather in the house of an Albanian Captain and talk much in mock-Italian about world affairs and politics. The Partisans wear solid intellectual blinkers, but the Captain is intelligent and vivacious. But he does not fight for Albania.

We manage to cross the Drin by horse but find no guide and little hospitality and so stay the night in Gorice. We must push on hard tomorrow.

25th January

The household seems to be poor but is by nature overwhelmingly generous. Albanian macaroni and *kungulli* (pumpkin) are cooked especially for me and I learn the art of making *misr buk* (maize

A mountain village destroyed by the Germans in retaliation for resistance activity.

bread) – one of the benefits of being hidden in the store room. There is a fine view of Dibra only a mile or two distant.[65]

A fine starlit night, and we make good speed along the Dibra-Klos road to Sopot. A good thing that I hired a horse to ford the river en route. Once more our march is too short. Perhaps that is to allow me to enjoy better the scene of a battle between Italians and Partisans, an engagement which can have been nothing more than long-range sniping.

The Germans were hunting communists in Gorice three days ago. Just as well that our dates did not coincide. Tirana or Durazzo was heavily bombed yesterday.

26th January

We wait all day at Sopot – very boring without an interpreter. My Partisan guides, Beshir and Riza, amuse themselves all day by talking politics and reading papers and pamphlets. Riza is a true schoolboy communist with a head full of slogans and a political catalogue in place of imagination. Beshir is older and steadier but not intelligent. Albania is welcome to its future generation.

It rains towards evening and we decide not to move before midnight.

27th January

We set out at 02.00 hours to march to Klos by the motor road. Six inches of snow have fallen, but we have a horse to help us. At dawn I am introduced to a household as an Italian. Soon we push on via Klos and Guribardhe. By 13.00 hours, feeling tired, we reach the latter village and hear more rumours about English officers. We have heard of Englishmen in Zolli with either Partisans or Zogists. Now a Partisan political commissar tells us that the LNÇ general staff has moved south and that Col. Nicholls or some

---

65 Now in Macedonia.

other officer is in Zibere.[66] My Partisans depart for the south. I go to Zibere and find after dark that I have stumbled on Lt. Smythe with Slender. He has all the news which I require – so my journey has ended successfully in a 16 hour march. Raki and cherry brandy and wheat cakes with honey form a pleasant reward for my labours. Our sleep is disturbed by bugs. It might have been disturbed by much more as I arrived under the patronage of a Partisan political commissar in a nest of Zogists. His *'Djeci Fascismi'* (Children of Fascism) was happily followed by nothing worse than silence.

28th January

I spend the day with Slender, living luxuriously, taking notes and messages, talking Albanian politics and trying to find how Abas Kupi stands in our area at Peshkopijë.[67] Thank God that Col. Nicholls is found. He has suffered terribly. The fate of our mission now looks more cheerful. In the morning Capt. Bulman arrives, complete with beard. He has acquired a violent and undiplomatic dislike of this people – not a very deep man but a very cheerful one. Smythe seems to be a wee bit idle but he knows better than Richard how to keep his H.Q. fit to live in. The four other ranks with him are very happy and are not put to the wall by mulemen and others. Albanians don't eat valuable *buk-grun* up here.[68] A good interlude in a journey.

---

66 Lt. Col. Arthur Nicholls (1911-44) was a Coldstream Guards officer and member of Brigadier Davies' Spillway staff at the Bizë HQ. He escaped the attack on Spillway but died on 11 February from the consequences of gangrene as a result of frostbite suffered while hiding in the mountains in severe winter weather. He was awarded the George Cross posthumously in 1946.

67 Abas Kupi (1892-1976) was born in Krujë and in his early years saw service in the Ottoman administration under Essad Pasha Toptani. He was appointed head of the Krujë gendarmerie by King Zog in the 1920s. After the Italian invasion in 1939 he fled to Turkey. In April 1942 he and a group of other exiles including Gani Bey Kryeziu returned. He participated in founding the LNÇ but broke away from the communists and helped found the Zogist Legaliteti group.

68 Perhaps Hibbert means *bukë gruri*, wheat bread.

29th January

I set out early on my return voyage under the very good care of Ali Koleci. A lovely day. At Zibere (Xibër) snow; but early spring mud and warmth in the Mati valley. We march hard and finally pass Patin to sleep at Lis. During the day we pass a local fair on the Klos-Burelë road. I am spoiled by my escort with special dishes at meals and fruit and coffee at frequent intervals. The Zogists are good travel agents. Even raki is provided. The only drawback is that they stop constantly to chat and smoke with acquaintances.

Tony Simcox, Reg Hibbert and Selim Nokë. Early 1944.

30th January

We move early across the Burelë-Peshkopijë road and reach Maçukull by early afternoon. The road is bad because it runs across muddy gullies before it runs bald-headed at the mountains. We climb hard into the snow. Behind us is a lovely view of blue mountains and brown valleys with occasional brilliance from streams and house-tops. From that direction heavy bombardments have sounded all day. But we have other problems. Our path plunges over 1,000 feet through a forest and thick snow. By night we are safely housed in Koleci with generations of the Koleci family to greet us. Oh for an Italian dictionary or an interpreter!

31st January

We move early from Koleci after being well feasted but after an hour up a steep valley we stop to eat again. Ice and snow are a nuisance. Then we plunge straight up the side of Mali i Lurës into the forests and thick snow. At the top the views and scenery are magnificent, but much sweat has earned them. I find that when the path is exceptionally hard my mind turns always to the luxurious and lovely things of life. So today I have dreamed of England, home and beauty. We rarely talk of things such as home. Our lives are very much stripped for action: but where is the action?

At the end of the day we climb down from the mountain into Lurës and stay the night in the not too comfortable house of Baftja Hoci. The weather continues to be superb – bright sun and sparkling snow. In the high forests the silence and splendour are perfect.

1st February

The day starts with a slight earthquake – a novel experience. Then I find myself led away by Baftja Hoci with no escort to carry pack and greatcoat. Baftja is afraid of his enemies in Lashkiz, so we have to march to Reç by the longest and worst route, an icy switchback. I goad Baftja to find some more men, which he does; but they prove slightly mutinous under a hot pace. By night we arrive very tired across the Drin and stay in Ibrahim Halili's. As usual there, our welcome is not overwhelming. But food of sorts and sleep make a tolerable night. At least I learn that Stables is not with Muharrem. I can know which path not to take tomorrow.

2nd February

I set out late from Reç and by good luck stumble on Tony and the [radio] operators in Kalis, only two hours away. Stables is in poor trim – Richard absent with Dan Kaloshi to negotiate with the collaborationists.[69] The radio out of action for lack of a charging

---

69 Collaborators with the Germans.

engine and the people of the neighbourhood very unfriendly. Tony is tired and unwell and our operators continually causing friction with the people through their bad habit of treating Albanians as 'wogs'. The other ranks move to another house by night, and Tony and I are happy to stay where we are, as both of us have some slight stomach trouble. We hope to call Muharrem to our rescue soon.

3rd February

The men of Kalis are holding a *besa* meeting in this house so Tony and I have to spend the day in an outhouse, away from prying eyes.[70] We discuss Albania and agree in a bad view of the situation. General H.Q. is destroyed. Col. Nicholls is in hiding with badly frostbitten and gangrenous feet after nine terrible nights in the mountains. Hare is going to Cairo to expound the hopeless Trotsky policy of declaring for the LNÇ, while Slender and Stables are both off the air and so cannot explain Nicholl's new policy of help for Zogist and all resistance elements.[71] Seymour is promised as our new G1 while Kemp is obviously fitted for the task. And there is no liaison between missions in north and south. The whole of this stupid business has been caused by the inflated messages of BLOs, especially McLean and Smiley, who gave Cairo a totally false impression of Albania's military value.[72] It will be a miracle if there is ever any effective resistance to Germans in Albania.

In our own area of Peshkopijë the Partisan forces are negligible and immobilised by their unpopularity. Tony and I both believe that the people here will never rise and that leaders such as Cen Elezi and Dan Kaloshi will never move.

Our only remaining hopes are in Muharrem Bajraktari and

---

70 A *besa* is a sacred and binding promise. It is associated with the preservation of honour and is an essential precept in Albanian culture. Such a meeting might involve commitment to a *besa* or discussion of the circumstances to which a *besa* relates and its fulfilment. A *besa* can represent a commitment of loyalty, for instance, or be associated with a blood feud resulting from murder or damage to a woman's honour.

71 Capt. Alan Hare was Deputy Adjutant and Quartermaster General to Brigadier Davies at Bizë.

72 Major 'Billy' McLean and Captain David Smiley.

Fiqri Dinë and his pro-German committee.[73] Neither of these offers brilliant prospects; but we are still negotiating with them. The people here fear the Germans but know they will not suffer at German hands if they stay quiet. And if they wish to see the Germans cleared from their country, they are equally sure that England and America can achieve that without their help. Their sole concern is to use British help to settle by force their own political quarrels and to prepare to claim parts of Greece and Yugoslavia after the war. Such is the attitude of the leaders towards us: the rank and file regard us solely as a source of financial profit and as suitable victims for alternate hospitality and robbery. It is essential to understand that there is no will to fight Germans in this land: only a display of allied force will persuade men to follow us – too late. All that this country is fitted for is a number of itinerant officers to collect information and spread propaganda: a major military mission like ours is a farce. And it is made still more of a farce by Cairo's failure to provide interpreters for us, interpreters with no political stake in the country. And there are too many regular soldiers here who are afraid to tell Cairo the truth and have no understanding of diplomacy and politics. This war we are supposed to be waging is a complete fiction – performed so solemnly by all parties that it makes very good comedy.

At the end of the day we find that the *besa* meeting was simply an agreement to drive us English from Kalis. We shall go tomorrow; meanwhile I exercise my French prose in an urgent appeal to Muharrem. Life is improved by some wheat bread and chicken, which fortify us in a dispute with the locals over our soldiers. These

---

73 Fiqri Bey Dinë (1897-1960) was Prime Minister of Albania from 8 July 1944 to 29 August 1944 in the pro-German Albanian government. Originating in Dibrë, he was chieftain of the Dinë clan and was associated with the Ballist and Legaliteti movements aiming for an independent Albania. Together with Abas Kupi and Mehdi Frasheri the aim was to coordinate Zogists and Ballists to create a nationalist anti-communist alternative for Albania's future. As the diary reveals, the initial German offensive against the Partisans in Mati was successful while the Partisans took the upper hand in later action. Dinë's contacts with the BLOs ensured his dismissal after only forty-three days in office. At the end of the war, Dinë fled through Yugoslavia to Brussels. For a while he was active with Muharrem Bajraktari on the Albanian Committee in Paris.

are what are officially known as trying conditions: with patience, tobacco and humour, Stables does not appear over-tried.

4th February

We wake to find that our host has unwisely shot one of the villagers who disliked us. A futile comic opera war begins at once. We are besieged and all our movement plans are ruined. It is ironic that an Albanian should shoot to kill when we least require it and yet would run miles rather than stand against a German or Halil Alia's men.[74] The situation deteriorates during the day. We are not allowed to move from the house – we stay, chiefly in Ali Dikë's interest, as he might be shot when we could move unscathed. As the blood-feud develops with an M.G. [machine gun] to help, the upper part of the house is hit regularly by bullets. Tony and I are sure the villagers will come no closer while we are here; but our host, the murderer, will not let us pass – an awkward situation where mistakes might easily happen. Towards the end of the afternoon our Fairy Godmother arrives, Muharrem Bajraktari himself. A truce occurs at once: water, food, fire and coffee suddenly appear. Mafeking is relieved! Muharrem talks at length with the villagers and tells us that the *besa* must take its course when we have gone. So Mersin Matia must expect more fire and shooting. It was a clear case of abuse of diplomatic immunity. He deserves what comes to him.

Muharrem reads us a lecture on our failure to take his advice and stay quiet and seems upset at the Major's absence. But he evacuates us by night and we sleep comfortably in a house in the hills. The procession thither is impressive – a large band of Muharrem's trustiest men, Muharrem on his horse, six Englishmen and their baggage mules and our servants – and all very silent. M.B means to impress us: we mean to profit by his political need of us.

---

74 Halil Alia was a prominent nationalist and collaborator with the Italian forces in Kosova earlier in the war and with the Germans in the summer of 1944.

5th February

Muharrem arrives early and feigns ill-humour over the Major's absence when arrangements are ready for the long-awaited meeting with Fiqri Dinë. We persuade him that Tony is better fitted to meet Fiqri as he now possesses the up-to-date news which I brought back from Nicholls and Slender. So M.B. calms down and promises us a quiet place for our radio and a happy life ever after. We hope that Richard will not arrive to ruin this negotiation. Muharrrem has a grand political plan up his sleeve and is evidently playing against Abas Kupi. But if we play him right, we may make him fight the Germans in order to win his political programme. At least he seems to mean business which holds out some hope for us. A miracle happens. My haversack, which was lost last night by carelessness on the part of our soldiers and mulemen, is found on the path by our host. Well worth a napoleon in reward!

We seem to eat too much when we are static; the soldiers are very gluttonous. We are well cared for, and an excellent shopping sortie returns from Peshkopijë with honey and sugar to enable us to make afternoon tea. Even then the soldiers find something to grumble about. They are very tiresome.

Peshkopijë in 1944.

6th February

We wait for Muharrem's guide to fetch us, living comfortably and quietly the while. I am annoyed all day by a maddening rash and an influenza head but manage to learn some Italian and study some Albanian maps with Tony. As usual we beat out our views on the situation and even on English politics.

We are feasted for lunch on a complicated Albanian dish of pastry and butter which is very good.

At evening we move for two hours up into the hills – very cold indeed and a cutting wind. At a house near Zenil Lita's we find Muharrem and his hosts and are feasted royally. The radio and operators are smuggled away and we are swamped by political personalities. Cen Elezi arrives and Mehdi, Islam and Xhelal Ndreu. They all retire with M.B. and soon we are called to join them in a dark and chilly room. The conference is on.

We attack Cen Elezi about our treatment in his area and that calms him down. M.B. has obviously tamed him and intends to make use of him. When M.B. outlines his plans we find them full of promise; and so all depart to sleep with a feeling that good foundations for some effective war and politics may have been laid. Once more we hope that Richard does not arrive to ruin all before the talks with Fiqri Dinë have had a chance to succeed. Tony and I think our position strong: Tony negotiates well, if not eloquently.

7th February (Monday I believe)

We breakfast with Muharrem who then departs. He hates to stay near us by day in case the Germans seek us. We retire to the secret room of our soldiers and radio, only for Xhelal to burst in and ruin the whole secret. All the neighbourhood will know of our radio's presence. Thereafter the day is uneventful: Tony and I try to amuse ourselves by talking but the soldiers eat too much, look miserable and doze.

At evening we move, Tony and I after Muharrem, the operators and radio to their secret H.Q.. As we set out, Michael arrives from Eles Bajrami's with a letter from Sherif Lita on behalf of Osman [Lita]. He claims Plosten as his area and waxes wroth that we should meet M.B (his foe) and Cen (hardly his friend) in it. He threatens to expel us in Aziz Biçaku style. Michael will meet Sherif tomorrow. Meanwhile we can proceed with our plans and await developments. We write to M.B. and hope that he has not been trying to pull a fast one on Osman Lita. More likely the pest Xhelal is half in the enemy's camp. We sleep at Ceren. A most hospitable house – milk, wheatbread, apples, mattresses, eiderdowns.

8th and 9th February

We wait M.B.'s summons at Ceren. Milk, apples, nuts, cigarettes, wheatbread and excellent food make Tony and me very happy. And by night we share a fine double bed on the floor. We chat and discuss but can do nothing until Muharrem moves. It is very cold and the snow falls thickly. Xhelal is still spying on our radio. On the 9th Richard arrives. He sports Albanian costume and is full of the good life he has led with Dan. He has been visiting collaborators and others (e.g. the treacherous Selim Xhetani, who provided him with champagne) in the Peshkopijë and Dibra area. Richard seems very confident of Dan Kaloshi and refuses to believe that Dan is like all other Albanians. Tony and I reserve our opinions and exchange news. We represent the Bajraktar's front and suspect Dan of being jealous of Muharrem.

10th February

Muharrem walks in on us early to announce that Fiqri Dinë is away from home and our meeting is to be postponed a fortnight. Tony and I are to return to the radio – Richard and Michael will tour the Peshkopijë and Dibra areas with Dan. We discuss our suspicions of Xhelal, the Ndreu family and Kalis with M.B. He is suspicious too. Then we arrange to move from Osman Lita's area if necessary into Lumë – a move to the good.[75]

---

75 Osman Lita was the son of the former Lita clan chieftain Mustafa Lita, referred to in the memoirs of Baron Nopcsa as having broken the rules of hospitality by holding his guest, the Baron, hostage in 1907 in his home in Kalis, his stronghold. Julian Amery describes Osman Lita in his diary as resembling his own house being 'dour, windswept, cruel, corrupt'. Lumë was Muharrem Bajraktari's area, today located partly in the Kukës region of north-east Albania and partly in Kosova.

Muharrem's report looms large. For the rest of the day we lounge and talk. Richard has made a crossword puzzle and I have to solve it – quite a good one for an amateur. For lunch we enjoy an excellent Albanian dessert and for dinner some first-class *kos* [yoghurt] – and always these lovely Ceren apples. He leaves to join Michael and Tony and I wait for Zenil Lita.

11th February

We hear from Richard that Michael is off to Prizren and Richard is on his way back to his friend Dan. Richard does not attach much importance to Muharrem and his report – he speaks of M.B limiting himself to an attack at Kukës.

Xhelil Lita comes and we are to move tonight to Muharrem via the radio – a matter of a few days. Ali Dikë flaps a little: he has a secret reason for not liking our arrangements and so takes two days leave. He can be very awkward at times.

As usual in this house we are excellently cared for: one of the sons has been a sergeant in the Italian army. It has left him much more alert than normal young Albanian men. At night the weather is very bad with wind and snow and sleet and cloud; but we tear ourselves away from Ceren and the home of Sami Isa and march via Xhelal Lita's to the secret station of the radio in the house of Malik Lita at Vanaj. A most uncomfortable march, but a necessary one. Tony and I were beginning to grow roots in the luxury of Ceren.

12th February

Tony and I enjoy a bath and delousing session: lice are plentiful. As usual the soldiers require more discipline. They were lazily trying to operate a schedule with only one and a half hours charging. They deserve something much stronger than a lecture. We are cursed with a very stuffy band of other ranks.

In the middle of the morning Tony and I find that we have been robbed overnight – Tony of 14 napoleons and sovereigns and I of 14 napoleons and sovereigns. We suspect the brother of Malik; but it is most awkward as only Malik and the brother and son of Zenil Lita slept in the room with us. All are offended: all speak of their family honour and there is no result but ill-feeling.

For the first time Tony and I had not slept with our breeches under our heads as they were soaked with snow. T. E. Lawrence had a sentence to the effect that in fighting for another man's country you lose everything, including yourself. The loss of myself is still to come.

Later we hear from Richard and Xhelal. The latter vows that Ali Dikë must answer for the loss of our stores in Kalis. Tony prepares to join Richard to clear this inter-interpreter feud once and for always. We have fallen among thieves today and stupid ones at that.

All day the batteries are charged but two broadcasts fail. Happily we hear some news from London and obtain GMT. The war still waits for us. I wish our signallers would help harder to make it end quickly. A little enthusiasm from them would make life much happier. Tony is a little unsure of his own mind. These men need to be drilled or nursed. Is he browned off or is he simply the detached type of officer?

13th February

Porridge for breakfast, chicken for lunch and an English book to read – H. C. Bailey's Mr Fortune stories – crime fiction and not very enjoyable for me. The day is very empty though Tony does his best to amuse us by making fudge-toffee.

In the evening Tony leaves with our pet civil-servant, Mersim, to join Richard at Eles Bajrami's to investigate the Kalis losses and the Xhelal-Ali Dikë dispute. The operators fail again in their night's sked, but we hear English and Albanian news. Otherwise charging and work on the aerial and a little conversation with our soldiers, trying to encourage them.

14th February (Sunday)

Goodier spoils the morning sked and earns a hearty rocket. Davis shows his usual bad manners at mealtimes and earns another. Everyone lounges instead of cleaning the room and collect the biggest of all. A good start to the day. A DDD (high priority) tells us that Slender has passed Nicholls' messages: my efforts to beat Slender have been beaten by our own radio and operators.

Ali Dikë returns with Maslan. For the rest of the day I work casually at messages and log-books and talk with Malik. He is an unusually broad-minded type of Albanian and very full of interest in the wide world and its ways. No doubt he is as little to be trusted as most of his compatriots. I profit much from talk with him – he gives me some apples and tobacco.

The night sked is supremely successful – three messages out and seven in. Tony returns with news that Xhelal has confessed to the theft of our material from Kalis. We should be able to make him squirm now. He deserves it. There is trouble on the horizon – we are going to be asked to move tomorrow. Malik is in full cry for money. Curse him!

15th February

Malik demands that we leave, pretending that we are no longer secret. Only bread and cheese are given to us to eat. It is best to go. All morning we rocket the signallers for their slackness and we decode Op. Order Underdone, an impressive document which suggests from its clarity and logic that a new hand is being felt in Cairo. Things are beginning to move.

Two brews of tea (army tea stolen and sold back to us) console us for Malik's incessant demands for cash. In the evening Tony and I plunge through thick snow to join Michael at Xhafer Lita's. Xhafer is a hearty and pleasant fellow and treats us well. Tony and Michael and I talk Albanian affairs until very late. Michael finally agrees with our plans for a strong British policy towards Albania and agrees in our condemnation of the futility of many BLO efforts and those of our late H.Q.. But Michael is not a man to pursue strong policies or to put a bold face on failure. He is too fond of life, comfort and words – an excellent mess companion.

16th February

In the morning a conference with Xhafer. He promises to fight, but not in company with other chiefs. He has an eye to our money; but he may serve some small purpose if properly played. If only Osman Lita does not overawe him in this area!

Maslan returns with sugar, oranges, raisins and tobacco. An excellent supply sortie. So we eat and psycho-analyse ourselves with the aid of Penguin Specials. Sherif Lita arrives and finds a cold reception from Tony and me. A large and excellent dinner and sleep.

17th February (Thursday)

A very cold and windy day. We pass the morning with an amusing incident over some stolen English tea which someone wants to sell back to us. And all the Albanians protest violently when we keep the English sack which holds it! A strange morality.

Otherwise we talk and argue to cheer the local populace. Michael tells me that Richard casts me for a role with collaborationists – very ironic since I think so scornfully of his relationship with them. This is not a regiment where various elements can be disposed of at will. Tony, Michael and I are left in the dark as to Richard's policy, largely because he does not know it himself. Some team work would be useful.

In the afternoon Xhetan Elezi and Bashir Sufa arrive and promise to fight. What does that mean? Two men and a boy shooting from 5,000 yards with rifles at nothing when the Allies have driven out the Germans? Shqipëri, Shqiptarëve! We can do little for this country.

Michael returns to Eles Bajrami. Tony and I return to Malik Likë, who is full of fears when we arrive in daylight. The snow is very thick and the wind fierce and cold, but the Korab range behind us and the Sllovë valley in front make a fine view.[76] We are frustrated by Ali Dikë's cunning delays from reaching the radio tonight. But Malik is very hospitable and there is *kos* to eat. These obstacles to our work are growing serious. Happily we do not let serious work hinder hearty lives.

---

76 The 25-mile-long Korab range lies on a north-south axis in the territorial triangle where Albania, Kosova and Macedonia meet. Mount Korab itself at 9,068 ft. (2,764 metres) is the fourth highest summit in the Balkan Peninsula.

18th February

We stay or rather we hide all day in a bare upstairs room at Malik's. Life settles down after some trouble with Ali and Malik about secrecy. Zenil is our only visitor; but he is a welcome one and shares our tea. He brings news of German plans to set Albanian against Serb in Kossovo. Everyone here rejoices at the thought of fighting the Serbs and Tito.

At evening Michael arrives with Sherif Lita's men – more trouble with Malik over secrecy. The evening is merry and we are well entertained. Strange how different Malik is when our soldiers are not here!

Villager with loaves of bread.

19th February

An early start on the road to Shkavez and M.B. – very thick snow and hard going, but fresh and pleasant.[77] Michael walks terribly, a result of disposition rather than infirmity. We stop interminably, wait hours for lunch and finally stay at Vilë, two hours from our destination. This is a most unsatisfactory way of travelling: it makes work impossible. But at least we manage to find a man to carry a message to M.B..

All the evening we argue fiercely about Albania and manage to persuade Michael that further British gold will be wasted here unless paid after fighting instead of before. In every case little resistance by Albanians seems likely; and further pretence and exaggeration to earn promotion for BLOs would be disgraceful.

Michael and I compete in the night for a single blanket and the fleas compete for both of us.

---

77 Many Albanian place names have several variants, in this case Shkavez/ Skavicë/Shkavec.

20th February

In the morning we walk two hours from Vilë to Shkavez – snow fine and thick and a powerful wind driving the snow against us. And Michael still manages to feel tired after only two hours – a bad hiking companion. At Shkavez we await Muharrem's pleasure. We are comfortable and well-fed and full of conversation. By late afternoon we hear from Muharrem that he will receive us in two days' time. This is no good to us, so we insist on moving nearer to him despite the opposition of all our guides. After a dinner of beef (the dried variety) we venture forth into a freezing windy night and scramble along icy ledges to a house which refuses us admission. On we move again, with Michael growing more and more tired and upset and peevish at the need for a long march. It ends as a steeplechase up a mountainside and we end in a poor house in Ujmisht where Tony, Michael and I have to freeze under a single cover. Michael is not happy.

21st February

My 22nd birthday starts badly: we are woken at five a.m. and told that we must move on as we cannot stay secret here. So out into the blast again for a short march to a third-rate house where we are not very welcome. We wait in the cold before being shut in a chilly store room with a tiny fire, countless draughts and no food. We freeze and sleep and finally manage to obtain some maize bread and cornflour. A lousy day but it ends excellently. Our messenger has managed to stir Muharrem at last and we can move to his house tonight.

A two hours march and we relax in luxury with real coffee, cigarettes, raki, carpets in plenty, a superb dinner, the Bajraktar's conversation and some bedding fit for kings and BLOs.

We hear that Andy Hands has been driven from Degë and that the Hoxha has been burned in his own mosque. How much of my stolen kit was burned with him? And did Mehmet Xoxha and the Partisans really fight? Trouble is brewing in Kossovo.

I hear that my *cingare* [cigarette holder] was involved in the blood-feud in Kalis. Ali Dikë and Gafur Nokë had quarrelled over the price and that helped to start the shooting. My *cingare* is something of a trophy.

A night at Muharrem's is a worthy birthday celebration

22nd February

We wake up to more luxury, milk and wheat bread and coffee. After a shave and some cigarettes we begin our conference with Muharrem. We reach a happy conclusion as to the report of M.B.. Tony has a copy and I shall remain to translate it. Then Muharrem is called away to confer with some chiefs from Prizren who come to seek aid

The original *cingare* bought by Hibbert with its metal container.

against Mihailovitch who is invading Kossovo. While he is away a huge pile of mail arrives for me from Spinster – thirty-five letters. News from home is an exciting event and some of the letters make entertaining reading. So Margaret [Hibbert's sister] is engaged. I shall be the odd man out when I reach home. All seems serene in England. All is serene here today. My father's guess that I am with Tito is fairly near the mark.

Apparently Andy Hands and Ian Merritt are safe near Berisht. Neel is ill and Kemp is being flown to Cairo from Montenegro. Hibberdine will have a large task left to him in Kossovo. Kemp's report to Cairo would be worth hearing.

A fine lunch of eggs and *kos* and wheat bread is followed by a conference with the chiefs of Prizren. Tony handles them very well and manages to persuade them to fight Germans rather than Serbs. German propaganda is very successful in Kossovo in setting race against race. We cannot intervene much. Tony manages to squeeze in some successful bouquets for M.B..

Then we begin again with M.B. and manage to whittle down some of his colossal ambitions to promises of practical action near Kukës. He ought to have been exploited months ago. Now we are too late to win anything really significant. But here is a glimpse of a chance of some action – circumstances throttle it. Michael feels obliged to congratulate Tony and me on our tactics and diplomacy: we manage to tickle M.B.'s vanity but have given nothing away.

So we pass on to raki and cheese and so to a magnificent dinner set off by Albanian wine – young but pleasant. Tony and I break into lively political debate (English politics to the wonder of all the Albanians) and at last we retire to our luxury beds again. It is good to be 22 if this is the luck which a birthday brings.

23 February

Luxury as before. M.B tells us some more stories about the German hunt for Englishmen in the Drin valley below Kukës. Hands is said to have lost his mules and radio; a new mission is said to be established with Ymer Bardoshi.[78]

I borrow an Italo-English dictionary and an Italian edition of Mignet's *French Revolution* and begin to learn some Italian. A French reader provides some happy glimpses of familiar poetry and prose. And always we talk busily about anything or nothing.

In the afternoon Tony and Michael leave to find Richard and the radio, leaving me in solitude. This semi-European room seems strangely empty when I find myself alone after months of communal living. But Ibrahim, Hamdi and Bairam join me by turns to drink raki and to talk. Dinner for a single officer is not so luxurious as for three but it is still very good.

After dinner Muharrem comes to talk and I manage to probe some of his opinions on Albanian domestic problems and on the post-war politics of the Balkans. He is a man of keen opinions, a zealous nationalist and a confirmed enemy of communism. A few men of his calibre in the Balkans, backed by a strong British policy, would strengthen Britain's position in international diplomacy. I feel that we are only now working on the lines which should have been

---

78 Ymer Bardoshi was a former army officer leading a group of about one hundred men. He was much trusted and liked by the BLOs.

taken from the start. But now there is little hope of organising this country for battle, and no Balkan front we can oppose to a Russian which may prove to be expansionist after the war. On the Russian question Muharrem and I agree, though his fear is of communism while I think of a nationalist and ambitious Russia.

24th February

Today I start translating the report with M.B. whose command of literary French is pathetic, even if he talks more busily than I. However, we beat the report out into our common diplomatic language and I try to write it in respectable French. Italian helps me to correct Muharrem's blunders by reference to Ibrahim, his son. I am left fairly strictly alone to work – which is a pleasant novel experience in Albania.

The report is ambitious in its scope and is of little use to us now – Richard will laugh it out of court. But it is interesting to speculate what it might have produced for us. And when I probe Muharrem about Albania's constitutional and political history, I obtain (with the report) a vivid glimpse of Balkan politics and conflicts. There is material for war here, against Germans and Russians and plenty of others. We have not known how to use it. Albania is now a lost cause; but I don't believe there was need to lose it.

I dine in state with Muharrem – an interesting new dish of boiled peppers and pickled cabbage stuffed with spices. We chat a little and then I exchange some Italian with his sons – and so to bed.

25th February

Rumours are flying that Partisans are surrendering in small groups near Valona: in this anti-communist neighbourhood much rejoicing.

I turn the report into English and it seems to read respectably enough. Ibrahim approves of it. A German plane causes a diversion by dropping leaflets to say how the wicked Englishmen are trying to create a civil war in Albania. Single-seat planes from Kukës keep this area well covered – looking for radio perhaps. Muharrem draws me his ethnic Albania on a map.[79] It is colossal, stretching from the Arta to Volos line, as far north east as Niş and Sofia and the frontier of European Turkey. Ethnography is an anagram of agrandissement in the Balkans.

Some extracts of verse and prose from a French grammar brighten the evening. And then raki and conversation with M.B. and sons, and finally a good three-course dinner. M.B.'s hospitality does not seem to weaken with time.

26th February

My efforts to read and learn Italian keep me busy most of the day, and a few stray ends of business are tied up. The chief of the Bicaj gendarmerie arrives in the room below asking for statistics of Italian damage in these parts; the Tirana government must be getting that post-war feeling. He also brings news that three German officers have arrived at Kukës to organise the Gendarmerie. We hope that they do their job well if the gendarmerie is to fight for us on the day.

Towards evening I leave M.B.'s amid hearty farewells (he reminds me of provincial characters in Balzac – a local boy who has made good, though a very superior type of local boy). To Shkavez through snow, slush and sleet to the house of Isak Kasani.

---

79 'Ethnic Albania' refers to territories within the Ottoman Empire traditionally inhabited by larger or smaller ethnic Albanian populations. It encompasses Albania, Kosova, western Macedonia, Albanian-populated areas of Southern Serbia and parts of Northern Greece. This irredentist concept in the Balkans has its origins in the reaction to the break-up of former Ottoman territories, previously with no internal boundaries, into independent states. This was the case particularly with Bulgaria and Serbia, as a result of the Treaties of San Stefano and Berlin after the Russo-Turkish War of 1877-78. The League of Prizren was set up in 1878 to defend the rights of the 'Albanian Nation', given the geographical dispersal of Albanian populations in Ottoman territories that might be divided by new international boundaries. The issue of national identity, where previously ethnic and linguistic difference had been preserved under a common Ottoman identity, was a major preoccupation of the newly formed post-Ottoman Balkan states. The territory of 'Ethnic Albania' was based on that of four Ottoman administrative areas or *vilayets*, Kosova, Yannina, Shkodra and Bitolya, although Muharrem Bajraktari's concept was even more ambitious, reaching as far as Sofia to the east and north to Niş.

These slow piecemeal journeys waste endless time; but the people will not let us move otherwise. Plenty of visitors arrive, including Soliman Ahmedi and son (the perfect Albanian dandies); but no one seems to bother about the publicity which this gives to M.B.'s activities with us. Fine food and sleep.

27th February

I am soon moved into a room apart where melting snow drips though the ceiling, where perpetual frost prevails and where I eat bread and cheese and smoke poor tobacco. A copy of *The Sphere* of 1936 is miraculously unearthed – what a reminder of England! No wonder Hitler expected a short war.[80]

Ali and I talk a little Italian and the two small boys, Xhelil and Muharrem, try to amuse me. Otherwise a dull day. No news of Tony or Baftja Latif, so that I cannot move yet. I can only watch a sunny day with white clouds which promises spring in a month or two. Slush and snow dull the pleasant prospect of the landscape. But the Drin valley looks lovely today – it was very grim yesterday.

28th February

Still no news of Baftja Latif, so I move to his house and find him recently returned there. Travelling is not pleasant through a drizzle of rain which has half-melted the deep snow. A hearty welcome from Baftja who sends me on my way to the radio and Tony. A very exhausting march – like marching up very steep steps for three and a half hours.

I find Richard and Tony crowded in a small room with hosts of retainers, and the radio and soldiers 'hidden' in a room below. A good meal and bad raki – a terribly crowded and stuffy night. Richard very fit and in good humour: Tony looks tired and is somewhat on edge. Richard brings good news from the Dibra area. Abas Kupi is apparently well ahead with his organisation: Mehdi Frashëri promises government support, Fiqre Dinë is in

---

80 *The Sphere* was an illustrated magazine similar to *The Illustrated London News*, aimed primarily at Britain's colonies and dominions. It featured pictorial news about royalty, society and sport.

line.[81] Gjon MarkaGjoni brings in Mirditë.[82] All these have been collaborationists at some time but may now prove useful. This puts M.B. in a new perspective. M.B is missing his bus: we must try to tame his ambitions by facing him with these other men. We can afford to be firm.

Richard also brings books. He is taking Michael south with him.

29th February (Tuesday)

Trouble in the morning with the owner of the house and Malik Likë – money and swindling and overcrowding of the house. All these people still claim to be terrified of Germans and us being seen by day. However we move away tonight.

I hear more of Richard's plans and learn much from the radio logbook. All this gives me a freshening new perspective. I think we can now begin to enlighten M.B. a) on British foreign policy and b) Albanian resistance movements. Then we can proceed to demand action to justify his fine words. Evidently we must give an instant cold shoulder to his plans for a Red/Slav peril. Only after taming him will Tony be able to try to mould him to our purposes. Meanwhile we must have an aeroplane in his territory. Cairo's plans show a welcome firmness; their insistence upon Partisan interests is illuminating. Last-minute resisters are not to have it all their own way.

Richard departs for the south again, leaving us to organise a drop and to deal with M.B. We amuse ourselves in the afternoon by running our petrol charging-engine: successful on a paraffin-

---

81 Mehdi Frashëri (1872-1963) was born in the last years of Ottoman rule over Albania and was associated early on with ideas of Albanian national independence, while holding various senior posts in the Ottoman administration. After independence, in 1923 he was Albania's delegate at the League of Nations. He was Prime Minister from 1935 to 1936. His strong opposition to Italy's invasion of Albania in April 1939 led to internment in Italy. On his return he acted as honorary chairman of the 1942 Pezë Conference of anti-German factions. His cousin Midhat was leader of the nationalist Balli Kombëtar movement. He was prepared to work with Albania's new German masters, however, and once again became Prime Minister in the pro-German government for one month in October-November of 1943.

82 Mirditë was a predominantly nationalist Catholic tribal area north-west of Peshkopijë. It is now a District of modern Albania. Gjon MarkaGjoni (1888-1966), also known as Kapidan MarkaGjoni, was a prominent Catholic clan leader and chief of the Mirditë district.

petrol mixture. It makes much noise and attracts the whole village to watch – an idle and annoying crowd.

In the evening we move with our new interpreter Jashat Bunguri and all the soldiers. A dreadful journey with rain and three feet of melting snow and darkness and mountain paths for five and a half hours. I win the record for spectacular falls by disappearing over the edge with the radio on my back. We arrive at last soaked to the skin; but some raki-punch consoles us and sends us swiftly to sleep.

1st March

A dull day spent in drying clothes and making arrangements for our stay and for a drop here. Tony, not well and a little ill-tempered, negotiates impatiently, but all is arranged. At night our material arrives but not Ali. An interlude day.

2nd March

Tony still very unwell; so I have to get things moving – routine clean-up etc. as the radio is out of action for a day or two. The soldiers are much more cheerful nowadays, Goodier and Elvidge are much more satisfactory than the other two. At least I find I can get under their skins – sometimes we even manage to be hearty together.

Tony and I write to M.B. about his drop and talk to Baftja Latif and wait. I find that I have a flair for making Albanian coffee and follow it up with a raki punch. Fernando makes a great business all day of making a macaroni – and a very good one too. In the afternoon I read the Book of Job in Gregson's Bible – a lovely and exhilarating prose, but strangely out of context in this hand-to-mouth life.

By night Tony and I move to Baftja Latif's, leaving Ali very disgruntled that we take Jashat Bunguri and leave him behind. All night we are devoured by fleas.

3rd March

We live all day in a nasty hole of a room. M.B. arrives in the morning. We sober his ambitions as best we can but as Tony has not prepared his conversation we are not over-successful. M.B. is likely to be a doubtful starter now. He might have been a favourite had we had more time and had the early BLOs not over-weighed the national balance in the Partisans' favour. M.B. refuses to allow an immediate drop here for fear of another Dardhë. This country is hopeless. Evidently M.B.'s only hope has been to gain British support and material and so to bribe and dazzle Albanians to follow him. But that is useless to us.

M.B. leaves us to a dismal day in our ground floor garret.

Tony and I work on a sit-rep for Cairo trying to present a true picture of the mil.sit. here. It will clash somewhat with Richard's messages; but it may enlighten someone as to our forlorn hopes.

From our garret we move to our flea-bound room upstairs. Ali joins us and is told to join the Major for a trip to Dibra (as Selim Nokë, at our next dropping ground, is his enemy) and returns with me to the radio house. There I use the end of a super-sked: 9 messages out and 9 messages in. The radio is up-to-date for once: we can listen to London news without fear of wasting batteries.

4th March

Trouble in the morning with Ali Dikë and co. who failed to leave this hideout by night. Later a few rockets for the soldiers. Some bargaining for a goat and a lamb leads to a very good lunch. With the help of the message book I get up-to-date with Albanian affairs. The picture is reasonably complete and very unpromising.

Life is not lively as the soldiers are as slovenly as ever and rather dull company. Without material comforts they lose all their vitality and all their raison d'être. But Gregson has some interesting things to tell about south Albania and his experiences with Major McLean and the Brigadier.[83] The vast H.Q. set-up makes a fantastic tale.[84]

---

83 Major, later Lt. Col., 'Billy' McLean (1918-86) had two tours of duty in Albania, initially from June to November1943 and returning in April 1944. He was particularly involved in trying to bring Abas Kupi and the nationalist Balli Kombëtar to the point of active rebellion against the Germans.

84 According to Julian Amery, the Brigadier had set up a huge organisation at Bizë complete with staff officers, NCOs, Albanian and other helpers. He would travel with up to a hundred pack mules when on the move and maintained the sort of timetable and discipline over schedules and uniform to be found in more conventional H.Q.s. He had 'the latest collapsible camp furniture and several hundredweight of stationery'. Amery, *Sons of the Eagles, op. cit.*, p. 68.

In the evening Tony comes and we leave the radio house with its host who is none too pleased to have us, due mostly to Ali Dikë's and the soldiers' lack of common sense: Ali is riding for a fall. We reach Selim Nokë's house and the new dropping ground, to find M.B and twenty merry men feasting and playing the filxhan game and sleeping all in one small room.[85] A hearty evening: it is always fun to spend a night with a chief and his men – a good time is had by all at the closest of quarters. These quarters are so close that Tony and I take up half a man's space between us.

Selim Nokë (in foreground in black) and Dan Kaloshi (in white) enjoying target practice in the snow. Early 1944.

5th March

We arrange for our drop with M.B. who departs. We recce the ground and find it good. Otherwise we live in an outhouse full of smoke and with glassless windows. Everywhere the thaw

---

85 A *filxhan* is a small coffee cup for drinking coffee prepared in the Turkish style. One game played all over the Balkans with such cups is telling fortunes in the coffee dregs. The cup is covered with the saucer, swirled round three times anticlockwise and the cup and saucer turned upside down. A personal object such as a ring or a coin is placed on the base of the cup. After some minutes the cup is reversed and the fortune is read in the pattern left by the coffee residue inside the cup.

goes slowly on and water and fog surrounds us. Yet we are very comfortable and Selim is very hospitable. He tells me more of the history of my cingare. He gave it to Gafur after receiving it himself from Xhem Gostivari as a reward from saving Xhem from prison.[86] And now Xhem plays with the Germans.

The smoke acts on me like tear-gas and even when we come out of our dug-out in the evening and move into the guest room, smoke still stays with us. The highlight of the day is a sweet specially prepared with our precious sugar. The lowlight is one of the usual attempts to swindle us from a distance over some slight repairs to a charging engine handle.

6th March

Crisis! A letter from Michael announces that our secret dealings with M.B. are known to Sherif and Osman Lita and Cen Elezi and finally Xhafer Dita. The latter name suggests that Ali Dikë has betrayed us – and so think all our companions. Sherif has threatened an action against M.B. if we continue with our drops. Another Dardhë seems certain. Here is the fruitful result of Richard and Michael's faith in the Lita collaborationists and of the universal faith in Ali Dikë. Ali and his man Mersin have never enjoyed much of my trust.

After some flap we find that our host is not upset by this mess and so prepare to meet our aircraft. Notes hum to and fro between the radio house and us and Michael joins us after dark. He is full of evil forebodings and yet still favours the Lita connection. His news for Cairo is unimportant. With us he mocks Richard's ambitious plans: no doubt with Richard he mocks our views and hopes.

7th March

We live fairly coldly all day and Michael takes our teasing very temperamentally. Since we cannot argue with him we have to tease.

---

86 Xhem Gostivari was the alias or *nom de guerre* of Xhelal Hasa who led the Balli Kombëtar in the western Macedonia area. He was deeply disliked by the Partisans who considered him a collaborator.

Our host is always pleasant and hearty and hospitable – will he prove to be one of the few reasonably dependable Albanians? At present we have most amiable relations with him – even to the extent of dirty jokes in Albanian. He is sobered somewhat by a dispute with the owner of our radio house (the usual petty troubles) but promises to find us better quarters for our soldiers.

In the afternoon we prepare our fires (ironically enough in the shape of a V for victory). Michael departs with much flap and flourish and we stand by. A perfect night but no aeroplane.

8th March

Muharrem arrives early with much news and leaves spectacularly with his escort after having reglé les choses of the drop and the radio. Afterwards we can start our day, with noblesse obliged.

M.B.'s news: Fiqri Dinë and Abas Kupi and Gjon MarkaGjoni and others are forming a power party to collaborate with the Germans and later with us in order to fight communism and keep power in their own hands. They have invited M.B. to join a new regency. M.B stalls and comes to us in the hope of receiving British support to resist them. Without British support, he and his nationalists will be in a poor position. Tony and I promise to do our best for him with Cairo. G.H.Q. should be fairly interested in these tidings as they do not wish to condone collaboration. M.B says that British prestige is involved here if Britain does not make some firm stand against pro-Germans. He plays on Tony's and my uneasiness about the lines which British missions in Albania have been taking.

Abas Kupi, prominent leader of the pro-Zogist movement.

At last the weather turns fine. After weeks of heavy snow and rain we hope to see the end of the snow and the thaw which alternate up here. From the back of the house we have a glorious view of nearly all Albania from Kossovo to beyond Lake Ochrid – a splendid panorama which seems unconnected to the men living in it.

During the day every man in the house disappears to hunt a murderer in Kalis. We have to steal wood to keep warm but have plenty of work writing messages on M.B.'s information. Message writing to Cairo is not easy: one has to picture so much of their piecemeal and unreliable information in order to make one's message intelligible. Tony and I do our best for M.B. but it is not easy to fit it in with the reports from Michael and Richard. We comfort ourselves with milk and coffee.

QTN tonight, so we do not stand by our fires.

9th March

The bad weather returns with snow and bitter wind and cold. In the morning a dispute over the soldiers' expenses with the host of their house. Tony waxes wroth and curses all Albanians; and it takes an hour or more to calm the Albanian gathering in our room which feels itself insulted – more or less justifiably. We can afford to lose our temper with individuals but not with the whole race. In any case half the swindling which we suffer is our own fault. All this talk of trust and friendship leads nowhere. Work amongst an alien race is a thankless business.

At least I can shake the lice of Albania off me. The luxury of clean clothes and fresh louse powder gives a vinegary feeling of invigoration.

Richard arrives with a small retinue of Dibra men, much to the distaste of the men of Lumë. We brew tea and drink cherry brandy and talk. He has lost much of his old hope for success in this region. Dan Kaloshi is out of favour and we manage to persuade Richard of M.B.'s sincerity and value. But he still threatens to ruin all by demanding immediate (military) action which could only produce the downfall of all pro-British chiefs. Little by little we may win our point, even if Richard refuses to admit it. Michael has fallen from favour.

A hearty conversational night with Selim Nokë – he is a powerful character and can be charming company. A formidable record as an outlaw adds to his charms.

10th March

Today we live in another, warmer room and read and talk and wait. The weather stays wintry although the thaw begins again. Richard handles Albanians with some of Hands' naughtiness; he is very tired of this country. Trouble seems to be brewing between the Dibra retinue and the men of Lumë. While the clouds gather we make tea. At night the clouds break on Richard and Tony. While I stay and chat with Selim and Javit, they go to move house with the soldiers. Their host demands three times his due payment, receives nothing and opposes the move with force. Jashat [the interpreter] turns yellow in the face of Albanian opposition and demands to be allowed to go home. There the matter stands tonight; but tomorrow will see a conclusion in the Dibra-Lumë affair.

11th March

The men of Dibra surrender and retire, leaving us only Jashat. I leave and march to Zenil's house in two hours (a good time). There I try to get in touch with Michael and Xhelal [Ndreu] and Sherif Lita and Ali Dikë. Whilst I wait for developments I practise some amiable Italian on the younger scions of the house of Ndreu. In the evening Michael arrives from Xhafer's and we talk between ourselves more than is polite to our Albanian hosts. Michael is very defeatist about our prospects. Xhafer [Lita] is apparently only interested in our money and any drop hereabouts would be a failure. Michael counsels an agreement with the Lita family. I cannot see how such a move could be possible while Osman and Sherif retain their evil fame as collaborators. Michael and I agree that we should make some rapprochement with the Ndreu family and cut our losses.

Zenil is very hospitable – I am beginning to smoke too much.

12th March

The weather shows a little improvement – the thaw is complete in Sllovë valley. Michael and I confer with Sherif [Lita], who makes many rude remarks about the British mission and its methods (many of them just). He makes it quite clear that he wants to force us into an agreement with him and his collaborationist friends. I still think it is in our power to force him into our paths if we proceed tactfully.

Islam and Xhelal Ndreu arrive. Cen Elezi is disturbed by reports of the Major's contacts with Selim Xhetani and Halil Alia and by reports that the Major says openly that Cen stole 1,000 sovereigns at Sllovë.[87] Some immediate action is needed here to prevent complete loss of confidence in us. Xhelal is anxious to raise men for Richard – and for money. With careful handling and M.B.'s help these Ndreus may yet prove useful.

Zenil takes Michael and me apart and warns us not to carry out our business in this area too openly and certainly not to have a drop. There is a lot of bad faith in this neighbourhood and our policy does not improve it. If we do not revise some of our methods and plans, we shall be in danger of losing all friends and supporters here. Local fears and suspicions are great: four villages have made a *besa* against communists (and, we believe, against us). We cannot afford to quarrel with everyone at once. The collaborationist party is trying to force us to favour it: we need some strong *points d'appui* to resist them.

I move to Xhafer's and do not meet a very warm welcome: he suspects, rightly, that we are only playing with him. He warms up when Ali Dikë arrives in the evening. Ali too speaks of possible trouble in this area – witness the *besa* made in the Bushrica valley against communists and ourselves. Germans and Gendarmerie and the natural fears of the people threaten to make our difficulties increasingly greater.

Xhafer's comfortable bedding gives an excellent night's sleep.

---

87 Halil Alia is described by Peter Kemp as having the reputation of a 'robber baron' who appeared as a 'small sturdy man with a hooked nose and merry dark eyes set in a fleshy face'. Kemp, *No Colours or Crest, op. cit*, p. 167.

13th March

In the morning a conference with Xhafer who declares openly that he cannot hope to raise men to fight without huge grants of money. The people will fight only for profit. And it is useless to organise a drop unless we can bribe the people to help us – which is useless to us as we did not come here to organise a mercenary army. In this country it is impossible to organise for war in the winter. We might manage to organise in the spring and fight in the summer. But the winter has been an insuperable obstacle to our plans and we are totally unprepared for an allied invasion in the spring. We have lost prestige and influence by our obvious failure to achieve the impossible. We can retrieve our position only by cutting all our losses and starting again from zero in the spring; but Cairo decrees that by then we shall be too late. G.H.Q. does not know this country!

I send Ali Dikë to try and find a place for the radio in Gjegje – probably a vain search. When I set out for Vilë it is warm and spring-like, but on top of the hills the wet snow is very uncomfortable for walking. We walk too fast and reach Vilë by daylight which disturbs Baftja a little.[88] He also announces that he is 'displeased' with the Captain who has under-paid his brother for under-work. In our present state it pays not to offend good supporters like Baftja even when their work is not 100%. As a result of Baftja's discontent and of the unhelpful profiteering attitude of Mahmoud (the radio host) it takes me four hours to cover the one hour's distance to Selim Nokë's. There I hear that the radio is again out of action. What with that and indifferent weather, there has been no aeroplane. Without a quick drop the local situation becomes very complicated.

14th March

A dismal day followed by a terrible night of roaring blizzard. We can do nothing except swap news and make ourselves comfortable. I do my best to boost the Ndreu family as possible good friends – we certainly need some besides M.B.. With the latter no progress has been made. We are still to meet him shortly.

---

88 Baftja Hoci. See entry for 31 January.

Damn Ali Solimani: he arrives to stay the night and as we must remain hidden from him we cannot move into the guest room to sleep. He is probably spying and looking for us. No doubt Selim *burrë i fortë* [strong fellow] can deal with him.

Much talking with Richard. He does not have much sympathy for men of other types than his. But he is a hearty companion and hot-gospeller for his idea of enjoying *la bonne vie*. I imagine that in a regiment he would be a model of efficiency and zeal and good military order and discipline and fine in a fight. Unfortunately this task of ours is very civilian and scarcely at all military.

15th March

A lovely dawn of orange and green-shaded blue over a landscape of perfect snow. Even the trees are unbroken in their whiteness; and light clouds rest in the valleys to hide the deep shadows of the rivers. The high hills and mountains are freshly smooth but the foothills look old as the snow outlines their wrinkles and bulges. Near at hand the wind has swept the snow smooth with wide brush-strokes and the whole land shines against the sun. The icicles begin to drip and birds to sing and Albania waits for spring in glorious stillness.

In the afternoon I have a slight contretemps with Selim. These people cannot tolerate jokes with any personal bias. At least they take advantage of such things to show displeasure and so to force us into awkward positions from which they hope we shall buy ourselves out. Selim is soon calmed; but my joke leads to a quarrel with Ali Solimani – we don't regret it in his case. But we have to be very careful in our idle conversation with this unsympathetic interpreter, Jashat.

Later John Hibberdine (Captain) arrives with Otter, Gjiko and Jemal, Orlando and Luigi and guided by Ram Hoxha. The north of Albania seems to be finished as far as we are concerned. The recent German drives have shattered the Partisans and scattered the British Missions. Hands with his party is in Montenegro awaiting evacuation (Hands ill). Neel is in hiding in the far north, ill and alone. Merritt with a party is hiding with Ymet Bardoshi (Merritt behaving most irresponsibly and strangely). And Hibberdine is seeking Abas Kupi to ask him to extract Neel. Hands has caused much trouble north of the Drin by

Crossing a mountain village stream

his excessive support of Partisans and he has not collaborated too well with 'nationalist' Neel. Kemp's mission in Kossovo has been cut short by his return to Cairo, by Cairo's fear of British officers being involved in frontier disputes when the Germans withdraw and by the jealousy of Tito's Partisans, with whom 'our relations are of overwhelming importance'. And now, after being hunted in very severe conditions, John tells us that there is nothing more to be hoped for in the north. Muharrem and we seem to remain the last outposts of an English party in the Drin valley.

At midnight we have a false alarm, light our fires, but hear the aircraft pass by to Yugoslavia. Terribly cold but a magnificent night.

16th March

Two troubles in the morning – one with our last radio host, one with Ali Solimani. Then we help John Hibberdine and party on their way – we have not been able to welcome them very heartily. Next we say farewell to Xhiko and Xhemal. In our condition we cannot afford to surround ourselves even with the most faithful retainers.

In the evening a message. A very cold night with a high wind and a starlit sky. We wait painfully until after moonrise at 1.0 a.m, and then, after several chilly false alarms, light our fires for our plane. It drops badly if spectacularly. But Selim Nokë is superb. He saves almost everything for us and disputes with the people on our behalf. By morning we can guess that the plane has failed to release half its load. For the rest we are sure.

17th March

A little chocolate, some Woodbines and V's and some bully beef and a tea brew cheer us on our weary way. We manage to check everything and find our radio, gold and food. The war material is very poor and Selim is disappointed, but 20 sovereigns cheer him. He well deserves them, *burrë i fortë*.

In the afternoon the village arrives in force to complain against all this pro-Englishness on Selim's part. He maintains our cause heroically and successfully. The village departs; and promptly Flt. Lt. Hands, Lt. Merritt and all the rest of our northern pioneers, bar Neel, arrive.

The snow prevented their exit through Montenegro, and now they are making for Valona. Their news from the north is depressing and feeling between BLOs there appears to have been poor. Feeling between Richard and Andy [Hands] is bad. And Andy is too used to luxury to think our hospitality other than mean. We should be more generous and Andy should be better humoured. Our position of 'secrecy' is difficult with these constant movements of English through us; but Englishmen deserve the best possible welcome. Andy has helped considerably to mess up our affairs in this country, but they would probably have been messed up in any case.

18th March

We do our best to entertain Andy; but between Andy and Richard the task is difficult as they bicker constantly. At last we make a good lunch of porridge and bully and pickles and cheese and a brew of real coffee and tea. Hands' party arrives unexpectedly and spoils my porridge programme – Hands' fault but it makes his opinion of our welcome lower. Then Hands goes and all is quiet again; but as he intends to stay for a while in this area, there is sure to be trouble between us.

There is nothing else of great interest – we take a Saturday night of irresponsible idleness. The 'quince' joke tends to monopolise conversation with Selim but we got on very well together.

19th March

In the morning I cook breakfast while Tony and Richard go in search of our mail, dropped in Kalis. We are disappointed as mail is very scanty – four letters for me. There are some magazines and books – just enough to remind us of another world. All at home seems uneventful; the war still seems to be very hard. Will it last longer than we think? We hope not if we have to stay in this awkward situation here.

A colossal European lunch, rather alfresco, and a hearty leave-taking from Selim and co., and we start for Muharrem's. At Ujmishte we find most good houses filled with gendarmes and therefore we move on to Muharrem's unexpectedly by night. Richard is an impatient marching companion and hustles the Albanians somewhat. Not a long march but a weary one. M.B's carpets are very welcome.

Muharrem Bajraktari (in cape) flanked by his personal guards.

20th March (Monday)

We meet M.B. and begin to enjoy a day of luxurious living. M.B. is difficult as we bring no definite good news for him and his party. Richard handles him a little tactlessly; he should be more silent and firmer. Some of the work put in by Tony and me is thrown away but matters improve later and stand finally where we started.

The Albanian position is not pleasant in view of recent Cairo messages. Their favouring of the LNÇ robs us of all chances in the north and encourages the defection of nationalists to the German camp. Today we hear that Cen Elezi has accepted German pay. Richard is at last coming to our way of thinking in support of M.B.. We try to write a report of the state of affairs, pulling some of the wool from previous BLOs off Cairo's eyes.

Otherwise I get pleasure from reading *World News Reviews*. It is good to be in the picture again. Our Balkan sphere is evidently a danger point for the allies – Britain versus Russia, with the latter on top. M.B.'s views appear strikingly up to date in the light of the articles in *World News Reviews*.

We drink raki and eat heartily and well and talk and sleep to our hearts' content.

21st March

We use bad weather and sleet as an excuse for staying longer. The morning brings a long chat with M.B. about communism and nationalism and family history and Albanian history. We give him 50 sovereigns as a personal encouragement and he responds very cheerfully. An excellent lunch is his first response.

In the afternoon we hear that Osman Lita has informed the Germans of our drop – a search party of gendarmes en route for Selim Nokë's calls on M.B. to enquire whether there is any danger of finding our material at Selim's. M.B. angrily denounces Osman to the gendarmes for harbouring Michael! Stables will soon declare war on Waggoner. Our drop is going to have some interesting repercussions here.

We hear that Hands and party have returned to Vilë. Our difficulties from that source are going to increase. Not only will Hands and Merritt queer our shopping market but also our political pitch. All very awkward!

At night M.B. is in a genial mood and tells us stories of peacetime Albania with its Ruritanian politics and the rival antics of Italian and English military and political advisers. Richard and Tony and I talk about English politics. For all our lack of news, we have a good view of the world and its affairs. At least we look at them from an interesting viewpoint, inside Europe.

22nd March

The weather is still bad, with plenty of wet snow falling. We read and argue about currency exchange values and what may happen to them when the allies come. Should we change our gold or not – Richard thinks yes. Economic problems baffle me.

I finish the last of our *World News Reviews*. That is sad as they make good reading and provide much information to think about and discuss. We need some informed comment on world affairs to put our work here in its right perspective. Richard is always keen to discuss things but he knows surprisingly little about them. He is a pleasant talker but with no skill and a very simple outlook. Tony goes deeper but is not so enthusiastic for discussion and word battles. M.B. lends me an old book on *La Question Albanaise*, written for the 1918 Peace Conferences.[89] It puts this country's case very well and gives an historical viewpoint which makes it easier to sympathise with the people and their ideas. There is no doubt that great things could be achieved here if Great Power politics permitted. After centuries of oppression this people offers a tempting field for king- and country-makers.

Once more I am convinced (despite the assurances of all the other BLOs) that Albanians are not hopeless and useless and that M.B.'s political dreams would not be entirely hopeless if our Russian ally allowed us to support him.

In the evening we hear a report that 50 Germans have entered Kalis – unconfirmed. What of our radio, and Hands and co. and Selim Nokë? M.B. fears an operation. We plan to leave by dark in the morning. We must do something about this rumour – I think something more energetic than the brief marches which Richard plans.

23rd March

A brief march to a poor house in Ujmisht. A dismal stay there all day, which I while away with a little Home University Library history of *The American Civil War*. Aeroplanes bring us some comforts even if they cause us too much trouble to no purpose. Tony is sick and Richard browned-off. We can get no reliable news of events in Kalis; we are very much at sea.

By evening we move to Isak Kasani's in Shkavec – snow and wind and bad paths do not improve our journey. At Isak's is a crowd of visitors but we eat and sleep well. Still we can get no news.

24th March

All day in a hidden non-public room, well cared for – even a chicken for lunch and some milk. We manage to send Isak Kasani

---

89 This may well have been F. Bianconi's *La Question Albanaise* (Paris: Hachette, 1913) which could not have been written specifically for the Versailles Peace Conference but may well have been used to put the Albanian case.

to shop for us in Prizren: our shopping list consists mostly of luxuries. I can't help thinking that we could succeed better here by turning completely native. Selim soon brings us definite news that the Germans have burned Ali Dikë's house and have arrived as far as Mersin Media's house in Kalis. Selim Nokë, with our property and the 'plane material and most of Kalis, escaped to Reç. Our radio was fortunately whisked away earlier to Ali Dikë's care: where Hands and co. are we have no idea. Is this Osman Lita's work or Cen Elezi's? Certainly it is Halil Alia's. If it develops we shall be in a very tricky position. Poor Ali Dikë! What will his relations with us be now? Better than ever if he is as anti-German as he has said. But Cen Elezi's surrender to the Germans is a bad example.

Richard and Tony leave to find the radio and Ali Dikë in the Bushtrica valley. I stay and move by night into Vilë to find news of Selim Nokë and our baggage and Andy Hands and the Germans. Baftja Latif's house is full of Germans, so I have to wait and freeze among the snows of Vilë until a peasant consents to guide me to the house of our doubtful friends Soliman and Riza. There my reception is cold to say the least – colder than their sour bread and beans – but at least I can sleep in comfort. Latest news is that the Germans and Halil Alia's men have left Kalis for Dibra with the loot of Ali Dikë's farm. Perhaps tomorrow I shall be able to find Selim Nokë and put our affairs in order.

25th March

Most of the day I freeze by myself in a room apart and finish *The American Civil War*. The small boy of the house, Shechir, is as much of a nuisance as an amusement with his constant gabbling Albanian. After lunch I manage to bribe some men to go in search of Hands and Selim Nokë. The latter is found in Kalis and promises to see me tomorrow. That tomorrow is not a cheerful prospect as Riza, the owner of this house, returns from Prizren and shows himself definitely hostile to English visitors. But even inhospitality is welcome as a mixture of gale and snowstorm rages outside all day.

26th March

Once again I am put in chilly solitary confinement with little fire and less company. Selim Nokë fails to arrive, and I have a stormy interview with the family who will not raise a finger to help me to any of my destinations. None of them speaks Italian and I have no interpreter; difficult to say the least. I am on the point of retreating to Baftja's when a note arrives from Kalis summoning me to Kalis. The gendarmes are still in residence, but no one seems to bother. I find Selim with a group of merry men in a poor, crowded house which still suffers from the effects of Italian ravages. Hard lying but good company. All our material is said to be safe; the only damage is from some pillaging in Mahmoud's house. But there may be further consequences of our drop to come.

27th March

After several days of severe snow and wind the weather dawns fine. Selim is involved in local quarrels and sending the gendarmes back to Kukës with an empty report. I am left to play with the children. When Gafur finally settles to business I find that Selim has things well in order and that he has received an instruction from M.B. to guard us and our radio well. So I promise to carry the good report of Selim's *çeta* to Richard. A short visit to Mahmoud's house confirms that our material is safe; and then a march to Malik Likë's at Vasaj through heavy snow and a tearing wind. Malik is away and no letter from Richard awaits us. But one lives very well here: work can wait until Malik cares to return.

Local conversation everywhere seems to centre on Cen Elezi's surrender to the Germans. The people dislike his move violently. There is much speculating whether M.B. will follow Cen's example; if he does it will be Cairo's fault.

28th March

No Malik arrives so I continue Mignet's *French Revolution* in Italian interspersed with dog-Albanian conversations. Malik arrives in the afternoon and trouble begins. As a reprisal for our drop in his 'area', Osman Lita with Sherif has inspired the people of nine villages to make a *besa* against us. Malik is afraid to keep me in his house but no one else will accept Englishmen here except in greatest secrecy. After a long dispute with Malik and his uncles I manage to obtain some reason from them and an agreement to break the *besa* secretly.

Then Richard and Tony arrive by daylight – a fatal step. The whole subject of Albanian affairs is reopened and Richard and Tony are utterly unconciliatory. We reach nowhere by growing angry and rude; whether rightfully or not we only endanger the few connections left to us. In any case Osman Lita not Malik should be the target of our anger and Richard and Michael have always pandered to him. Fortunately Malik does not lose his temper and sends us safely and secretly to his uncles' house. A lovely night but bitingly cold – and not a very comfortable room for sleeping (the house of Shaban Tota-Gjegje).

29th March

Richard, Tony and I are established in a reasonable room and are well cared-for. We have to buy for ourselves but we can buy plenteously and well. So we feast all day and talk Albanian business and other idle things. We receive some messages which praise Hands' pretended achievements and give us no line at all on which to work M.B. – Cairo considers him queer [odd]! McLean

Major 'Billy' McLean (later Lt. Col.) and Enver Hoxha at a Partisan rally at Labinot in July 1943.

is coming back into Albania – to suffer the results of his pro-Partisanship; we must wait and see what he will do.[90]

In the evening Michael arrives looking much better and very proud of a march over the Korab. He has been staying in the Lita H.Q. and has much inside information about Cen Elezi's surrender and Lita politics etc. We all agree that we are now in a good position to negotiate officially with the Litas as we have proved by our drop that we do not depend absolutely on Lita support.[91] If only Richard and Michael don't give way to Sherif Lita too much.

Much merriment is interrupted by Zenil, Malik, Ismail and Ali Dikë. Friendly talk is spoiled by another outburst between Richard and Malik. We adjourn to a communal bed for four and sleep like happy sardines.

30th March

In the morning Zenil and Ismail assure us that the local *besa* is meant only to fool the Germans, not to hinder us. Malik refuses to meet us. The mission's position seems to be temporarily improved by the coming of the Germans and our drop. But we hear from Cairo that an invasion is unlikely here in the near future, that Underdone is postponed, that the Russians are growing interested in troop movements hereabouts. The people here are terrified of Russia and her advance. At least we shall be given a few months' more grace for success or failure. Michael decides to ask to be evacuated: we all give him home addresses to write to, in hope that Cairo will approve his withdrawal.

---

90 In 1943 McLean worked to help the Partisans to form the 1st Partisan Brigade and then attempted to amalgamate the anti-Italian resistance by bringing together the Partisans and the nationalists. On his second tour of duty in June/July 1944 he adopted the line of favouring the nationalists.

91 The Litas were an influential and somewhat notorious family in Kalis and the surrounding area. Baron Nopcsa (Baron Franz Nopcsa von Felső-Szilvás 1877-1933), the Hungarian adventurer and enthusiast for Albania, told of an encounter in 1907 with an earlier family member Mustafa Lita and his son Osman (possibly the same Osman). These two deceived him, took him captive and attempted to ransom him. See *Reisen in den Balkan, op. cit.*, pp. 124-36. http://www.albanianhistory.net/1907_Nopcsa2/index.html.

A veering wind fills our room with smoke. We either freeze without fire or asphyxiate ourselves with one. Happily it is warmer today. We are at a loose end and try to amuse ourselves by eating odd snacks and making brews – rather a shabby existence.

In the evening Richard and Michael leave for the Lita H.Q. and Tony and I march to the radio – an uphill but pleasant journey. There Fernando [their Italian cook and steward] has prepared a magnificent chicken stew with wheatcakes. No wonder that our soldiers look very fit and contented. Ali Dikë is in pleasant mood too – despite loss of his house. And Qasim our host is very affable; so all goes swimmingly here.

31st March

First, a bold decision to have my shirt washed – God knows when it last saw soap. Then a slight rocket for two Albanian henchmen who think that *grosh* [traditional white bean soup] is not good enough for them and demand constant sugar and European food. Class or race distinction is not very commendable, especially in a land of communal dishes; but our soldiers lead a fairly dull life and we must reserve all our small stocks of good food to boost their morale. In any case Albanians have always eaten *grosh* and therefore do not need to add to their pay by luxury feeding (strange what constitutes luxury here!).

Some new messages from Cairo seem to indicate that G.H.Q. is at last seeing some daylight through our messages about the Tirana Group and M.B. and about the true situation of parties and BLOs in this country. Brains are at last threatening to baffle bull-shit! Tony and I keep the attack going by beating out some more forceful messages on the present state of things. Until McLean arrives from Italy we shall be able to do no more.

We live lazily and well here; but Fernando's camp-fire cookery, though excellent to eat, is a weariness of the spirit to watch and wait for. The soldiers cannot complain of lack of comforts (Albanian ones of course) but they lead a drowsy life. Tony may envy them sometimes, but I don't.

At night we hear that Russian troops are near the Czech Carpathian frontier and sweeping towards Odessa and so to

Bessarabia. Goebbels has appealed to us to help Germany against the Red menace. These Albanians would answer that appeal cheerfully: we shall have a hard task to teach them otherwise.

1st April

The charging handle is broken, so we do nothing all day but cook and suffer smoke fumes and talk. As Gregson is going home we write letters for England, in the hope that they will ultimately get there. The weather grows worse and finally shakes Tony's and my resolution to move back to Isak Kasani's. So we stay and feast well and sleep. It is cold – we were wise not to move.

2nd April (Sunday)

A charging handle arrives so charging restarts. Ali (Kasani) arrives to announce an extraordinarily successful shopping party from Prizren – he tries to persuade us to not bring Ali Dikë into Lumë, but we insist on our need for him. We amuse ourselves by cooking *tetli* [honey and walnut cakes], eating, teaching Fernando to make fires, writing home and exchanging badinage with the soldiers. In the evening we march along the mountain tops to Shkavez where we meet Richard. It is a lovely night with hard snow underfoot. At Isak Kasani's we are lodged in a room apart, a very pleasant change from crowded guest-rooms.[92]

We hear that the Germans have burned the house of Haziz Dine Hoxha near Peshkopijë. Because of Englishmen seen in that district by daylight? Hands and party are now with Dan Kaloshi. Richard and Michael have made some sort of arrangement with the Litas, and it seems to favour them more than us. Richard and Michael grow dangerously fond of individuals, so fond of them that they begin to believe in them. Belief is a dangerous element in this job.

---

92 Most Albanian houses maintained special rooms to receive and accommodate guests and to keep them separate from the family quarters. This was particularly important in Muslim households where women would never be seen by guests, except perhaps occasionally pre-pubescent girls and old women. Host and guests would be expected to observe strict customs and courtesies associated with their roles. Guests might not be acquainted with each other but would still be expected to share the guest-room at night.

3rd April

At Isak's we make the most of the luxuries from Prizren – even some sweets. We decide to organise a landing ground for planes at Kastriot (half an hour from the Germans). Probably the local population will not tolerate it; but it will be great fun if we succeed. And evacuation will become very easy.

In the evening Selim Nokë arrives in high spirits. It looks as though his *çeta* really will be with us in the mountains when spring comes. He paints a glorious buccaneer picture of life in the Gostivar hills. This seems to be a substantial proof that M.B. means business. Yet Cairo sends us still more messages with much doubt of his value. We determine to keep our pro-M.B. propaganda machine working hard.

We try to de-louse; but we are too lousy to have much effect. Still it does help to give a really sound night's sleep.

4th April

Another uneventful day in which we make ourselves comfortable and make odd negotiations with odd people. We hear a new directive from the radio, which seems to suggest that Cairo is appreciating our point of view. Richard and Sgt. Gregson move to Zenil Lita's to join Michael and the Hands evacuation party. Selim is awkwardly possessive and moves Tony and me to a house in Reç, near Mehmet Troci. It is useless to us: it serves only to show the flag in Reç. Awful night in a hot room full of men (some sick), with no bedding and devoured by fleas. We are very angry with Selim but we can do nothing about it.

5th April

A lovely spring day which persuades us to sun ourselves on the local terrace. A vague day in a very poor house – only maize and cheese water to eat. We meet one of Cen Elezi's prospective gendarmes and give him an anti-gendarme pep-talk – to no effect. Money alone speaks loudly to this people. We have a little trouble in discussing with Selim the payment of his *çeta*. We shall have much dispute over our little mercenary army.

By night we climb steadily for five hours to the radio through soft melting snow. The mountains look lovely in the moonlight with clouded shadows in the steep valleys. A good meal and sleep at the radio house.

6th April

We rise to eat porridge and so start a day of good living (somewhat crude by civilised standards). With the eating goes a thorough de-louse, of which I find plenty too many. I am kept pretty busy chasing our soldiers and Fernando who are all disorderly. The soldiers are astoundingly lazy. Cairo tells us that Hands has reached Slender. He is behaving very badly toward Richard, his conduct guided by personal whims and not by interest in the job. Some trouble between Selim Nokë and Ali Dikë. Selim must be taken down a peg before his 'commandant of çeta' ideas grow too big. A good meal and sleep at the radio house.

7th April (Good Friday)

To suit all tastes we manage to find a rare (a unique) tin of fish for breakfast. And afterwards I mortify my flesh by taking my fourth bath in this country. A lovely spring day, so we spend as much time as we can scanning the far mountains for suitable dropping grounds. In fine weather this job of ours may become very pleasant. Some cookery experiments and some Italian while away the time as we wait for news from Cairo which does not come. Jugged chicken is a dish to remember. Tony is not a very communicative companion at present. We try hard to hear BBC news but with little success. What lousy operators we have – no Mendoza link, no BBC!

8th April

The morning schedule brings us puzzling news. First we are asked for May sortie requirements which implies a longer stay here than we had hoped. Then we are told that an Anglo-American occupation of Albania is a very slight possibility. It looks as though Russian troops will be coming this way in which case our task here will grow very difficult, as Slavs and Albanians hate each other above all else. The situation grows interesting but it does not offer much encouragement for our work. Our only hope now lies in McLean who will have to decide whether it is worth supporting our policy or not.

After some payment problem with Qasim Jata (unintelligent rather than malicious) Tony and I leave late. Without a guide and with a badly loaded horse we make bad going but reach Lapa and rest comfortably. It has been pleasant to stay at our radio H.Q. but there is a depressing lack of life there. Goodier becomes more and more of a problem – an awkward type for whom Tony and I are ready to start gunning if he grows any more insolent and unruly.

9th April (Easter Sunday)

Our feast day is a day of abstinence. We want to move onto the mountain tops to recce dropping grounds; but the householder is afraid of the local *besa* and refuses to let us leave in daylight. So we stay for a long colourless day and divert ourselves by reading and smoking and making brews. I come to the end of my Italian nursery stories and begin to dip into Tony's book, an insipid sort of novel *Chaos is Come Again.*[93]

In the night we march to Çaja, a long steep climb through a grimly impressive gorge and valley. A good house and a fair welcome; but tomorrow we shall see how friendly our host really is. We shall want him to walk with us by day – the acid test of friendship in these parts.

10th April

The morning is cloudy so we postpone our recce in the hope of being able to see more tomorrow. We are promptly shunted into a siding i.e. a chilly upstairs room where we brew tea and porridge and do our best to keep morale high. I read and am too absorbed to notice the chilliness of this hill-station. At night we are allowed to venture downstairs. Tony and I talk for a long time about English and European politics and society. We share a none too optimistic view of post-war affairs, of Russia, America and

---

93 *Chaos is Come Again* by Claude Houghton, 1938.

the Commonwealth and England. A lively conversation and an interesting one. Tony's opinions are often conventional but he is always open to new ones. One can sharpen one's wits with him.

11th April

Again the morning is wet and we are shrouded in clouds. A letter from the Major and the radio only shows how static this area is at present. We set off to look for dropping grounds on the mountains and find only one fair-weather ground right on top, still sheeted with melted snow. It is a very stiff climb up and down again, but pleasantly strenuous. The scenery through drifting clouds is spectacularly massive. This is like a day in Wales, with everything magnified in size and splendour. We climb down again to Daut Xoxha's house in Çaja and then descend further to Ibrahim Abdia's house in Lapa. A very good day's exercise with a comfortable night to cap it.

12th April

Another of our frequent empty days, this time without anything to read and no porridge, tea or sugar. A bit boring but it is lovely weather outside and plenty of people come to see us. And Abdi brings us a message from the radio, indignant to have seen that the soldiers eat eggs and *petullas* [fritters] while we have only beans. So he promptly produces four eggs to console us. Cairo at last makes clear our position vis a vis Muharrem – an important man, but he can have only small-scale help, due to our commitments elsewhere. At this stage that seems just enough, we can now go ahead in negotiations with him. A sheaf of messages from Richard strike an ominously pro-Lita note. Sherif is doing his best to seduce this mission to his profit by using Michael's 'intuitions' and Richard's impulsiveness.

By night we climb up steeply to find the radio, losing ourselves on the way. In the last two hundred yards our horse takes a bad fall in deep snow off a path – and stays there. We recover him after some flap and settle down to some good living with our soldiers. These are as strangely dull as ever and are due for a large rocket for their careless behaviour of late.

13th April

A chaotic day. A little law and order is beginning to appear in our domestic arrangements when Selim Nokë and Baftja Latif and their following appear. A troublesome interview begins with Selim. He is offended by our protests at some stolen material and chooses to turn this against Ali Dikë. A tricky situation which ends only with an unsatisfactory compromise. We hear that M.B wants to make a move against the Germans. We must visit him and clear this static situation.

Amerigo (Hands' old cook – a superb one) joins us and cooks himself in with distinction. And I receive some clothes from Limjan. Life is growing luxurious! The weather is superb and we have a fine vantage point, with a view stretching far beyond Kukës. It sustains us in further boring bargaining over Latif's mule. A sleepily comfortable evening without even notable world news. Only a snatch of *I know that my Redeemer liveth* raises the night above the ordinary.

14th April

A bombshell arrives in the morning – a letter from Richard who writes excitedly that the Lita family is going to declare against the government and that he is going to back them to the hilt. Tony and I do not like the look of this as we have a very low opinion of the Litas. I can only presume that the new nationalist front of the government threatens the safety of the Osman Litas and the Halil Alias of the land and that they are now ready to drop their collaboration and call on us to save them. Tony and I must wait and see but in the honest interests of M.B. we both hope to find a red herring.

Amerigo cooks us a *dolce* – a very good one – and Tony and I join Richard and Sherif in a Lita house near Vilë. Richard is bubbling over with hope and expectations – doomed I should think to disappointment. Why should we rush into the arms of collaborators rather than stick to Muharrem? Only because Sherif knows how to seduce Richard and Michael. Curses on Michael.

15th April

A lovely warm spring day with the first flowers appearing and lizards basking in last year's leaves. We sunbathe and talk and confer with Sherif. At first all is friendly but as we get down to details his financial ideas appear more and more impossible. Richard still refuses to see that we are being asked to buy a following for Osman Lita in this area. He is too keen to impress Cairo with results. Our conferences end very coldly with all Richard's card houses collapsed (thank God!). I have had to interpret in Italian all day. As Sherif is a shit and Richard is very impatient, I have had the hell of a time. In the evening we return to the radio, Richard downcast, Tony and I weary of foolish disputes but happy. We hear that M.B. has surrendered to Tirana but don't believe it. We shall see.

16th April

All is confusion, as Richard puts a finger in every pie and cooks none. But fine weather and a grand panorama soon draw us out sunbathing. A Prizren shopping party arrives with several luxuries – honey and triple secco [orange-flavoured liqueur] and sweets and oranges. In the midst of a consequent orgy the Partisans arrive, showing all the traces of their hard winter. All are unusually amiable and I get to know the pleasant French-speaking Stefan. In the late spring we should be able to do something with these Partisans. Their talk and a letter from M.B. suggest that they and M.B.'s party may begin to draw together against the pro-German government – a very good thing. Meanwhile M.B. does not wish us to come to his house. The Germans have been burning in Bicaj. M.B. was ready to defend himself. Good for him! But if he does not see Richard soon the Lita lures may still prevail.

Amerigo prepares a sumptuous supper. We are beginning to recapture the ghost of the Degë days.

17th April

Neither the Bari nor the Cairo skeds are successful nor does a letter come from M.B. There is nothing to do but organise our H.Q. and sunbathe and nothing to read but trash. Life with Richard is wearying as when he has nothing to do he can never amuse himself without inventing a thousand useless tasks which always involve everyone else who has no interest in them. Tony is in one of his reserved moods. It does not matter. The weather is lovely and we can lie in peace and watch the war fly past in force to Belgrade and Sofia – an impersonal war.

18th April

Today is like others recently, except that we receive plenty of messages. Apparently the long-awaited McLean is now in the country.[94] Richard and Tony will be going to meet him at Xibër while I stay with the radio, keep an eye on our war and try to find means of receiving a plane. A letter from M.B. announces that we can see him tomorrow. It will be possible to tie things up again for a few days. We amuse ourselves by building an oven for Amerigo and Fernando. The latter is doubtful whether it is hot enough to suit a master-baker but it looks superb. Such innocent amusement makes our day almost lively – much livelier than Michael's days would seem to be to judge by his latest dismal effort from *le quartier* Lita.

19th April

We have to rise and march before dawn to Vilë to meet M.B.. Annoying but we use a lovely crescent moon climbing over the Korab with the first light. We are shut in the usual chilly and damp store-room where we all doze fitfully (i.e. Richard, Tony and I) until M.B. appears. Richard tries to force things but M.B. shows himself very urbane and courteously firm and refuses to commit himself to anything until the allies promise to support his party in force. He is prepared to make an entente with the Litas but he makes us see that he sees himself as senior partner. We end in a compromise; everything will wait until McLean comes hither. If M.B. does not realise soon how large are Allied commitments elsewhere, he and we can do nothing. If he stays too righteously inflexible, his and our plans will fail completely. The Russians and the Partisans cannot be played with.

Tony grows a little sick – one of his chills. After a rotten day we all return to the radio – Tony on a very feeble Azzi. Ali Dikë

---

94 McLean parachuted into the H.Q. at Bizë on 19 April.

used Azzi without permission. Richard is raging about it. Ali Dikë will suffer an uncomfortable half-hour. Otherwise all quiet and colourless on the Stables front.

20th April

Tony grows sicker and finally cannot leave with Richard to meet McLean at Xibër. Richard plans to move fast. His anxiety to have a plane written down to Stables in H.Q. books makes him very anxious to have a drop at Gramë. Tony and I doubt the wisdom of a drop to Partisans. But a drop it must be.

In the afternoon much trouble over horses – they have been sadly neglected. Richard flies off the handle but they will still be neglected. Richard goes to the Lita houses and Tony goes to bed – temperature 103.5. I become nurse and the day ends with dull domestication.

A message from Cairo shows that H.Q. is attracted to the Lita-M.B. plan as drawn by Richard.

21st April

Tony is the order of the day. He is very feverish and ill and we can do little to help him, having no drugs and no diagnosis of his illness. He takes only milk and we can obtain only one and a half kilos of it, watered and at famine price. Let us hope that Nature keeps him going.

I send our signallers out on the hillside in the hope of improving their signals, with little luck. Not a Goodier day I feel. He spends most of it bringing rockets on his own head.

In the evening Michael arrives with no doctor and plenty of excited advice. Between us and a bottle of triplo secco we devise possible means of improving Tony's condition. Our resources are poverty-stricken. We leave Tony to sleep and retire downstairs to talk Albanian politics. Richard appears to have handled the Litas somewhat tactlessly again. Trouble threatens to brew there. .

Qasim Pristina has joined me as we should move with him to Gramë for a Partisan drop. But a drop of any sort here may have very bad results in the present state of our relations with M.B. and the Litas. If Tony's illness gives me any excuse, I shall avoid the drop.

22nd April

Tony still at 103.5 when I clumsily break the thermometer. Now we are quite out of touch with his illness as he himself has fallen very silent and admits himself very ill. A man in that state seems to exist only as a body.

We await the doctor who does not come. At last we have a letter from him: Osman Lita will not permit the doctor to come as Richard has trodden on Osman's gouty self-importance. So churlish an action is typical of the house of Lita, but it is really Richard's fault as he should understand them better. Michael must travel back to Kalaj-Dodë tonight to solve the diplomatic problem or else to withdraw himself and Gregson bag and baggage from the Lita hospitality.

Michael and I talk much, mostly criticism of Richard, the *enfant gâté*. Michael's position especially is now made very difficult by Richard's stupid wilfulness.

Davis, Elvidge and Goodier are promoted acting paid corporals, saith the decree of Cairo. They do not all deserve it but to prove their virtues they manage to contact Bari for the first time – Bari using a wrong call sign.

Michael departs. Tony remains very sick. I manage to persuade Abdullah to let us use his main guest room for Tony. He is willing to do plenty for us in exchange for more money but he rejects any suggestion that our soldiers should move to another house to leave Tony in peace. Fear and cupidity are the ruling motives of these people in relation to us.

It is very difficult to nurse Tony here. He must be terribly uncomfortable but nothing much can be done about it. We have no comforts.

23rd April

Tony is still in high fever after a bad night. The doctor arrives with Michael. Michael says that a night-long dispute with the Lita's has finally gained Osman's consent to the doctor's visit to Tony. The doctor is about as ill-mannered as Osman himself. I am sure he is more of a commercial-travelling pharmacist than a doctor.

He certainly has a strong hold on the neurotic Michael; as M. says, he and I will never understand each other properly.

The 'doctor' fills Tony with a lot of injections and pills and us with a lot of self-important talk and instructions. Tony begins to show signs of improvement by the time that Michael and the doctor leave in the afternoon.

I send the soldiers away to Qasim Jatë's house. Abdullah's desire for profits must give way to Tony's comfort. We re-install Tony upstairs, give him his pills and settle down to a very hard night on the floor.

24th April

Tony's condition is better, but he grows a little more feverish and more discontented and bad-tempered as the day goes on. We have plenty of trouble with men and horses and material and payments during the day. But everything manages to get settled. Amerigo and Qasim and I talk Italian, not much to Tony's liking I fear. Tony blows up at me at night. I blow back as best one can at a sick man. Not very pleasant but it clears the air. This is not the country in which to be either a patient or a nurse.

25th April

Tony is a little better in the morning. We begin to give him something to eat. Amerigo works like a Trojan to keep the happy home together. Michael arrives, talks a lot, does nothing and keeps the party gay. As he hopes to leave for evacuation any day, I cannot leave Tony and so have to send away Qasim to tell the Partisans that our promised drop is off. An awkward conference with Qasim and two more conferences about money with Abas and Abdullah and some long-drawn bargaining for milk and eggs fill most of the day. No world news or messages of note. We treat ourselves to an excellent roast chicken and *bomboloni* [filled doughnut]. The war is suspended.

26th April

With Qasim leaving, we are left with little to do for a few days except look after Tony. He is much better and therefore more restless. He gets some sleep which is good. Michael and I lounge and watch the distant scene through binoculars and talk and read thriller stories aloud. The radio does not seem to be doing too well. I must pay a call tomorrow to see how much slackness has crept into our new corporals.

27th April

A dingy day of mist and rain, so Michael and I decide not to go to Kalaj-Dodë to talk to Sherif Lita. Tony is much fitter and becomes convalescent. The day is very empty. In the afternoon Tony and I dispute with Michael about local politics and policies. Michael's opinions are narrow and prejudiced and his advocacy seems to me to be childish in its unreason. Michael is cosmopolitan in formation. He judges everything by personal taste and advantage, although his intuition gives him a good appreciation of persons and things which interest him. He seems to have no rational standard in life. In this he has much in common with Richard; but M is more pleasant than R, even if he is a neurotic case. Both can do harm in this job, while achieving popular applause by their own skilled self-advertisement. Their combination here has been unlucky for the British Mission.

In the evening I visit the radio to stimulate our new corporals. They don't need so much encouragement as we thought, even though they are muddling along as ever.

Later I read *The Hunting of the Snark* to Tony and Michael. We fell asleep on a chicken *a la diavola*.

28 April

The weather switches back into winter again. We spend a day killing time domestically. Michael is splendid when he cares to keep the party going. I have a busy mid-day chasing our large Italian mule Cleo who runs away. It leads us up to the radio house where I collect a message saying that Abas Kupi refuses to fight unless the Allies recognise Zog.[95] The Tirana Group is pushing its

---

95 Abas Kupi was a leading figure in the Balli Kombëtar nationalist resistance movement. Its political compromises with the German occupation, driven by fear of communism, and the impossibility for that reason of cooperation with the LNÇ, had, by April, led them to seek accommodation with the monarchist Zogists. See Hibbert, *Bitter Victory, op. cit.*, p. 139.

programme to a conclusion. Nice for McLean to come in and find the situation so clear cut!

Tony and Michael play plenty of cards which is a little boring for everyone else. But the day passes and we watch Amerigo make spaghetti, rather as an English crowd of loafers watches workmen dig a hole. Our resources of work and play are low at present.

29th April

A better looking day with Tony making plans to leave his bed and Michael making plans for a march to Mati. No radio news. After lunch Michael and I take the small charging engine and walk to Kalaj-Dodë. The engine is to be given to the clamorous Litas. Why, I can't think – nor can Tony. But the welcome which Michael and I receive soon tells why the engine was promised by Michael and Richard. The Litas have seduced both of them by careful personal attentions, whilst never raising a finger to help the mission as a whole.

We hear that Xhafer has gone to the Germans at Gostivar to take some money off them and then come back to us, as he hopes. The rest of his family entertain us with raki and garlic and the doctor provides a good wine and excellent cigarettes. The doctor has bought us several good things and a heap of medicine. Michael coos with joy over the latter. The evening is pleasant and sleep is comfortable here. Evidently our politics have been biased by R and M's physical luxuries. These Litas are clever.

30th April

We wake to a filthy day, with a great wind and ice and powdered snow. We decide not to move and settle down to a chilly series of conferences, conversations and horse-play. Sherif is domineering as ever but by replying nothing to his diatribes we manage to tame him and leave our Lita ties suspended more or less satisfactorily. He (and, we are told, his father too) is mollified by the sight of the long-promised charging engine in action. The atmosphere is patiently cordial. Michael and the mysterious Serb doctor are more friendly than I thought which gives the doctor a finger in our pie. I am not fond of Zoti Doktor. Perhaps he can be useful to us but perhaps we are being even more useful to him. Who knows? The local buffoonery grows a little tiring, especially the Doctor's wearisome homosexual pranks. They grow very boring after bed-time. I suppose they are included in our duties here.

1st May

The day is nasty. Icy winds blast many of the first leaves and blossoms of spring. Michael and I move from the Litas to Eles Bajrami's where we are feasted with a lamb. Michael has certainly worked up a following in the area with his lavishness. Later we walk fast against a freezing wind and through patches of snow to the radio house and thence to join Tony. The soldiers need no remark. Tony is much better. I begin to feel unwell. Michael reminds me of a Tolstoy character, Golokhov, as he plays cards with Tony. Michael's message comes from Bari that an evacuation is planned in Slender's area. So Michael plans to march away tomorrow. We have a farewell dinner and I retire to bed feeling very feverish.

2nd May

I take Tony's place in bed with a temperature and take little interest in life. Tony makes a first-class fruit cake. Michael makes a great fuss of his departure. Michael and Gregson depart. I turn over and sweat my fever away.

3rd May

I am much better and leave my uncomfortable bed-carpet. A letter comes from Sherif Lita saying that he has declared against the government: what are we going to do for him?

We decide that I shall go to deal with Sherif and tell him that that there is nothing that needs to be done for him. Tony will contact Muharrem to see if this alarm has any basis in fact.

4th May

A hot walk to the Litas where I soon grow cold in a damp chilly room. Sherif's declaration proves to be a damp squib. The doctor is as boring as ever. In the afternoon Richard arrives back suddenly from Xibër. Col. McLean is not coming here until the 20th and when he comes he will ask for actions before we can start pouring in supplies. Does this mean the end of BLO make-believe? I think not. McLean wants success, like the other officers here.

Richard brings interesting news of the outside world, of the withdrawal of important formations from Italy – the impending invasion from England.

Mrs Hasluck is no longer in our section [at Bari].[96]

Richard brings a good new riding horse. He plays havoc with Rames' hospitality by making our host drunk.

5th May

We talk with Zenil (some childish trouble) and then leave with the doctor to join Tony. A hot journey and I feel ill again. After lunch I go to bed with a high temperature. This is going to ruin the northern recce on which Richard had wanted me to join Tony. Illness in Albania is boring.

6th and 7th May

I am still feverish – probably influenza. Two dull days as Richard and Tony leave me largely to myself. Some Somerset Maugham diverts me and we begin to live on excellent food. Otherwise there is nothing to do but sweat away my fever and chat idly with all comers.

8th May

I seem to be normal again in temperature so I get up to a warm spring day, feeling unusually weak in the knees. Our usual pastoral-bucolic life continues in the best splendour which we can gather round us. Nothing else to note.

9th May

Much movement of horses and stores, much lazing and then much flap as Richard moves off with most of the H.Q. to Gramë to open our dropping ground there with the Partisans. Richard is as full as ever of fantastic hopes and plans.

---

96 When Force 133 moved to Bari from Cairo in April 1944 Mrs Hasluck remained behind. In 1945, already ill with leukaemia, she moved to Cyprus and from there to her city of birth, Dublin, where she died in 1948.

I find the remnants of a copy of C. S. Forester's *The Gun* and swallow it swiftly with relish.

10th May

A fever overtakes me for a third time but as we have to change our house today I refuse to start sweating. Muharrem arrives and I have to interpret – not the happiest of tasks today. But M.B. is friendly and cheerful and all passes off well. At night we move – a bloody horse-ride which ends in the discovery of a temperature of 104. So I start the work of sweating and sleeping.

11th May

A sweaty and starving day – best ignored.

12th May

Qasim Dalipi, our new host, seems very anxious to please. Why? For the present his house is good. Ali Dikë has arrived and Tony jumps him into marching north tomorrow. All is full of Lita talk about weak British policy – that these people are willing to help England if they are paid plenty. We tell Ali violently what we have told him before – that we don't need Albania but that Albania needs us. But we waste our breath as usual. It grows very boring in bed but a drink or two and one of Amerigo's excellent dinners cheer things up; and we sleep with no Albanians to wake us early. All is very well.

13th May

I certify myself as *shëndoshë* [fit] and get up. A lovely day of spring. We have trouble with the charging engine and Davis has trouble with the radio. Then we hear that Richard has the same troubles at Gramë. Ali Dikë starts to cause trouble – the usual growth of interpreter's ambition to become master of our fates. Tony has to tame him to persuade him to move north. Tony is overwhelmed with arguments but finally wins through. I move off to Lapa to collect our third charging engine for Richard. A long six-hour ride there and back. No moon but a fine night. Maslan is very tired – so am I. But with a horse such a march is enjoyable.

14th May

The morning is very busy with Tony's departure for the north. He manages to drag Ali Dikë with him and they set off with the faithful Zeneli in beautiful weather.

Another Italian arrives from Sllovë, Fulvio, by profession a barber. I use his professional services at once. Short hair is a great luxury. Fulvio has all the gestures of a hotel barber. He is a pleasant man but rather broken down at the moment by Albanian treatment.

Some lounging and bargaining and then I ride our new horse, the Bajraktar's Dori, up to Abdullah's house. He is a good animal although a little lazy and wilful. Abdullah beats him in wilfulness, however, as he refuses to sell me our old oven in the hope of forcing us back into his house. When I return, Qasim defeats Abdullah's plan by finding another oven for me. As ever a fantastic price.

The day ends with a painful lecture from me to Maslan and Qasim about Albanian war and politics. The sentiments may have been good but my Albanian was awful.

15th May

The morning is busy with stones and mud, building our new oven – Amerigo approves of it so it must be good. Then Mehmet arrives from Gramë with a broken charging engine which has seen little mercy at Goodier's hands. Work on the motor is hot and vain.

We are a sober party here. Davis is quiet and I am too lazy and inefficient to speak Italian and Albanian unnecessarily. But a small party is much more welcome in this land than a big one. We are on very good terms with everyone here – nothing worse than a slight financial quarrel with Qasim. I start the abridged edition of Pope's *Iliad* which has appeared in our H.Q.. The age of reason seems nearer than the age of heroes but I enjoy the make-believe.

16th May

A sweaty and sunburnt morning of work on the charging engine and the problem is solved at last by a despairing resort to sweet cold reason. I calculate quite simply that a slow-running and a progressive jet are not necessary and that a broken jet will suffice. So I re-place the despised broken jet and the engine runs more smoothly than ever. Very proud of myself – even though the solution was accidental.

Then I retire to a private Olympus to finish the *Iliad*, only to be distracted, like the gods themselves, by endless human troubles, all of which are finally quieted by a good dinner and sleep.

17th May

Abas awakes us before dawn with a load of material from a drop at Gramë (Richard has been highly secretive about it). Some flap, some more sleep and then more flap. We find plenty of kit and plenty of mail. Family letters are very pleasant and cheerful and some lively other ones too. I go out and shoe Dori and get a vivid response.

The rest of the day passes in sorting kit and re-equipping ourselves. The task of keeping our personal kits down to our poverty level of one haversack is not easy with the temptation of the new kit.

Ali Dikë returns having gone with Tony as far as the Drin. He is as spineless as ever.

At night I test our new sleeping bags. They are American and very civilised – superb.

18th May

World Press Reviews, stomach trouble and stocktaking occupy the morning. The world is already preoccupied with the peace – the first years of peace will be an ugly time. Letter reading and magazine reading keep us busy and Amerigo obliges with some excellent *pan di Spagna* [sponge cake].

Qasim Dalipi guides me by night to Isak Kasami's house where Ali Bairami has arranged for me to meet Captain Abdurrahman Guri, commander of the Bicaj gendarmes. We talk until two in the morning and then I snatch a couple of hours' sleep and move back to H.Q. before dawn. Spring sunsets and dawns seen from horse-back are lovely: there is no feeling of weariness in them.

Abdurrahman is not foolish but like most Albanians he fails to understand what he is doing. No one can persuade him into new paths but he is ready to connive at all our activities except our relations with the Partisans. There are two obstacles to all our work here – the red star and the gendarme's uniform.

Views of the heights of the Korab massif where Stables mission spent the summer of 1944.

19th May

A late reveille worthy of G.H.Q. troops.

The day soon develops into a dispute with the local *tregtar* [tradesman]. I win a childish battle. Then our usual peace is shattered by a report that Germans are coming from Kalaj-Dodë. I pack Davis off with his radio and try to send out scouts. The flap is colossal. Then a man arrives shouting that the Germans are ten minutes away. Ali Dikë runs away with Maslan. The people begin to shift their belongings and pillage one another. Qasim Dalipi and I can do nothing but retire up the hill and wait. Everything is hopelessly panic-stricken. We come and go and achieve nothing and Ali Dikë rarely consents to let me into the secret of what is going on. At last we settle down into a forest hiding place, only to be recalled at once by a messenger who says that the 'Germans' were Kossovars running away from Valona and that Abas has arrived with material from the Major. So back we move by a painful path to find just before dawn a room pillaged and ruined with material scattered to the winds. We wait for day to start work.

21st May

Qasim does wonders to win back our kit: very little is lost. We restore order, sort the new kit from Gramë, quarrel with a few local robbers and recognise H.Q.. Everything has to be tied up and handed over to Davis. Some more of my personal kit is lost – thanks to the plane there is more at hand.

In the evening I ride with Maslan and Zajm to Zenil Lita's where we sit and talk. Zenil accuses us of pro-communism. Whatever we do, someone is displeased. Whose war is this? By darkness we move to Gramë – a foul and long and steep and pitch-black journey. Thank God for Dori! Then a few hours' sleep among the horses and then a new day.

22nd May

Lack of sleep and cold weather spoil the first taste of *la vie champêtre*. Plenty of checking of stores and exploring of the camp area keep the day busy. We live under parachute lean-to's – fine weather is needed. It is cold and I have just jettisoned my warmer clothing.

Qasim Pristina is here – he makes good conversation. Goodier and Elvidge are not very lively but are cheerful. Fernando is overworked. The scene is alpine but I am in no alpine mood today.

23rd May

A filthy day – cold, snow, sleet, rain and mist until night falls. We are soaked and very cold with no resources except an open-air fire. Whenever the rain stops we dry ourselves: when the snow stops we try to keep our mules warm. Fernando has a rotten job in this weather: our camp was not made for it. I start reading *Under the Greenwood Tree*, a rare pleasure here, but I am far busier running round the camp, making a fire or keeping warm. Qasim and I talk politics, Goodier and I talk army and we all gabble with Fernando. A happy party exasperated by the weather.

24th May

The weather is much more pleasant. The morning passes in distributing material to men the Major has sent. Richard has had a close shave with a German patrol by the Drin. Col. McLean has not arrived yet but we receive a long sitrep for him which seems to suggest that we may soon see a civil war if we can't persuade the nationalists to fight.[97] Richard's recent enthusiasm for Kupi seems to have been misplaced.

In the afternoon I climb with Qasim to see the Partisan *çeta*. There we have a long political pow-wow with the whole *çeta* thrusting proletarian democracy at me. Interesting but unconvincing, though probably I would be of their party were I an Albanian.[98] In the evening I bid farewell to these Spartans and return to my own Athens-in-exile. There we eat well, smoke round our fire and sleep.

25th May

A cold day which slowly brightens. I take Goodier through his paces with the charging engines. He is clumsy and inexpert, yet claims to have been a tank driver. Then I rebuild Fernando's oven and produce a super clay-padded affair. Fernando eyes it dubiously but I think it will work.

A day passes quickly here. *Under the Greenwood Tree* is finished. Hardy is a good open-air companion.

26th May

A sunnier day which almost persuades us it is not cold. We soon find ourselves mistaken when we cease physical work. The mules keep us busy today – saddles and shoeing. The animals do their best to knock us about, getting their own back for the rough time they have had with the Albanians. Then Fernando's cheerfulness collapses as his oven needs adjustment: these Italians are very volatile. Fernando works hard but not intelligently. He and Goodier and Elvidge turn officers into nattering cub masters. We always end our days gaily, trying to keep warm at a fire. But this life out of doors has not yet proved easy: there is still snow fifty feet above us.

---

97 At that moment McLean was marching from Bizë to Xibër and would arrive the following day. His task was to convince the Balli Kombëtar nationalists, not only to fight the Germans but to cooperate with the LNÇ. Furthermore, the British missions in the north needed re-organising.

98 Hibbert said this several times and post-war it was used to accuse him of communist sympathies.

27th May

A little rain at intervals – plenty of cold. We are so busy with the physical problems of living here that this diary seems ridiculously out of place, something belonging to another life, irrelevant and strange.

Haxhi comes from Vilë to say that Sqn. Ldr. Neel has arrived there with three tame Germans, Nik Sokoli and all. The other Germans, the untamed ones, chased him to Shkavez and then broke off the hunt. Our region will soon be as full of English officers as Mati.[99] No news of Richard and Col. McLean.

I begin *Blood and Sand* and enjoy it although it is not a particularly engaging book. Otherwise we tease Qasim and keep warm, itself a day's work. This cold sunshine makes me think of the grass patch by the tulips under the windows of the cottages at Worcester College. Such lazy heat and pleasant leisure are unbelievable here. And still we sit waiting and doing nothing, gloomily expecting the war to overrun us and toss us aside without any achievement on our part.

28th May (Whit Sunday)

A freezing wind melts later into a warm day. The pine forest below is full of cuckoos and our valley soon grows sleepily hot, with pine scent and wild flowers. A pleasing spot where these is no war but where war is our preoccupation. I finish Ibañez's *Blood and Sand* before I can start work but there is little work to do. The daily routine consists of keeping things running and reasonable. We acquire a dog, handsome but starving and often cringing – not a patch on Lulë who ran with us from Degë.

Little radio activity. Good news from Italy via a BBC reporter, Wynford Vaughan Thomas. But there is a lull and silence while we wait for the second front and for Russia and for Tito and for all European resistance to break out together.

As the night falls coldly we gather round our fire and Qasim and I break into one of our frequent arguments on Albanian

---

99 Mati district with its principal town of Burelë (Burrel) lies south-west of the Kukës region where Hibbert was located most of the time.

affairs and the war. I am coming to believe more and more in the Partisan movement as the only hope for action here. The war is shaking out the social and cultural creases in Europe. And nationalist chiefs, landowners and industrialists fear they will be shaken out with the creases. They will not fight (certainly not together with the Partisans) because they know that the violence of this war will crush like a bulldozer the positions, privileged positions, on which they stand. They cannot bring themselves to rise with the bulldozer and learn its new techniques. So we are left with the Partisan movements who can lose nothing by violence or by the bolshevising power of bombs. Their political programme offers a future which falls far short of the liberal standards of Western civilisation, but perhaps not so far short as Nazism? War never was an instrument of progress. We should go along with the Partisans not in the hope of a brave new world but because they alone seem to have the will to stand up to the German occupiers and to extract something from Europe's ruins.

Muharrem could raise the north of Albania, but Muharrem is afraid. He does not see that he is sure to lose if he does nothing; and he may be foolish enough to gamble with civil war if we support the Partisans. Yet the Partisans have been and seem bound to be the basis of our policy. M.B. cannot expect us to nurse him any longer (although it might have paid us better if earlier BLOs had nursed him better). M.B. is a good patriot but not a wise reader of the European scene. If he fails to fight he will suffer the fate which has overtaken the fate of the rest of pre-war Europe.[100]

29th May (Whit Monday)

Our bank holiday is peaceful. Qasim goes away to a Partisan conference. We find odd jobs in the camp. Maslan returns most annoyingly without having found the Major. Esat [Ndreu] arrives, pleased with his talk with Col. McLean, begging more material and talking busy politics. He has to be stalled.

My horse is growing wonderfully fit. Dori and my sleeping

---

100 Hibbert, *Bitter Victory, op. cit.*, pp. 85-107. Chapter 6, 'Stables Mission: Stagnation in the North' draws heavily on the diary for a summary of Stables Mission and its difficulties.

bag are my best possessions at present. They lift me out of the proletarian world and make living less hard work.

30th May

As usual when I prepare to write to Richard, a messenger arrives from him bringing me all the news. The other H.Q. is moving out of doors. I hope it finds as pleasing a spot as this one. Col. McLean is said to have a 'good line'. I hope it is so. Tony has been successful in the north – I am pleased to hear it as he has not had much of a break until now. Tahir departs in a great flap to Vilë with two mule loads of material.

It is very hot and mosquitoes begin to appear. Are they going to spoil our lovely camping site? Its loveliness is much greater when I wander up the river and cross into the brilliant meadows beyond and above. Flowers and bushes and grasses and even May-trees abound and no one to look at them but myself – I enjoy being surrounded by so much beauty in a ring of solitude.

Corporal Elvidge (left) and a crewmember of a crashed/shot-down US aircraft (right). Richard Riddell is in the background.

31st May

Qasim disappears for the day. We perform the usual round of odd jobs. Dori gives us some knocks when we try to shoe a front foot, but we win. Only a little of my blood is drawn. A passage of arms with Goodier and so end the little thrills of my day. All the world seems uneventful at present. It sounds as though there has been some blundering in Italy. 'A major effort is now needed to crack the German line before Rome' – Wynford Vaughan Thomas.

Fernando comes out of his shell round our campfire and manages to convey dirty jokes in three languages eked out by dumb-show. Men do not differ much under their nationalities.

Much thought of sunshine in England, brought on by the sunshine here. Oh for a day in the warm grass by the Cherwell! Just one day and then back here again.

1st June

The glorious first really is [glorious]. I celebrate it with a bath in our ice-cold torrent nearby. It is so cold that I have to curtail the luxury of nudity to five minutes. It is the first time for five and a half months that I have been able to get rid of my clothes with ease. Otherwise the liberty of lounging and doing nothing but supervise.

Esat arrives with a strong escort and strains our lunching facilities. He demands material for his *çeta* which is growing. I talk long and vehemently about our policy and the situation in our area until he begins to fear that he has offended and so becomes amenable. These Partisans deserve help if anyone does in this country but they can't have it without the Major's permission. Esat leaves to find the Major and seems contented enough with our talk.

In the evening an XXX message. Off we rush to Gramë dropping ground, a hot and hasty climb.[101] No sooner settled on the ground than a DC3 arrives. The pilot is brave and clever, skims over and under the mountain tops and through valleys and drops his load excellently. Then the Partisans arrive and we soon have all collected. Two containers are nowhere to be found. Did they drop? We send our mules off to our camp, overloaded, and we hire more horses. The shuttle service lasts into the morning. The night is cold but we have a huge fire and I snatch a chilly hour or so in a parachute. The Partisans are very good. No stealing and all is done in order. Only Dori breaks ranks to run back to camp to join his mule friends.

3rd June

A hasty wash when I reach camp at sunrise. Then three welcome but undistinguished letters from home. Then work. All day we sort

---

101 A few hours' climb to the Gramë dropping ground suggests that the campsite was on the eastern side of Mali i Gramës, a peak on a south-western spur of the Korab range.

material (plenty of comforts, too much explosive, not enough war material). By evening a load is ready (with a letter written of course) for the Major, whose whereabouts are unknown. Just then Tahir arrives from Richard with a letter, so everything stays put until morning. Goodier is to go to Xibër which adds complications to our affairs. The other H.Q. is also open-air now. We need more planes.

By firelight I read about happenings at home, which seem quite pale in these surroundings. I would like to hear from friends as well as family.

4th June

All day we sort and examine material and prepare to be rid of it. The Partisans come to collect some clothing and plead for some weapons. I stall them. We have little time to read our letters and magazines. It is hot and we sweat like quartermasters. Then comes the warning for another stand-by. So we all forget that the allies are at the gates of Rome and all move up to Gramë. There a Partisan concert of their strong melancholy music full of thoughts of Russia. A Dakota comes and the routine starts again. All is swiftly collected. The plane is very impersonal with no flashing dives and turns. So we load the horses and sleep for an hour before dawn – cold and aching.

5th June

We return to camp in high spirits, eat, read a fragmentary mail and start to work. All is soon in order – heaps of clothes for Partisans, plenty of weapons and ammunition and enough food for us. But our 'comforts' are lost.

Then Richard arrives with a new interpreter called Suliman, a nasty, ingratiating type. The Partisans come and collect their clothing and Richard allows a few arms as well – and off they go, rather suspicious of our intentions with the rest of the material.

Richard has plenty of news. Col. McLean hopes for great things in the north and has a good threatening line for the chiefs. Tony is now in the Has area for a meeting of M.B.'s friends with McLean. A general meeting may be called at Lurës soon. And German troop subversion is to become an important part of our work (Neel already having been successful at this). Meanwhile we stay as we are and wait for all McLean's policy to develop.

Rome has fallen. Fernando is delighted and we are all very pleased with ourselves and one another.

6th June

All morning we sort material for M.B. and others – enough to encourage nationalists and plenty to supply Partisans. Richard and I talk plenty: Richard is in good form and is good company today. We manage to pack the mules off to H.Q. and Richard goes to the Litas. It turns cold and wet, but we clear up the camp and the atmosphere is a bit hang-overish.

Then first class news – the second front. Much rejoicing – a stick of 808 in local tradition – and the Partisans exceed all bounds in celebratory waste of ammunition.[102] A French-speaking Partisan from Pezë, one of Michael's friends, arrives. We argue far into the night about Albanian politics. He is a man of 'moral' principles, impossible to argue with, obviously a future ruler of Europe.

I find a new way of feeding our wolf cub, letting him suck my fingers full of condensed milk. He is a powerful little brute, full of attack.

7th June

A Partisan day. First they come and collect material – then Esat comes and talks. Only at the end of the day can I begin to read letters from home and papers and magazines and world news. A busy day!

Esat has news from the Partisan congress in the south about the formation of a provisional government. He says that the time for definition between Partisans and others has come. Where do we English stand? I reply that we stand in the same place as ever: that we give vast material help to Partisans and none to others, that the initiative rests with the Partisans, that we support Partisans to the degree that Partisans fight Germans and strengthen themselves. Esat seems happy with my answer and we part on good terms. We

---

102 Nobel's Explosive No. 808 had been developed by the British company Nobel Chemicals Limited before the Second World War. It was green with a smell of almonds and was used widely by SOE for sabotage missions.

lunch together. The Partisans sit like children at a party and enjoy everything immensely in preoccupied silence.

At last our camp is cleared of the crowds and we settle down to our own simple society. My particular pleasure is two copies of the *Observer* – a very rare experience.

8th June

Emerli and Tahir take more material to Richard. Therefore much fuss over mules and plenty of kicking and swearing. Then a routine morning – some reading is possible in the afternoon. I teach some Partisans to use explosives. These men are neither hard workers nor keen listeners. They are far more anxious to outwit me by getting Fulvio to cut their hair. They succeed and I indulge some righteous wrath. Much talk of Partisan discipline but slight signs of it.

Good radio news. Then Qasim and I start arguing about Marcel Déat, Fascism, Communism, the 'crisis' of democracy in England, the relative values of institutions and theories, only to find at the end that we disagree fundamentally in philosophy – he a materialist and I an idealist, he linked to Slav culture and I to Latin.[103] We are both satisfied and retire to sleep.

9th June

A large and pointless quarrel over Fulvio begins with the Partisans. They try to threaten when I refuse to make him cut their hair. They shout about 'freedom for the people' (the common Partisan phrase of greeting, replying to the phrase 'death to fascism'), but I enforce freedom for Italians. Poor Fulvio is very upset and so too is Qasim. The Partisans try to disown their messenger but it does them no good.

Later Tahir and Emerli arrive with news from the Major that the M.B. scare is temporarily off. We relax and read and talk with one Selim Begu who arrives to see us – the first nationalist I have

---

103 Marcel Déat (1894-1955) was a former French socialist whose thinking took a right-wing, 'neosocialist' turn in 1933. Ejected from the French Section of the Workers International, he became a leading collaborator with the Germans, openly promoted fascism and later became a minister in the Vichy government. He created a French branch of the Wehrmacht, the Légion des Volontaires Français. After the war he was sentenced to death for treason but died in exile in Italy.

met who allows the Partisans a case. He gives me a good Serb rifle in exchange for a Marlin; we are both happy. The rest of the day peters out in wolf cubs, world news by radio and *World Press Reviews*. Qasim is nervous about a Halil Alia rumour.

10th July

The Lieutenant rides forth to the accompaniment of much fuss and bother. Tahir guides me to Limjan. It is excessively hot and Dori is a little restless but the woods and mountainsides are very lovely with hosts of wild flowers and butterflies and birds. Tahir tries to inveigle me into his home at Duqak and when I refuse forces me to hide in a willow copse outside Limjan for fear of Germans (though there are none near). Some of Dan's men appear, all begging for rifles, ammo etc. Then Dan [Kaloshi] appears the biggest beggar of all. He has a Lita approach to affairs which makes it difficult for me to tread in the major's footsteps. Dan speaks of leaving his house and taking to the mountains; but as usual he

and his friends, Hylmi Karasani, Ali Maliqi, Jusuf Xhelagu etc. demand strong assistance guarantees from us before they decide that they are patriots. I try to leave things in the air. Dan brings a serious warning about an intended operation here by Germans and Halil Alia. We wait and see: will the Partisans fight?

A lousy night full of fleas and disturbed.

11th June

At dawn Tahir and I start back to Gramë. A lovely morning and a delightful ride, especially through the high forests. I find the Partisans manning their defences in fear of an attack. But there is no danger today. Back in camp a cheerful welcome

Dan Kaloshi with
his new weapon.

and a good breakfast (I have lost the *misr buk* – maize bread – habit very quickly). Tony has arrived back from the north and is returning thither at once – he is evidently successful and happy there. He demands Dori as his white horse is exhausted. So farewell to my horse! At the same time I have lost my gold pencil – all my luxuries at once!

An icy bath in the torrent marks the afternoon. Much letter writing to Richard. Much talk to Fernando. Much sleepy relaxation.

Abas is back from Tirana: what wealth does he bring?

12th June

Qasim runs away to the Partisans for a conference of sorts, so I become an artisan. We fill Bren magazines, smoking continually to keep the mosquitoes at bay. Then I make some demolition charges in case we ever need to dispose of spare stores in a hurry. The 808 gives me a foul headache. As rain and thunder develop, the day itself is a foul one. At night Abas arrives with the Tirana material – he has done his best to swindle us and has brought only half of what we want. I suppose that is a good result in this country, a fine compromise between Abas and us.

The radio receiver which he brings is great fun, but it seems strangely flat and unconvincing among these resonant and powerful mountains. Civilisation speaks through it with an unconvincing and undistinguished voice.

I am suitably sick in the night – what shall I be when I am really back in civilisation?

13th June

A day of *festa* with broadcasts from the radio receiver and Chianti and some of Fernando's best *pizzacotti*. Yet our day is not so satisfying. Our *festa* is soon worn out. Perhaps the best part of the day is a speech in Albanian (inspired by Chianti) which I deliver to the Sheh of Ceren, all about war and peace and Albania. Really a work of art! It makes me feel more at home than all the luxuries of Tirana.

14th June

Some early trouble with Abas – not unforeseen – all the usual attempts to squeeze cash from us and all the usual sulkiness when he fails. Abas cash problems give rise to plenty more cash problems from our other men but some light radio music silences them like children. A strange rumour comes that Dan Kaloshi has killed Halil Alia but the rumour is to too feeble to be true. Thousands of mosquitoes – swarms of them – and uncomfortable, stuffy heat. Nothing to do and difficult to read peacefully.

I am reconciled to having the radio on when I hear the BBC Symphony Orchestra but I like to listen by myself.

15th June

Still the weather is oppressive and full of mosquitoes. We hear that an aeroplane is to be expected tonight and so occupy most of the day in preparation for it. Xhetan Elezi comes from Faik Shehu with news of American airmen bailed out in Reka. I set the wheels working to get hold of them if they are genuine.[104] They have not chosen a very healthy spot to drop in.

We move up to Gramë and wait. It is cloudy and misty and cold. We hear a plane and light our fires but have no drop. And in the morning we stumble back to camp with the feeling of having survived a physical ordeal.

16th June

We sleep the sleep of the just until midday when Fernando calls us to eat – menu as usual. Thereafter a casual round of putting things in order and of odd preparations for nothing in particular. Then Elvidge fails to connect with Bari. So back we toil to Gramë to chill ourselves in a long pointless wait, this time with no certain hope of a plane to cheer us. Very clear and fine. A merry party but very cold.

---

104 Faik Shehu was a local chieftain from the Dibra area.

17th June

Once more a morning of sleep. One more afternoon of odds and ends. This time Q.T.N. reaches us strength five. We settle down to Chianti, beer and raki and have a party. Qasim falls asleep and Maslan turns surly. Otherwise the party is a great success.

18th June (Sunday)

A foul and rainy day. We sit and talk; we make a fire and stop talking; we try the radio and find nothing worth having. A man comes from Faik Shehu with letters from the Americans near Kicevo. They sound unhappy and worried and in bad circumstances. It must be a sad day when one is forced to bail out into the land of maize and beans. We can do nothing until Faik Shehu's men return from Kicevo. Then I may have a chance to go myself.

In the afternoon a stomach agony lays me low – curse Albania and its bloody diet and climate!

19th June

A hangover feeling and nausea so I don't go to see Faik Shehu. Torrential rain so I don't go to see the major. As usual we sit and wait for something to turn up and make a cake until the sun shines – the best trial cake so far.

The radio keeps our evening busy. Voce d'America proves to be an excellent – the best – propaganda programme from the allies, being a very subtle confidence tonic for free Italy. British foreign broadcasts suffer from too great a directness, too open a determination to let the facts speak for themselves. Here in Albania, at least, no one knows the language of facts. Here we need a ministry of oratory not a ministry of information.

Tosca from Sofia and folk music from Germany leave the Forces' programmes standing, though some Forces Programme 'flashes' are brilliant.

Qasim and I fall into an argument about Russia and Europe. Qasim cannot be persuaded to regard Russia as a normal great power. Always his communist faith makes debate impossible. I find myself having Spenglerian thoughts about the decline of the West. And as modernity in Albania seems to mean unreason and barbarism, I do not welcome modernity. It looks as though the post-war world will belong to the leaders of unreason. Which side shall I be standing on – the failing but true one or the successful but repugnant one?

Here end six months in Albania.

20th June

A bright, hot day again. An attempt to read pleasantly and lazily is defeated by the charging motor and a decarbonising job. Then Richard arrives and turns our state topsy-turvy. We start climbing Korab to discuss the situation: Tony [Simcox] with Gani Bey [Kryeziu], a general north Albanian nationalist meeting on July 4th, everyone still marking time except Sherif Lita who seems to be intriguing against us again.[105] McLean seems to be chiefly concerned with his own ambitions for some sort of glory. Richard digs into the Tirana material and I find myself the recipient of a camera. We start straight in on snapping.

An XXX message – we stand by, freeze and shiver and nothing comes. Possibly light cloud overhead is the cause of our disappointment. Back to camp and sleep.

21st June

Richard awakes in lordly style calling for servants and radio and breakfast and loudly criticising the layout and efficiency of things. The he gets going on the camp. I like it better in its primitive and communal style. This country was not made for sitting rooms.

I set off with Maslan to find Faik Shehu. After thirteen and a half hours we reach Grevë just before dawn. Sometimes a lovely journey with stars and bullfrogs, sunset and dim mountain shapes. But man, in the shape of two dim and inefficient Partisans, manages to ruin all by their bungling on non-existent paths and by

---

105 Gani Bey Kryeziu (1900-52) and his brothers, Ceno, Seit and Hasan were from a leading clan from Gjakova in Kosova. Gani Bey was a former officer in the Yugoslav army, a nationalist and a Zogist and Ceno was brother-in-law to King Zog. He was closely associated with and supported by SOE officers in the field as an effective resistance leader, yet attempts to persuade him to work with the communist Partisans failed. His Yugoslav citizenship was to be his undoing when Enver Hoxha handed him over to Tito's authorities at the end of the war.

their fear of meeting villagers on all the larger paths and roadways. In the end I must be a day late in meeting Faik Shehu.

22nd June

Hospitality is excellent at Grevë – pleasant people and a pleasant house, even the delight of curtains in the window. Jashat greets me effusively but soon fades out, as he always does. Faik has some intelligent followers and their conversation can be pleasant – especially the elegant Shaban Strasimiri. Though only one hour from Peshkopijë, we move about freely outside. Here is a chief who runs things well and wisely. After an excellent dinner, we leave Grevë (some dispute over horse and mule and material first) and move to Trenë where Haxhi Lleshi joins us. Then a weary wait and conference and we move back into the hills of Grevë, just over Peshkopijë. A cold and aching wait for dawn and then for the sun before it is warm enough to sleep. I regret much that I am wearing tropical kit. It turns this weather into an agony.

24th June

All day we sleep uneasily and are made miserable by rain. Armies of men bring us food and we manage to pass the day reasonably well. I don't know these men very well yet – so I am a little cut off from society. As evening falls we prepare to move, when suddenly word comes that the Americans have been brought to Maqellare. All plans change at once. Jashat goes to fetch our allies. We wait until midnight for dinner to be carried to us. It rains and we flee to shelter in Grevë. Once more we fall asleep at dawn.

25th June

Today is a day of comfort. The Americans have been brought to a house nearby where they sleep all day. We are bitten by fleas and make much ceremony of tea and coffee. A long political talk with Shaban and Curi Strasimiri keeps me amused and awake, the more so as I do most of the talking. At evening, when we move out into the garden, David and Steve arrive, very tired and Steve a little ill. Hasty greetings and some trouble over rewarding the men who have helped them to escape.

By night we march to the Partisans. I really do march as we put the new boys on our horses. One attempt to ride our already laden mule results in a popular fall. It is an easy '*kadal, kadal* [slowly, slowly] march, and we are escorted by at least fifty men. A romantic introduction to Albania for these two fliers.

26th June

Day finds us toiling up to the Partisan camp. There we find hosts of visitors come for the conference of non-collaborationist chiefs. We halt and fraternise and some mass photos have a popular effect. We climb away with a storm of farewells and a fine Partisan chorus echoing after us. A lovely day into the bargain – good for our guests.

A man with a letter tells that there has been a drop with none but Elvidge present. We press on and find that Qasim has registered everything admirably.

Down we drop to the camp and then we work on the material all day – a dull business.

David and Steve settle down shyly. We soon work them into our routine by making them help us sort material. Piles of ammunition and shirts: no thrilling finds for us. Letters from home are largely very old but pleasant and cheerful.

27th June

We work tentatively until the major arrives then we stop pretending and turn to beer and skittles. Richard is as careless of Albania as ever and insists on good living. He has made an excellent mess here, much better than I could ever bother to make.

Late in the afternoon we hear that Faik Shehu and his friends wish to see Richard. After dark they arrive and we have much turmoil to provide fifteen unexpected men with bread without delay.

Hibbert with two Italian Alpini, of which Capt. Vito Menegazzi (centre) was attached to the 1st Partisan Brigade.

Corporal Elvidge with the radio set.

Faik keeps us busy until morning. He now heads a Dibra Council which recognises the Partisan Congress in the south.[106] Esat heads the local staff. We have the usual sparring over our nationalist contacts but our position is strong and we part happily. Raki and chocolate help us.

28th June

Shumë kalabalik [much hustle and bustle]. Fifteen strangers in camp are a tall order. Fifteen Albanians near a plane-load of material are explosive. We manage to steer through the chaos. Richard keeps the Americans entertained while Qasim and I keep Faik, Esat and co. on play. All is finally settled with a small award of material to the Partisans. No trouble – so peace falls on us.

Richard and David climb Korab. As I have broken my glasses I am cut off from the world and stay at home with Steve. A luxury day, especially at night when Cpl. Davis arrives and brings our crew of Albanians and Italians to a huge total.

But I prefer a small H.Q..

29th June

The major leaves us to meet M.B. and the Dibra committee at Zenil Lita's. Qasim springs a fast one on us by leaving – fed up with the situation here. Obviously Partisan trouble is brewing and Qasim does not have the courage either to face it or to say plainly to us that he does not want to. We must wait and watch developments. Our relations with this people can never really be satisfactory.

Sunbathing and odd jobs occupy the rest of the day. Our Americans settle in to the habits of our moments of boredom. We have quite a party in the evening to enliven things. Fernando is great fun.

---

106 A Partisan Congress had taken place on 24 May in Përmet in southern Albania attended by all leading leadership of the Partisan military and political movement. The purpose of the Congress was to assert the military and political ambitions of the Partisans and set up the executive of a Provisional Government in waiting. Baba Faja Martaneshi presided and attendees included Enver Hoxha, Spiro Moisiu, Ramadan Çitaku, Sejfulla Malëshova, Ymer Dishnica, Liri Gega, Islam Radovicka, Mustafa Gjinishi, Haxhi Lleshi and others.

Abas come from Peshkopijë with plenty to eat and drink so we have another party, our stand-by being cancelled. For tonight we'll merry, merry be....

30th June

Pay day for Albanian staff and horseshoeing day. I am growing into a perfect quartermaster. The Partisan trouble begins to develop in a strange request for explosives. They get half of what they ask. The rest can wait.

Richard returns from the Litas with nothing but an unsatisfactory letter from Muharrem. It looks as though our July meeting may be a farce, in which case evacuation would be the most honourable course.

1st July

A Partisan wakes me angrily and early. Hamdi failed to deliver my letter – the Partisans are not in a good humour. A letter from Esat is an unpleasant ultimatum – either the Partisans must have all our material or they will receive no planes.

Richard leaves to find M.B. and I go to argue with the Partisans. A broiling hot journey and still hotter disputes. The Partisans are obviously trying their hand at some local power politics. They agree with all our logical arguments but always insist on their unreasonable conclusions. Now our relations with the Partisans can depend on only one thing – Partisan action. Will they risk fighting?

A pleasant and lazy evening back in camp. Good American society and a lovely night.

A sudden scare due to Zybair Lita's arrival at Radomir with gendarmes. The usual frightful flap, followed by uncomfortable sleep. It is time Richard rode these Litas with a high hand.

2nd July

A morning of travel preparations, an early lunch and then we set off to join the Major to find the Colonel. Davies comes to go north to the Captain (Tony). Not a pleasant journey as the mules are troublesome and throw their loads continually. We join Richard at the Litas' and move on together to the Drin. Richard is impatient today.

Zybair Lita's men stop us and treat us somewhat discourteously, but let us pass 'this time'. We beg some maize bread and cheese and settle down for the night on a stony valley floor by the Drin. A good sleep in spite of the stones.

Stables Mission on the march with Richard Riddell leading and a runaway mule. Two of the Mission's Italians, Amerigo and Fernando, are on the right.

3rd July

An enjoyable day. We ford the Drin with water up to our horses' necks. Being wet we decide to swim and swimming is good despite a powerful current. Then we quarrel again with our mules and push on to Ali Solimani's house where we find the Bajraktar and Zenil Lita and Tasim Spahir all gathered with their escorts on mats under a huge walnut tree. Much talk and sleep and lunch and we all push on up the mountains in the heat. Poor Fernando is very tired. Through hostile Dardë and then down through a lovely bowl of mountain meadows to Fushë-Lurës. There we find no Colonel [McLean] and Lam Bajraktar has no news of him. We hope there will be no fiasco. A long and painful wait for a midnight dinner: finally a very welcome sleep with not too many fleas.

4th July

We hope to produce a Colonel and give a great impression of indifference by eating vast quantities of cherries and reading in the sun. A colony of well-dressed Jewish refugees appears – a crowd of unfortunates. Sharif goes home, Muharrem and his son grow restless, Islam goes home. All very awkward for us. Where is the Colonel?

We return to the cold yet generous hospitality of Lam Bajraktar. There we are flea-bitten in earnest. Selim Nokë comes and tries to make capital out of the Colonel's non-appearance. A terribly boring wait for another midnight dinner – and then hot and itching sleep.

5th July

We prepare to make a recce to find the Colonel when a letter from him is delivered a whole night late. With curses we set out to find him. Richard and I push ahead all day without food. The ride is long and enjoyable and Richard without responsibilities is a charming travelling companion. We finally reach a camp in the evening to find the Colonel and his staff and Merrett and others all living in luxury with swarms of Kupi's men.[107] The atmosphere is all-Kupi. To add to our interest we find that a Partisan division is across the Shkumbini coming our way. Fun may develop at any time.

A quick but good meal and off we move to Kupi's conference camp. An impressive scene in a fine valley, the wooded slopes all dotted with fires and whole sheep roasting over enormous fires. It rains a little but a blanket and a coat guarantee enough sleep. The H.Q. atmosphere is a bit ambassadorial. They are welcome to it.

---

107 McLean had travelled from his H.Q. on Mount Bastar, north of Tirana to attend Abas Kupi's conference camp at Lurës.

Abas Kupi and Lt. Colonel Neil 'Billy' McLean in discussion at Kupi's Lurës conference. July 1944.

6th July

Conversations start early and are soon ruined. News arrives that the Partisan division has clashed with Kupi's men somewhere, that they have burned Hysni Dima's house and are moving on Dibra, that Faik Shehu and Esat's *çeta* have taken Peshkopijë and killed Miftar Kaloshi. All the Kupi fans start talking vociferously about civil war but I wonder if one clash can be called that. The reaction of the Germans will soon prove who is their friend or their enemy. I reckon the Germans will go for the Partisans.

The Colonel and Amery are very exclusive in their negotiations but Richard and I gatecrash them and find Kupi playing for time and Muharrem going back to all his old grandiose schemes after seeing the support given to Kupi. Dan Kaloshi goes home, obviously hoping to have a crack at Faik Shehu. Sherif Lita disappears mysteriously and is obviously interested in nothing but anti-Partisan front. The Colonel and Amery seem far too much on Kupi's side, all because Amery thinks we need a nationalist Albanian on our side. But who can be sure about sides in the future? This is policy conducted in the subjunctive mood. It would be better to grasp the facts of the present situation. The action is coming from the Partisans.

Heavy rain and the situation cause the meeting to be called off and we move back to Merrett's camp to wait for Major Victor Smith who drops in tonight with important dispatches. Merrett's camp is lousy.

Victor Smith drops (a bad drop and most material stolen) and brings an attempt to make a truce between the Partisans and Kupi, calling to Italy three Partisan delegates, Abas Kupi and, to represent Muharrem, Said Kryeziu. Kupi and Muharrem jump at this – a sure sign the Partisans won't like it.

An uncomfortable night in an anarchic camp.

7th July

I talk much with Victor Smith who gives vivid facts about Partisan activity in the south. They are evidently fighting well and deserve help. Richard and I put to the Colonel a new pro-Partisan policy for our area and Billy McLean agrees. Our nationalists deserve to be dropped: they have had enough chances and have taken none of them. In any case I think the Partisans are now strong enough to force our hand – to oblige us to help them.

Perfunctory talks with odd people and then our convoy leaves (light) for Fushë Lurës. A pleasant ride followed by a great political talk with our hosts in Fushë Lurës. They are full of the pro-German anti-Partisan point of view. I think we manage to open their eyes a little about Partisan activity.

Bugs and fleas!

8th July

Richard finds a Franciscan friar and goes to Mass. I shoe horses. We join Islam Elezi and march back to our Korab camp. More fun in the Drin, a superb lunch, pleasant conversation with the Elezis and ten hours in the saddle. A good life.

Islam and Gani Çeni seem to disagree with their father's policy and yet not to dare to oppose it. A pity as they are good men and could help us much.

Back in camp, plenty of beer and talk. We have a new American pilot brought from Librashd by the Partisan division. A line shooter but otherwise a good chap. Elvidge has let the camp slide somewhat. Tonight we are merry – tomorrow we must work.

9th July

An early rise and we are soon at work writing sheaves of telegrams and putting across to Bari our new line for working with the Partisans. There seems to be endless admin work to do and admin is no one's strong point in this country. We hear Zenil's tale about Tony Simcox and probably Tony Neel surrounded by Germans in the Bityes area. As usual Zenil and his companions were too cowardly to enter the area and contact Tony. Yet Zenil gives relatively intelligent information and is optimistic about the Partisans and Gani Kryeziu in a most un-Albanian manner. Then we have money trouble with Zenil and he deserts us – true to type!

We send our American officers off towards Beranë. Sorry to see them go. They promise to write to our families. We have just heard that Michael and Sgt. Gregson are in Bari – some letters should be home soon.

In the afternoon a scare. Halil Alia on his way to chase us. We don't believe it and are justified by nothing happening. Then two Partisans come. We hear news of the battle of Peshkopijë where Miftar was killed and where a handful of Germans were engaged. Then on the 8th a battalion of the 1st Partisan Brigade arrived with Haxhi Lleshi at Peshkopijë, marched with Esat overnight to Fushë Alijë and attacked Halil Alia at dawn without heavy weapons. They were driven off to Gramë with some casualties. There they stay. We sleep at action stations and try to devise means of helping the Partisans.

10th July

A lull in the proceedings while we wait for Haxhi Lleshi and Esat to come. The wounded Partisans begin to come and Richard and I dress them – none very serious as Italian bullets make very clean holes. Most of the patients are in good spirits. Pouring rain fails to furnish a suitable backcloth to the tale of grave Partisan defeat. Their attack on Halil was rash and ill-considered though courageously fought and clear evidence of a will to fight. Esat's *çeta* and 1st Bn. of 1st Brigade. were involved, about 300 men, who suffered casualties, mostly dead and missing.

Xaxhi Lleshi is stiff-necked and dogmatic but otherwise reasonable enough.

We promise to give full backing to the Partisans. First we must try to get Halil Alia bombed, to destroy the public support which makes him strong. After that we may be able to make a permanent base of Peshkopijë and finally deal with Dibra. Alternatively, if reports are true that two Macedonian brigades and five battalions of 1st Vengeance Brigade are near Dibra, they may manage to hit straight at Dibra and then work backwards to Halil Alia.

In any case the attack on Fushë Alijë on the 8th was unsound. For the present Peshkopijë should be our target until the activities of the three brigades near Dibra are clarified. I think the Partisans now realise that they would have been wiser to confide in us before trying operations in which we could have assisted, perhaps by arranging bombing or at least by calling for heavy mortars from Bari. But then the Partisans have an old quarrel with us. Some Partisans have now died for that quarrel.

Great trouble feeding the many Partisans who arrive. Those from the south are largely in rags and many barefoot. Yet their spirit is excellent. They show up the well-dressed, nationalist two-timers. When our day of doctoring and talking is over, we still have to help Elvidge with some cyphering. An energetic day.

11th July

Richard leaves early to move with Haxhi Lleshi and Esat and a Partisan force against Peshkopijë. News all day is very mixed. Are the Partisans in Dibra or not? Cen Elezi has returned home. What is he calling men together for? We can only wait and see.

We have a full hospital round here. Two more wounded turn up: two seemingly lucky men with clean holes through the outer cage of their chests. One has a hole through his ribs plugged with gauze with the help of a rifle cleaning rod! A cheerful lad.

We play with cyphers and the charging engine. Nothing vital happens. A dull day, yet plenty to do. I feel we ought to try some diplomatic pressure on the local chiefs to stop them thinking of fighting the Partisans – also some persuasion on Bari to convince H.Q. of the strength of the Partisan forces here and the desirability of giving them some help.

12th July

Richard has moved off with the Partisans to attack Peshkopijë. As Haziz Kaloshi is in occupation there without Germans, this does not seem altogether wise. Elvidge and I stay to keep the information moving to Bari; but the most interesting things come from Bari. G.H.Q. has stopped all supplies to Albania pending civil war. Dali Sufa and his two brigades seem to be putting pressure on Kupi. They have interned Major Hare for two days, refusing to negotiate with him. The situation is bad. The Partisans in this area deserve some help but have weakened their position seriously by attacking Halil Alia unsuccessfully. If we are not to support the Partisans we might as well be evacuated; but the Partisans have made it hard for us to persuade Bari that they merit help.

Two more wounded arrive, one with a hole in his chest, one with a gangrenous toe. I cut the toe off: poor devil to be brought to having his foot butchered by me! He is stoical about his shaky prospects. Most of the Partisans are brave.

Abas brings a letter from the major. No exact news of Dibra Partisans. Richard seems to be plunging into a battle with Haziz Kaloshi. Opinion is hotly divided in this camp; it seems to go against Richard's intervention. More news from Sllovë way points to nationalists grouping around Halil Alia. This is the real danger in the situation. Are we going to be moderate enough to cope with it, for instance with Dan Kaloshi, who is drawing all too close to Halil Alia.

A letter to Richard by hand of Tahir leaves here just before Richard arrives at dawn. A warrior home from an indecisive battle, and not a very glorious one for an Englishman.

13th July

Richard's story is not too good. This is the second Partisan failure and our hands are tied against helping them. They need very early reinforcement. While Richard sleeps I write a review of the situation suggesting immediate vigorous action such as bombing against Halil Alia, with a view to separating nationalist chiefs from him or, failing that, the people from the nationalist chiefs. To my surprise Richard approves. He is a BLO with the Partisan forces these days. The excessive pro-Kupi-ism of McLean has played a big part in bringing this about.

We call Haxhi Lleshi, Esat and all to a very rainy conference. Morale does not seem to be shaken by defeat. (Richard says that the Partisan battalions fought most steadily yesterday). We explain the Kupi situation and the supply stoppage and read a summary of the situation to show it would be wise for the Partisans to take some action which would make the case for supporting them more convincing. Everything is very cheerful and informal. Then Haxhi and the battalion leave in a hurry to join the division at Dibra. It is impossible for the Partisans to find food up here and, tough as they are, they can't live on nothing. The reaction against them is running strongly and they cannot hold out here if we cannot supply them. But the Germans are still standing by Halil Alia!

Flap follows. We evacuate the wounded: they suffer plenty. The Partisans disappear very effectively into the landscape. We pack what little material and kit we have left in camp – we have cleaned ourselves out for the Partisans. Abas deserts for fear of the anti-Partisan reaction. Some men stay by us, but our evening turns curiously desolate and silent and lonely. Richard sends Elvidge and Qasim to sleep with the radio at a safe distance. We recce a sleeping post for all our party a little way from camp. Then we turn to a little jollification of an artificial sort while the atmosphere of abandonment surrounds us. But the eery evening turns cold, so we go to bed

Nothing happens.

14th July

In the morning all proves to have been a false alarm. The mountains still have an air of emptiness about them but we ignore it and cypher frantically (i.e. frantically by Richard's and my standards). We ride gaily down to Radomir and meet Sherif and Zenil Lita. They report that Cen Elezi and Dan Kaloshi seem to be siding thoroughly with Halil Alia. That will have to be dealt with. My

Italian has improved much and Richard leaves me a fairly free hand so that I can talk to Sherif as he deserves. We mix it strong for him; and he and Zenil, as representatives of frightened Lumë, are inclined to eat out of our hands. But they insist they will defend their neutrality with arms. Sherif even confesses that the people will not follow their chiefs. On the whole it is a satisfactory talk. It is rounded off by a report that Mehmet Shehu holds Peshkopijë with a Partisan force and that all the Dibra chiefs are fleeing – news neatly presented by Ali Solimani at a psychological moment.

Back to camp and to a rumour that Zybair Lita has captured our Americans. And so we wait.[108]

15th July

All the morning and afternoon we cypher and talk politics. In the evening I ride down to Sllatinë to see the wounded. Two are very bad – especially Abdul Lleshi with a gangrenous leg, who once was so hospitable to me.

A night of rumours and fleas, crushed next to Esat in a crowded room.

---

108 Mehmet Ismail Shehu (1913-81) was born to a Muslim Tosk family in Southern Albania in the Mallakastër area. He became sympathetic to communism in his twenties and after a brief time in formal military training he fought in the Spanish Civil War, rising to company commander in the International Brigade. On his return to Albania he joined the Albanian Communist Party and in 1943 joined the Central Committee. A leading member of the Partisan resistance, he became Commander of the 1st Partisan Assault Brigade then Divisional Commander in the National Liberation Army. After the war his military career took him to the highest levels. He was a close associate of Enver Hoxha for forty years promoting Hoxha's anti-Titoist line. From 1954 to 1981 he was Prime Minister of Albania with ongoing responsibility for defence and internal security. He fell from grace after his supposed suicide in December 1981 after which he was denounced as a Titoist spy, vilified and his name removed from official accounts of Albanian history and politics. While Hibbert and other BLOs admired his military efficiency which was critical to the success of the Partisan forces, he had a reputation for hardness and brutality noted even by his own co–combatants such as Liri Gega. Peter Kemp describes him as a 'sour, taciturn man of ruthless ambition, outstanding courage and sickening ferocity' (Kemp, *No Colours or Crest, op. cit.*, p. 95). Hibbert too described him as Enver Hoxha's 'iron hand' in the future regime. Kadare's novel *The Successor* re-imagines his rise and fall.

16th July

Four hours steady wound dressing – rather depressing. Then a hot ride up to Gramë with Esat and some Partisans. We hear that Mehmet Shehu and five battalions of 1st Brigade have been chased out of Peshkopijë and up to Gramë by the Germans. I rejoin Richard in camp to find him also dressing wounds. We strike camp tonight and move with the Brigade to Macedonia.

Evening finds us striking camp in chaos and night finds us led astray by Esat seeking a non-existent Brigade in the wrong place. We climb 'red rock' and walk round it, down it and up it. Finally we sleep under it, cold and tired.[109]

17th July

We send futile search parties up Korab to look for the Brigade. Then Richard and I go up and glimpse it as it disappears. I chase it at speed and Richard brings up the mules. Then we go down into Macedonia and halt and eat lightly while Mehmet Shehu persuades villagers not to fight us. By night we continue our long march, lose our way and finally settle in a wood at dawn. These Partisans are tough, especially the *çeta* girls – no food and very tired. Richard and I offer our saddles to some sick and dying *çeta* girls. The Partisan men don't appear to suffer from the same scruples.

18th July

No food so we sleep – we are not even allowed fires, so great are Partisan fears of reaction hereabouts. Heavy rain soaks and wakes us but our indomitable Italians have made a parachute tent and there we endure a peaceful penetration of water rather than a soaking. We are joined by our *çeta* girl friends and later by Mehmet Shehu and his pleasantly feminine vice-commissar. A happy party: we are allowed to light a fire and scrape together some rice and chicken. So we live luxuriously by comparison with the starving Partisans. Later, trouble starts with Ali and Hamdi and Tahir – too much work, discomfort and fear make them want to go home. We take them along by force.

---

109 This is probably Crvena Karpa ('Red Crag' in Macedonian), in the Šar Mountains. The Šar range extends from the Korab massif on the border between Macedonia, Kosova and north-east Albania. With an elevation of 922 metres, Crvena Karpa is now within the boundaries of the Mavrovo National Park, Macedonia, and part of the Brezovica ski resort.

We move down to the Gostivar-Dibra road, miles down and then miles up to a village where we stop for an hour or two of sleep. We are woken by bullets smacking into the column on the paths above us. Gendarmes are firing across the valley at us. We decamp fast and arrive at a false crest at dawn in time to see the Italian Mountain Battery (1 gun) bombard the offending village which sheltered the gendarmes. An interesting if tiring journey – and very hungry.

19th July

On we push, up and over the Bistra plateau, with a lovely view of the Dibra-Gostivar road far below us and mountains all around. At last we reach the prosperous village of Gebenek, a Macedonian pastoral village living in fear of Xhem Gostivari. Our welcome is colossal. The village is a delightful one. Everyone presses us to visit them and all the little girls kiss our hands. So Richard and I shave and eat hugely and drink tea and coffee in the village 'NAAFI' and talk all available languages and decide that life is excellent.

It lasts for a few brief and glorious hours and then work begins under a hot sun. Our mules are sick and we lighten the load. Then our mulemen desert us and we must be content with a crowd of useless pressed men.

At evening with much flap we move and march all night to another Macedonian village across the Dibra-Kicevo road. On our way we see signs of Xhem Gostivari's barbarism as the villages are deserted and destroyed. Nationalism has its terrors in these frontier regions.

In the village we struggle in a shadowy crowd to unload our mules and then all drag ourselves exhausted to a nearby house where we eat ourselves to sleep. A poor house, made poorer by Xhem, but hospitable. We can't talk to the inhabitants but Ahmed Jegeni can. Fortunately food and sleep are international.[110]

---

110 The march into Macedonia was no chance event. After a failure to hold ground after the fighting in Peshkopijë due to a lack of ammunition and supplies, Mehmet Shehu, leading the elite 1st Brigade, decided to withdraw to Macedonia on the eastern side of Mount Korab. The idea was to circle round to approach the Dibra region from the east. Riddell and Hibbert accompanied them. The situation was made worse by Bari HQ refusing to send supplies for fear of exacerbating a civil war situation as they perceived it.

Stables Mission on the move, led by an Albanian muleteer. Corporal Elvidge is on the white horse, followed by Italian chef Amerigo. At his side is chief steward Nazareno with Richard Riddell bringing up the rear on a mule.

20th July

We wake luxuriously late. Amerigo prepares a fine meal and we cypher. The Macedonian women watch us silently but sympathetically. A pleasant village with an air of civilisation.

Suddenly a flap begins. We pack everything in the middle of lunch and rush off to load our mules, while Mehmet (Shehu) tells that he has found a dropping ground so that we can supply his brigade. We must keep moving: so our Mission goes up with a Battalion to occupy and inspect the ground. We march up through lovely mountain meadows where the peasants are scything the hay, with a chorus of grasshoppers and flies and always a boiling sun. We come out on top looking over Kicevo and all Macedonia and back toward our own Albanian mountains. A superb spot for dropping.

Back we ride to join the column and camp in a wood below. It is cold and tempers (especially Elvidge's and Fernando's) are frayed by fatigue. Mushrooms are discovered. We eat delicately and sleep.

21st July

Lovely sunshine, so Richard and I sunbathe. As we are now among more sophisticated people, we can afford these little liberties. Life is much more enjoyable with the Partisans than in savage Dibra and Lumë. We vow not to return to the old conditions there.

Promptly to time Mehmet Shehu and the Brigade arrive. He seems a very good soldier and he has certainly learned something about officering in the Spanish Civil War. We have plenty of news for him. The Partisans have occupied Gjirokaster and Delvinë in the south and the Germans are attacking the 1st Division near Martanesh. So the Germans are fighting the Partisans, which makes it reasonable for us to support the Partisans. We become all the more impatient for a quick drop so that the Brigade can move on and support the Division. Pro-nationalist sentiments seem to have fallen out of fashion among the senior officers of British Missions.

We argue long and loud about communism and other things with Mehmet. I suppose that, if I were an Albanian, I should be a Partisan.

Good world news. We are all very contented in this lovely spot. Even Fernando is cheerful again as we talk round our night fire.

Partisan morale is good and high. Yet the Partisans have hardly eaten. We eat our own supplies and are joined by a few Partisan guests. One feels terribly selfish and unkind to eat when others have nothing even though our supplies are coming to an end and we must work while the Partisans sleep.

22nd July

We are turning into cypher clerks. We code for the morning sked and then quickly decode a futile message asking why we want supplies in Macedonia. We encode a lightning and furious answer, demanding an instant drop and just fail to send off by the same sked. Very disappointing to our keen sporting senses.

Mehmet is more stand-offish today: no wonder – where are the supplies we were to produce? We hear that BLOs are with Macedonian Partisans only four hours away. We cannot communicate with them yet. After the drop we may pay them a social call. Those BLOs have had seven planes in two days: very tactless of Bari not to send us any.

We eat well and have a freezing bath and then back to cyphering. Nothing world-shaking comes in.

By night we talk to odd Italian officers of the Brigade. They are in an unhappy state: old soldiers of fascism, they now try to look as though they never had anything to do with it.

I finish the day with a long talk with Gafur about Partisans and BLOs' sympathies with both sides in Albania and never fully with either. In the last war Lawrence of Arabia knew something of this sort. On a minute scale our tragedy is like his. We observe rather than live this war: we are in the middle of it, yet we cannot fully share it, neither begin it nor end it.

23rd July

We have been writing vehement messages to Bari demanding planes for the Vengeance Brigade. So far Bari routines have baulked us. We hope the morning sked will bring us good news. All it promises is one plane tonight. What is the use of one plane to a Brigade? We have to apologise helplessly to Mehmet Shehu and his staff who leave to meet the Macedonian Partisan staff. This situation at the crisis of the war and at the crisis of the evolution of the war in Albania is hard to bear. Richard and I are both worked up about it. The plodding of our Italian and other followers brings us back to the fact that the war can plod on without us.

We ride up into the mountain hayfields to choose our fire sites. A lovely day and a fine ride but our horses won't play much on the open country. They have to work too much on mountain paths for them ever to be really lively.

A strange medical case of a man completely unconscious, probably from poison from eating fungi. I force no. 9's into him and hope for the best. He recovers.

We stand by in half a gale and don't see anything drop as the wind takes all the 'chutes over the mountains. So Richard and I go back to camp to sleep and leave it to the Brigadier to deal with the material.

We are fed up with all this inactivity. Either full supply or movement are essential for the Brigade. At present we have neither.

24th July

In the morning everything is brought to us in excellent order. As we feared Bari has sent us a maintenance plane, despite our request to the contrary. So the Brigade is still without supply, while we have more comforts than we can deal with. The Partisans are fortunately very reasonable about it.

We do our best by inviting Brigade and Battalion commanders and commissars to dinner. Until then we lounge and eat chocolates and read a very good mail. Evidently they know at home where I am which is some satisfaction. My most valuable mail package is a pair of glasses. Ugly glasses but 100% functional.

Still no satisfaction from Bari but our dinner party goes excellently. We talk world politics and Albanian politics and Kupi and civil war. We are impressed by the ability and intelligence of these Partisan leaders and they use moderate language. I think we managed to make some impression. I am getting quite eloquent in Italian and Richard tends to let me have a freer hand in talking these days.

25th July

I am sick in the morning and the day is boring when I do get up at last. We lose four horses and sweat in vain to find them. They finally turn up. We decipher messages frantically: there is nothing of interest. Even world news does not thrill today. Richard writes a recommendation in generous terms for me to be promoted. I am doubtful about its chances of going through

Once more we entertain – this time a member of the Brigade political department and commanders who could not join us yesterday. We pull their legs rather cruelly about commissars and politics but we finally draw from them some valuable information about Partisan organisation and discipline and the political scheme of things. We find our respect for these men growing as we get to know them.

Our command and the public at home and the BLOs have failed to understand that this war in the Balkans is political in nature and that commissars and political departments play a leading part in it. This is a war not only to destroy Germans but to build a different Albania. The commissars are one of the sources of Partisan strength. They are essential to the Partisan war effort and in this sense are useful to the allies.

26th July

The morning is brightened by the news that we can have four planes in the next three nights – but Q.T.N. tells us not tonight. At last we are getting somewhere.

We entertain the two Italian Captains of the Brigade artillery to lunch. They are charming and tragic and uncomfortably overwhelmed by our hospitality. Our hands are partly tied against helping them, due to Partisan suspicion. The tragedy of these Italians must be being repeated all over Europe. No wonder we British are constantly being told that it is our responsibility to re-establish Europe. Europe is in no state to help itself.

In the evening another tragedy looks in on us in our comfortable tent. A pleasant young Italian lieutenant volunteers to be a mule-man for us: he can no longer stand the life of a simple Partisan. We can sympathise with him; but we also sympathise with the Partisans. The latter have condemned all Italian officers as fascists. Apparently they have an Italian battalion and it contains no officers – very much on the party line. We can talk to Mehmet about it, but we can make no promises.

Finally 2nd Lt. William Schmidt of the U.S. Air Force turns up, having bailed out near Dibra. New guests are always welcome, although this one is not very lively.

A very cold night and no room in the tent. *Shum i keq* [very bad].

27th July

A letter arrives from Mehmet Shehu hinting that we are not very forceful with our H.Q. about these planes, just as we have a telegram that three planes are due tonight.

We have one of those recurrent quarrels with sensitive Albanians which always crop up in this country. Ahmed raises hell because Schmidt joined us before the Brigade staff had seen him. Plain nonsense: when treated firmly by us, it subsides.

In the afternoon Staff Sergeant Melton joins us, also of Schmidt's plane. Neither is very lively.

A dull day and a brilliant night. The three planes come according to routine and drop according to the pilot's fancy, the first good, the second bad and the third moderate. I suppose it is the same with bomber pilots – some have guts and some don't.

We go home to sleep.

28th July

In the morning we check material and find plenty of Italian ammunition to please the Partisans. We lose our horses and search hotly and in vain for them. At last they turn up after ruining someone's wheat field. As a result some local trouble. We read as many papers and journals as we can but we are all very impatient with this uncertain halt here and mostly slightly stomach-sick. So we are bored, but a plane is coming so there is rejoicing in the camp. Richard stands by and I go to sleep.

29th July

I ride early to the dropping ground. A plane-load of purely Partisan material is soon handled. We strike camp and prepare to move with much fuss and bother. Finally we get away and make a long and tiring journey to find Donald MacDonald and his Macedonian Partisans. We have a lovely view of Struga and Lake Ochrid and then plunge through some fine forests to meet Mac, living lonely and uncomfortable and disillusioned. It is dark but I can see how his terrible winter has altered him. He is quite in the Partisans' power so he has no political problem. He is fed up but both of us are delighted to see each other and we talk far into the night.

30th July

All day long we talk shop, Richard, Mac and I – interrupted only by an excellent lunch in Mac's honour well prepared by our Italians and a spate of photography. Mac is very sensible and helpful. Here as a Tito BLO he can call unlimited planes. He helps us with some propaganda to Bari to

Capt. Donald MacDonald with two Macedonian Partisans. July 1944.

try to obtain the same for us and our Partisans. We send Bari the strongest ever pro-Partisan signal. Richard's pro-Partisanism now has to be restrained a little. He is over-enthusiastic about things. At night we hear from Mehmet Shehu that an attack on Dibra is planned for the first of August. So we shall move up to Dibra to join him. Poor old Mac stays behind in his loneliness – luckily soon to be evacuated. We say farewell, leave our Americans with him and move up to sleep with our mules.[111]

---

111 The visit to Captain Donald MacDonald was unusual insofar as the Dibra-based SOE officers were 'trespassing' on SOE's Yugoslav area under the command of Fitzroy Maclean, who was working with Tito's forces although the two areas were next to each other. SOE had therefore assumed the restoration to Yugoslavia of territories, in this case Metohija, that had been lost with the partitioning in 1941. At the time Bari was supplying the Yugoslav Partisans with generous deliveries while hesitating to supply the Albanian Partisans who appeared still to be a more uncertain quantity. Indeed, in his final report to SOE H.Q. Mac reported that the 'last week of Jun. and first two weeks of Jul. were splendid with drops from 50 planes. Jul. saw all our Partisans fully equipped with arms, amm., clothing.' (Capt. D. S. MacDonald report, National Archives HS9). MacDonald's activities were thus reduced to acting as 'quartermaster', receiving and distributing the materiel coming in with frequent drops which left little chance for close involvement in front line action or opportunities for initiative, hence his isolation and boredom. MacDonald and Hibbert had become good friends during their training in Cairo and their friendship continued throughout their post-war lives.

The 1st Partisan Brigade standard bearer with Mehmet Shehu on the right.

31st July

We march early and we march all day. It is terribly hot and dusty and I am feeling sick and tired from stomach trouble. We leave our mule train in a village under Nazareno's care and Richard and Elvidge and I march wearily on with the radio. Elvidge confesses to being very fed up. I can believe it as Richard and I cannot entertain him and he needs entertainment. The BLO signaller problem is a serious one.

Very late we reach Gorenë (but we have halted for skeds during the day). We join Partisans waiting for zero hour and then we call the village elder to find us food. This he does with great success. We eat well and settle down to sleep among the fleas. We are too tired to notice their bites.

At 03.50 firing begins and continues sharply for some time. The battle has begun just below us. We decide that the Partisans are excellent fellows, turn over and sleep.

1st August

We breakfast well while the Partisans fight below. We can see very little detail of the battle. We toil upwards through colossal heat to Mehmet Shehu's command post, high above the Dibra road system. There we have a fine view and hear the story of the battle. The Partisans have penetrated the town and intend to hang on all day and make a decisive push tonight. I am doubtful of their chances as they lack assault weapons. We hear that other troops of the Division are probably in Peshkopijë and beyond – a pity that there is not time to get everything tied up properly before making a big set piece push.

All day we talk with Mehmet and write telegrams and cypher and watch the battle. The Germans mortar the Partisans fairly steadily but the Partisans do not press the battle too far.

We are too late to go down into the fray so we finish a huge indent for material to Bari (a test case) and then eat à la Partisanne half-roasted mutton.

It is cold, so we curl up in greatcoats under some rocks and try to sleep. I succeed so well I miss the attack. Richard fails miserably.

2nd August

A cold misty morning. To our chilly eyes it is clear that the Partisans have begun to withdraw. Soon we hear that they intend to attack again tonight, so we spend a sunny morning dealing with radio traffic and talking to Partisan personalities. All our meals are alfresco these days so our days are entirely free from timetables. Under a sweltering sun we go down to Gorenë, meet the staff and interrogate three German POW. My German rises to the occasion. Here is more of the folly of war: young Germans who know the war is lost for Germany but who have to fight and are really only interested in writing pornographic verses. I expect these men will be shot and all for no good reason.

In the evening plans are changed. The rest of the Division is occupying Peshkopijë and shall move to Burelë to cover its flank. Richard is disappointed to learn that Major [Victor] Smith has had the luck to corner the Divisional liaison post – not really surprising given his past record with the Partisans.

We march easily to Kosisht and sleep out in the cold for fear of the fleas inside.

3rd August

We camp busily in a blazing sun all day. This is a poor village and we eat meat indifferently and are all very uncomfortable from old flea bites. The radio does not work well. Life is not at its best.

By evening we march again (having sent sad farewells to Mac by courier). Across the Drin, where our Partisan mule-men are stricken with water fear, and on and on and up and up until we finally reach Ostren I Madh in the early hours.

Mule train and BLOs crossing the Drin river.

We are all very tired and the mule-train is very awkward tonight; neither Elvidge nor anyone else seems to be able to keep it in order when Richard and I have to be elsewhere. So we pass the Dibra road system once again. We steal hay for our horses and settle in our sleeping bags under a lovely sky just before dawn.

4th August

Again we cypher all morning while Elvidge signals and while the Italians flap at the thought of having to work at quicker than routine speed. We have some difficulty in moving steadily with the Brigade as our work needs a careful and exact timetable, which the Partisans don't have.

I suggest to Richard that I should go to Peshkopijë to liaise with Victor Smith. Richard jumps at the idea. He hopes to win the Divisional liaison post yet. He deserves it on seniority but he has not played his cards right.

In the afternoon we all walk pleasantly to a village near Ternova. The march is enjoyable and we reach a delightful, secluded camping ground where all is excellent.

The radio works, we eat very well and we sleep on a grassy terrace while the moon shines down through apple trees. The Partisans sing us to sleep with some of their poignant melodies.

Up by the mosque there is a perfect film setting – Partisan fires and songs and voices, with the sounds of horses, moonlight on the mosque and an atmosphere of camaraderie all around.

We have greater hopes of plentiful plane supply. That rounds off the satisfaction of the evening.

5th August

We rouse to the sound of Partisan trumpets and with our new organisation we are breakfasted, loaded and ready to march exactly on starting time. But the Partisans are delayed by an hour of photography and parade and conference. And Mehmet has to say farewell to Fiqret.

I leave with Haxhi Lleshi while Mehmet and Richard move off towards Mati. We move easily and mostly walk. In every village Haxhi has a good welcome and at Hamesh, where we lunch, we have great fun and feasting. Hysni Dema's house has been burned by Aqif Lleshi and we rejoice in his well-stocked garden – even water-melons. Hamdi Dema (a deserter from the Macedonian Partisans) and Hysni's friends all give us a trembling 'vdekje fashismit' ('death to fascism') to prove how friendly they have always been in secret. But this cuts no ice with the Partisans who know their power now and intend to use it. The Partisan position is good and at present they are using it well.

We move gently to Haxhi Lleshi's own home village – a great welcome. All the Partisan battalion accompanying us (Ferit Radovitsky's) has a roof over its head. But our house is dreadful. We start to itch and a torch reveals myriads of huge red bugs manoeuvring on the walls and climbing up above to parachute down on us. We eat hastily and evacuate the house to sleep outside. There we grow cold in our greatcoats and remaining bugs still eat us steadily. Little sleep in spite of our tiredness.

6th August

Up early for a long wait while Haxhi settles local affairs. Then we move on only to wait for several hours while Haxhi meets Aqif Lleshi and his own very charming wife and son and daughter. I grow browned off with this dawdling method of progress. Alone like this with many Albanians one begins to feel a foreigner's isolation, the biggest enemy of this type of work.

On we push, down and across the Drin. We are so late that we decide to halt in Peshkopijë for the night. Freed Peshkopijë is an interesting sight, with its half ruins and brand-new Partisan slogans on the walls and plenty of idle Partisans and townsfolk about in the square. This is the first Albanian town which I enter and Faik Shehu gives me an excellent welcome in a large and very pleasing house. I meet and am impressed by Mustafa Gjinishi of the Divisional staff. We have a large dinner of Partisan leaders and notables. The gathering seems welcomely civilised. And then another very sleepless night troubled by sandflies.

This situation certainly needs to be clarified. I hope contact with Smith will help. Here is the 18th Partisan Brigade being formed and we still have only two missions with the Partisans in north Albania to deal with this expansion. The department in Bari is still taking the situation in but still does not seem to appreciate that the time has come for large-scale operations and large-scale supply. With the right backing it would be possible to cut off and reduce the whole German garrison in Albania. But the war will end before that is realised.

7th August

A lazy awakening in pleasant surroundings. Peshkopijë in early sunlight is a cheerful sight. I go shopping for the first time for eight months. And what would anyone in England think of our shops? For us they are better than Bond Street.

Xaxhi and the convoy leave while I am still buying Chianti; but with the grand discovery of a real road under his feet my horse soon passes the others and, walking and riding, I reach Sllatinë for lunch. Victor Smith is away but Carpenter and a bailed-out American give me a good welcome. Here they live harder than we do. I wish we copied the living problem in the same way. The Partisans seem pleased with Smith's work.

Victor returns from a day with the 4th Brigade, very happy with the world. Over cigars (yes, cigars!) we talk Albania. Victor Smith knows his job and has the war situation tied up. His cooperation with the Partisans is very close and he has won their confidence. It appears that we and Smith are working broadly on the same lines. We hope that together we can persuade Bari to see the situation as it is and not as McLean says it is. I think I would be happy to work with Smith.

8th August

The day passes with lounging, coding and talking Albania. Last night we stood by to no purpose; but a stand-by here is a luxury business which does not interfere with the day's work. I learn a lot about Bari and the divisions on policy issues. It seems that the BLOs in the south have been caused much trouble by the activities of missions in the north. Smith and others are bitter about it. They think we should have come out clearly in favour of the Partisans months ago.

We stand by again and this time a plane comes. Even this hardly stops us talking. We have many issues on which to exchange views and many tales to swap. But finally we sleep.

9th August

More and more stories about Partisans and BLOs in the south capped by my stories about Stables mission and nationalists in the north. Bari has been at fault in not understanding the political nature of this war in Albania and not giving us a directive for handling political questions. We have wasted eight months here.

Smith declares plainly that he is no politician, but he comes near to handling political questions authoritatively. He and I agree that Albania is going left and we have to go with it. It cannot be stopped.

We meet Islam and Zhetan Ndreu who want to make peace between Cen, Xhelal and the LNÇ [the Partisan-dominated resistance alliance]. Membership of the LNÇ seems an essential condition. At last there is something firm to say. Victor writes along this line to Muharrem Bajraktari. With him there is no need to be brutal, only firm. I hope the Litas will be rolled up without negotiation, just as Lam Bajraktar is being rolled up today by Dali Ndreu and the 4th Brigade.

Mehmet Shehu arrives to take over the Divisional command. He says that Richard should stand by tonight. All is going the Partisan way. Burelë has been cleared of Kupi's people. There needs to be a reorganisation of the northern missions, to include the withdrawal of McLean and Neel and instructions to Simcox not to oppose the Partisans.

No stand-by, so plenty of reading, including a good paper called *Transatlantic*.

Mehmet Shehu at the head of the 1st Partisan Brigade.

10th August

Today we hope to show off the new Piat mortar but no crew from 5th Brigade show up to train, so we are frustrated. We hang about today as always but we talk a little less. All of us find inactivity oppressive. Our only stopgaps are endless reviews from England. I now know how unsatisfying reviews can be.

We have a telegram that Dibra will be bombed today. That is excellent especially as we hear that the Germans and Xhem Gostivari are gathering there for an attack on Peshkopijë. We react by asking for more bombing tomorrow and afterward.

I find I am beginning to hope for a change of atmosphere. These eight months of restricted society have been enough. It will be hard if it lasts much longer.

11th August

Tahir appears, so I pack him off to shop for Major Smith. Soon I have my marching orders – off to 1st Brigade and Richard with a squad of reinforcements. It has been well worthwhile meeting Victor; it opens my eyes to the way in which six whole months have been wasted. Perhaps we shall do better now. Perhaps!

We wander slowly to Peshkopijë. 5th Brigade H.Q. tells me that Dibra was bombed yesterday and today and the barracks were destroyed. It gives a big kick to everyone here and will probably guarantee Peshkopijë's safety for some time, at least until 2nd Brigade materialises.

I take a hot sulphur bath – delicious after nine months without hot baths, then an excellent evening with Faik [Shehu] and his friends and an excellent dinner. Sleep, as usual in an Albanian house, is not so good and this is the best house I know!

12th August

Waiting for my Partisan escort to organise itself, I sit with Faik Shehu and his friends and hold court in the clean cobbled yard of this delightful house. Here, where civilisation makes a truce with the barbarism of the mountains, is plenty of material for painting. The white yard with the blueness it takes from the sky would have made a picture for Utrillo.

Like H.Q. men in all the best houses everywhere we converse about the war. Everyone is very pleased about the bombing of Dibra. Perhaps we shall yet be able to deal some strokes against the Germans if Richard and I take on the liaison with the 2nd Division. I used not to feel particularly strongly against the Germans but a glimpse of their crop-burning and the shattering demoralisation they inflict on the people here and everywhere in Europe bring on something near to hate. And yet one knows all the time that individual Germans cannot be blamed for the war any more than we, as individuals, can take credit for victory. This is a Tolstoyan theme. I feel that my mind is at sea and as long as it stays so I am happy to drift along as an army lieutenant. But the time will soon come to start thinking and doing other things and to grow out of soldiering and living in a lawless way.

We march through colossal heat and with long and frequent halts to a village above Zogat – not very interesting. I insist on sleeping outside and, for once, I sleep well.

13th August

Up early and straight up the mountain above – so steep a climb no one can mount a horse. I get little enough riding as it is, due to my enthusiasm for walking.

It is so hot that we are only too glad to eat cheese fresh from the sheep and then to halt in a most lovely cluster of trees, meadow and springs to skin cook and eat four large sheep. These Partisans take some of the romance from the scene by their colossal appetite for meat but, on the other hand, they express their appetite in a lively, human way. They have no western sensibilities.

Trouble with villagers over horses delays our march and we no sooner reach the main Klos road than we stop to sleep – I outside again, much to the amazement of the Partisans. They know how to live comfortably (in houses) when they can and they recognise only necessity as an excuse for suffering outdoors. They have a Home Guard spirit.

14th August

We march early from Klos and arrive with only one alarm en route at Richard's recent dropping ground. There we taste Mati cooking and grill in Mati heat. By evening we push on towards Lis. At last I leave these slow Partisans and go on alone to Brigade H.Q. and thence to Richard's camp, arriving before dawn. Partisan society has been pleasant but the welcome of familiar civilisation and a flea-less sleeping bag are pleasant too. A bit tired.

15th August

Much talk with Richard and much message writing to shake up Bari. This Brigade is getting material now but Bari refuses to be elastic. In Mati one sees a vivid picture of the contradictions into which we have fallen. Here Kupi and the Partisans have been and are fighting each other. Mustafa Kaçaçi of the Mati battalion was very bitter about it when I met him yesterday.

The heat is colossal. So we ride on to bathe in the Mat River and recce the main bridge into Burelë. If we have to blow it, it will be easy.

We have a lovely field as a dropping ground, wonderfully level. But two planes miss it altogether in a drop tonight. We curse them through our new S-phone.[112] We lose most of the material.

Life in Mati is luxurious, with plenty of fruit and other good food. Fighting can be heard from Mirditë and Krujë. Shall we manage to stay here long?

16th August

The usual bother of hunting for badly dropped material. We have lost a lot. Some cyphering and some reading: German, French and

---

112 The S-phone was a directional two-way radiotelephone developed specially for the use of SOE operatives behind enemy lines, allowing conversations between the operative on the ground and a friendly aircraft up to a range of thirty miles. It allowed field agents to communicate by voice with aircraft dropping supplies and personnel. It consisted of ground and air units but although it had a range of thirty miles it was only functional up to a height of 10,000 feet. Ground monitoring stations could not pick up the signals. It was not a navigational device although the agents could provide directional guidance. It also allowed pilots to pass on up-to-date coded messages and instructions to the agents in the field.

Italian books have all come for me but only one letter from home.

Terrific heat and my own thoughts fill the day – thoughts about ends and means in this war in Albania. But thinking is interrupted by camp trivia. Two more planes drop to us and this time drop well. But all the artillery shells are the wrong size.

17th August

Another idle day but an annoying one. Little piecemeal conversations and negotiations all day long with several stupid Albanians. And the heat does not improve one's temper.

We are waiting for Bari to answer us. Until then we can do nothing. We contact the commander of the Mati battalion but can only talk to him and not help him practically. Our work holds fire. Social bavardage keeps the home fires burning.

18th August

A day of great sun and much rain. We read and chatter for most of it. I read *Chant de Bernadette* – dull stuff but good for my French.

We are hoping to move soon so we throw a dinner party for Hysni Kapo and the Division's Commissar.[113] An excellent dinner. All goes with a swing, aided by excellent news from France.[114] These 1st Brigade men are jealous of our move to the 3rd Brigade. We are soaked by a Mati storm – magnificent lightning.

19th August

We go in search of material which was dropped on the 16th and which has been discovered in a distant village. All our mail has been lost except for my new pair of glasses; all our money is lost too. Some hundreds of boots are found but many remain hidden. These Partisans are not very good at psychological persuasion. The peasants are playing with them which makes us so angry that we ask for the head man of these villages to be beaten until the material is produced. The Partisans promise strong measures tomorrow.

---

113 Hysni Kapo was a senior Partisan commander, highly placed in the Communist Party.

114 The Allied invasion of Southern France, Operation Dragoon, had begun on 15 August.

Richard and I are soaked and frozen in a furious hailstorm. But we ride back to camp and dress for dinner. A Decca radio receiver has been found for us. Our evening passes with music and the Voice of America in Italian.

20th August

Up early for the luxury of a shave by Fulvio and to the sound of firing close at hand up the road. Stavri tells us that we must move up to Brigade H.Q. in Lis. We pack up, watched by a wolf pack of scavenger peasants, and climb in great heat to Lis. There Richard and I lunch with Brigade H.Q. and hear that the Germans are striking from Perlat in some force (five or six hundred). Some good fighting should break out tomorrow; hitherto it has been patrol clashes only.

When we find our new H.Q., wicker chairs and a table have appeared from nowhere. So Amerigo can have a good birthday. He dines with us and we give him a sovereign as a present. Then we relax to a broadcast of Figaro which is delightful. The atmosphere is unusually English – summer nights on the river, etc.

Finally I hear a broadcast in English from Sofia in which the Bulgarian prime minister does everything except ask for peace directly.[115] The European collaborators are coming on their knees now. We need to keep them there until the Partisans and other fighters can consolidate their power.

21st August

We keep on receiving telegrams from Smith and Bari which keep us running up and down hill to the staff. The Germans have advanced from Dibra against the 5th Brigade at Maqellarë. Near Burelë we are hoping for a German attack to give us a chance to smash them. Two planes of grenades and battledress are coming today or tomorrow. Then we hope to move to the 3rd Brigade in

---

115 This was Ivan Bagryanov (1891-1945), Prime Minister of Bulgaria from 1 June to 2 September 1944. Three weeks after this broadcast the Soviet Red Army invaded Bulgaria from Romania. A pro-Western, independent politician, he was executed by the new communist regime in February 1945.

the Shëngjergj area.[116]

Our radio receiver works overtime on news bulletins in sundry languages. But radio programmes are poor. Our propaganda to Albania needs plenty of attention. We must see what we can do about it.

Elvidge is at sea with his radio these days; we are very out of touch with Bari. And the charging motor causes some trouble round about midnight. A nice chap Elvidge but not very positive.

22nd August

Inspired by Richard, I resolve to shave daily – a compliment to returning civilisation. We hear that the 5th Brigade has driven the Germans back on Dibra and that the 2nd Battalion, 1st Brigade, is following up the Germans who have disengaged before Burelë. This news, together with two planes expected tonight makes us all very pleased with ourselves. As Elvidge finds communications a little difficult still, our work is at a standstill.

The limping *Chant de Bernadette* sees me through the day – a dull day. We are all very bored here. In the evening our planes are cancelled due to some indecipherable emergency. This gives us some trouble with Brigade staff, who are very keen on clothing sorties. We fall back on our usual defensive line '*nesër*' [tomorrow].

We fall asleep to the sound of commentaries on the French Maquis. There they have planes and make good use of them.[117] Perhaps our turn will soon come.

23rd August

Still our radio causes trouble and still the time drags slowly here. Even the charging engine begins to crack up. At least the weather seems to have improved a little.

---

116 Shëngjergj is located in a mountainous area south-west of Dibra on the edge of Tirana district, near to Bizë where Brigadier 'Trotsky' Davies had held his headquarters until January 1944.

117 After the Allied invasion of Normandy in June, the Maquis (armed Resistance) had become particularly active. Supported by SOE agents in the field and supplied by airdrops of weapons and supplies, they were effective in holding back German troops from reinforcing the Normandy area.

High spot of the day is news of the fall of Paris.[118] All here are delighted. Morale should be high if the Germans do come to attack us again.

Louse powder in my sleeping bag gives me a bite-free night – quite an innovation.

24th August

We wake to the sound of gunfire but attach little importance to it until we find that the Brigade command post is almost entirely evacuated. Then we ride down to Zog's castle at Burgajet, find the Brigade H.Q. there about 1 kilometre from our camp and find ourselves in the middle of a battle.[119] German shelling is heavy but ineffective and a Partisan attack drives them and the Zogists back from the hills and towards Perlat. We can hear the 4th Brigade having fun between Lurës and Mirditë. At the same time comes news of considerable Partisan success around Dibra.

Back in camp, radio communications are still bad. We hang around trying to devise means of improving it and reading in restless fits and starts. No contact with Bari in the evening but, as the night is clear, we decide to stand by and are rewarded by two planes full of battledress, boots and grenades. In spite of high wind and the Germans over the hill, they drop well and we lose nothing. The 1st Brigade are delighted with the goods.

25th August

A ride round the hills and valleys where stray parachutes dropped and talks with Tuku and Patriot fill our morning. One letter from home is a welcome find up in the hills. We prepare to move and say our farewells to the 1st Brigade. Richard likes to make them elaborate.

---

118 On 19 August the French Resistance in Paris mounted a mass insurrection against the German occupation of the city.

119 Burgajet castle was the birthplace of King Zog (1895-1961). It was situated in the large settlement of Burgajet in the Mat valley, a few miles from Burelë, in what was the Lis Municipality. It was the citadel of Zog's forebears who had been the feudal chieftains of the Mati area. It was completely dismantled later by the communists. Its marble is said to have been used for paving stones in Burelë.

We march past Patin and camp for the night. A good march and a pleasant meadow for camping. A simple, animal life, disturbed only by man.

It has been fun with the 1st Brigade. I wish we could have helped them more straightforwardly and with less concern about point-scoring between Missions.

26th August

Up so very, very early after a night spent dozing and nursing the charge engine. We push on to Bejn, find our guide and climb down and up to Guribardhë.[120] There a squad of the Mati Battalion meets us – new boys, very keen. English field rations brighten our lunch and we climb up into the mountains through lovely woods and weather with a road underfoot.

Another halt for the radio and we march on into the cool, clear night with Shëngjergj in the shadows below us and a dark vacuum towards Tirana. At last we go down into the huge meadows of Bizë, cupped among the peaks. There we unload and fall asleep to the sound of shepherds' rifles as they guard the sheep.

Our mules and Italians are very tired and sorry for themselves. I can't think why. Richard and I have walked all day and are far from dropping. It is hard work cheering these volatile Latins along the flinty paths; but they deserve their grumble now and then – they serve us very well.

27th August

High in the mountains again we are very cold by night as autumn is coming. We send off couriers to hunt for 3rd Brigade and try to pull our little unit together. Our charging engine dies on us (never touch regulators and cut-outs). At last we are forced to settle in the old camp of Brigadier Davies for lack of smooth patches in the woods. There we write anxious signals calling for our four last planes when we hear a squad of Partisans arriving. A company of 3rd Brigade marches very smartly up our hill and presents arms to Richard, every man in his own time as Partisans should. They are a pleasant crowd

---

120 Guribardhë is in Elbasan district, about eighteen miles south-east of Tirana.

and we talk interestingly with them far into the night. They give no points away to 1st Brigade for morale and bearing. They have been fighting in the Tirana suburbs. Let's hope they let us in on it.

28th August

In the early hours Ulysses [Hulusi] Spahiu, the Brigade Commander, appears with his Commissar. Ulysses is an old International Brigade man and an impressive character. We talk well into the morning and get on excellently together. He talks very good French. He and I can chat easily and proceed to do so when he returns for lunch. Our position here is clearly a good one: two planes straight away and then 2nd Division.

Plenty of message writing as a result of our conversations. No plane comes. Richard has insisted that Bari should know how to find Bizë without the help of map references. *Nesër*.

29th August

A diplomatic problem because the planes did not come last night. We give the usual speeches about the difficulties of supply and dropping etc. They seem to believe us and our position is much relieved when an XXX message comes. Elvidge receives well and all the afternoon we cypher except for a halt for bathing. Life becomes pleasanter as we recover from cold and chills and grow used to the autumnal mountains.

A lovely night – a lovely dropping ground – two perfect drops – and a good mail bag. A good excuse for a lazy sleep.

30th August

Early in the morning we walk down to see what the planes have brought us. Plenty of weapons and ammunition and the Partisans are very pleased. Richard spends a long time chatting them up but we finally get back to our tent to find it in chaos and to hear that we are condemned to cypher all day and Elvidge has had some good skeds. We get down to concentrated work while the Italians build our house of parachutes and put up our pin-up girls. This time we add some war scenes and propaganda photographs and, *pièce de résistance*, a cinema poster for *I Married a Witch* which turned up by luck in our propaganda package for use with Germans. The results of our cyphering are pretty negative – a batch of unimportant messages.

My mail is a good one including one from Charmian. She keeps up the feminine touch in my correspondence delightfully. I have always tended to fall in love with her – I definitely do at this distance! I have a new nephew born on 19th August.

Thanks to our new charging engine we hear plenty of news. With magazines etc. we get too much commentary. Ulysses comes to dinner and we chat pleasantly about war. He cannot understand how difficult it is for people outside occupied Europe to understand the political nature of this war.

Two more planes – moderate drops. Thank God for our parachute house. We can now sleep warmly.

31st August

Some anti-tank rifles have come – not very popular – but there is plenty of other good and popular material. I collect some new breeches and puttees for myself and turn into a smart officer again. The gentle Captain Menegazzi arrives from Martanesh at lunch time. We entertain him as best we can and enjoy some shade of civility again. With these educated Italians a new atmosphere enters our camp.

Odd jobs around camp (we are become so soldierly that we institute a neat, regulation trench latrine) are interrupted by the old-style magnificence of Baba Faja who wants material from us and feels himself slighted in his capacity as Vice-President of the LNÇ by our excessive intercourse with mere Divisional and Brigade Commanders. I have to speak to him in Albanian and just about manage it. He leaves us fairly happily. Perhaps Radio Bari's praise of Mehmet Shehu and his boys cheered him somewhat.

Another plane is due. But before it comes, Tahir, Commander of the 2nd Division, arrives. He and his Commissar are a new type of Partisan leader in our experience – not so highly educated as most we have met. He seems put out on meeting us; we cannot think why. But the plane gives us something better to think of – our best drop yet.

August total – 17 planes!

1st September

The morning reveals a dropping list of grenades, M.G.'s and ammunition – very satisfactory. Our camp is growing rather boring for lack of much daytime activity except cyphering. Bari is beginning to talk of German surrenders but for us the practical task is for us to get these Partisans equipped and down on the main road to hit the Germans.

The Divisional Commander and Commissar and Spahiu dine with us in the evening. All soften up considerably. The superb world news makes everyone happy. Tahir is going to settle our status once and for all with the General Staff.[121]

I have a lot of stomach trouble so I have to starve. Stomachs are a nuisance in this country.

2nd September

We wait most of the day for Spahiu to come and escort me to the 3rd Brigade down near Tirana or for Tahir to bring the list of 2nd Division requirements. Neither happens so we decipher and lounge and read and talk. A strange deserter (a German 2nd Lieutenant) is brought before us – he has been in McLean's service but his tale sounds very odd. Even if he is honest we can't use him. He will have to suffer for being a German.

At last the list comes in the evening – far too large a list in some items. Spahiu has gone without letting me know. These people are always unpredictable.

Our Italians are going down sick like ninepins. How much is genuine, how much is scrounging and how much is Italian emotion no-one can guess.

The radio fails us so we have to stand-by but to no purpose.

---

121 Hulusi Spahiu commanded the 3rd Storm Brigade. The 1st was commanded by Mehmet Shehu and the 4th by Myslim Peza. Shehu was particularly proud of the 1st Brigade, being the first that was put together. (See Peter Lucas, *The OSS in World War II Albania: Covert Operations and Collaboration with Communist Partisans* (Jefferson, North Carolina, and London: McFarland & Co., 2007) p. 146.

3rd September

A very heavy dew shows how near autumn is. Richard and I are so stimulated by it that we even do some extra cyphering for Elvidge. Then a conference with the Divisional Commander. To our surprise we are met on our return by an English Major who is coming to relieve Donald MacDonald in Macedonia. He is an old and wiry, pipe-smoking, regular soldier with foreign climes written all over him. I wish the Macedonians luck.

After lunch I set off with Fulvio to join 3rd Brigade near Tirana. We march and ride on very bad paths and just fail to cross the last ridge before dark. So we eat in a house full of bugs and retire hastily outside to sleep. Although we are moving through country new to us, there is nothing much new in the scenery. It is still as wickedly up and down as ever.

4th September

We rise before the sun, only to be soaked by heavy storms as soon as we start to move. Two or three more hours over filthy roads bring us to Priskë. We can see Tirana which looks a pretty town in a fine setting, two hours away. Ulysses Spahiu joins us, shows me the bad state of the equipment of many of his men and generally treats me as though I was a visiting elder statesman. Plenty of recruits seem to be coming from Tirana every day. Fiqri Dinë has resigned, confessing publicly that he cannot keep order. The people of Tirana seem to be becoming restless under the rule of the Gendarmes and what is left of German rule.

Like many Partisan days, most of our day passes in doing nothing but in the evening, after admiring the electric blue of the distant Adriatic under the sunset and hearing that Brussels is free, we move off before the capital which really concerns us – Tirana. We stop to eat in a semi-Ballist's house and then ride on through broken valley country to a point about twenty minutes from and slightly above Tirana. Just in time to witness a skirmishing demonstration on the outskirts by the 1st and Dajti Battalions. Plenty of firing to little effect but very good for Partisan propaganda against the gendarmes. If the Partisans keep this up the Gendarmerie will not bother anyone much longer.

5th September

This is the way Partisans would like to spend their time – food and sleep. We have nothing else to do all day except doze and eat, both of which we do very well. We manage to send off two shopping expeditions. One load of food comes back in the hands of a voluble peasant woman whose two daughters were arrested by gendarmes a few weeks ago and have now been carried away by the Germans to an unknown destination. She dramatizes her tragedy to us but she shows how sympathies lie in the town: they are turning to the Partisans.

We dine and wine with much demonstration of Partisan joy through strength and when the moon rises we go out to join a three battalion raid on Tirana. I, with the brigade staff, find myself caught between the Partisan and gendarme fire. When it dies down we see some positive results for the Partisans – two gendarme posts ablaze and plenty of German fire coming over. Just as the Partisans begin to disengage, a German plane lands beyond the town – a pity we can't be there to receive it.

6th September

We are not very energetic in the morning until some rapid fire close at hand wakes everyone up. All through the day sporadic fire continues but gets no-one anywhere. We talk and doze and send off our first Tirana shopping parties and look boredly at the city through binoculars. Then in the evening the Germans make a push to rescue some war material which fell into Partisan hands yesterday. They take the hill across the dip from our house and bullets fly fiercely for a while. Then the Partisans retake the position and only firing at a distance reminds us that the Partisans intend to disengage tonight. An ugly wound to deal with, with very inadequate materials. German bullets make quite a mess.

By moonlight we march back towards Priskë and sleep in a peaceful, dusty olive grove, all flap forgotten.

7th September

The sun is well up when we wake and move to Priskë. My poor old horse is very sick, but he manages to stagger the distance.

We are met by multitudes of new volunteers come from Tirana and joining the Dajti Battalion. They are fairly well educated and should be a good leavening for the Partisans. Hulusi tells me that he will be distributing them among different Brigades. I tie up all the ends of my business here and prepare to leave. As I depart a courier announces that the 3rd Battalion have bagged a German Major and a car in working order.

Fulvio is ill and makes the most of it, but we march through the evening and night to Shëngjin, a tough and tiring road. There fleas and bugs drive me outside to sleep, but even outside there seem to be hordes of insects in ambush. All the better for waking me up at dawn.

8th September

We flog our animals up through Shëngjergj, but better our horses exhausted than us. I meet Richard on the road going to meet [Victor] Smith and Dali Ndreu at Priskë. He does not know what is brewing. At Bizë, Fernando and Amerigo are still sick, Amerigo very. First the luxury of being clean, then of eating at leisure, then of hearing the news. Mac's replacement lieutenant is still here, ill. Cyphering keeps me too busy to deal much with the sick. An XXX message – the first this month. How does Bari expect a mission to work without planes? Given the weapons, we have enough men here to take Tirana. Perhaps it is the supplying of Tito which holds up our supply. All is rather vague to me as Richard has ridden off with the message book.

Elvidge and I dine sedately together, both pleased with the peace which has descended on the camp. We stand by and are dew-soaked by the time the plane comes. Not a brilliant drop but it brings a letter from Ann, a charming letter. When she does not write I believe it does not matter but when she does her letter fills my whole post-bag by itself. She and I are both fantastic to each other. Will there be an end to it?

9th September (Saturday)

Richard's birthday, but no Richard to find the goodies which last night's drop brought him. There are not many comforts or supplies for us but two bottles of gin (not Bolanachi) make this a distinguished drop.[122] The Partisans are very pleased with six Piat mortars and eight pairs of binoculars among other things which means that I don't have to explain away the lack of planes overmuch.

Cyphering and routine occupy the day. Then I find that my mail is a very good one. Some of it is addressed to 'Captain' Hibbert which tickles my ambition.

Graham Tustin is still ill – also Amerigo and Fulvio.[123] Fernando is the bravest of that group – he is already staggering around. It is easier to deal with the sick who have courage.

10th September

Richard signals via Carpenter that he does not intend to return yet and indents heavily for supplies of comforts. We do our best for him and throw in a bottle of gin which may annoy him as he will have to square it with Smith and co.. Bari sends the good news that I am promoted Captain w.e.f. [with effect from] 15th July. It all seems too easy – except for the Italians who can't forget the *Signor Tenente* formula.

An interesting message announces that McLean intends to go out to report. We must persuade Bari to keep him out. Bari is improving a little for Radio Bari broadcast our farewell communiqué on 1st Brigade almost without alteration, suppressing only our rude remarks about northern chiefs and Zogists. But then Bari lets itself down on the evening sked by announcing that there are only ten planes for us this month – hopelessly inadequate but largely due to trouble with Enver Hoxha over Richard's 'reactionary' past – or so it seems. That winter activity still haunts us. I feel that Richard will still hear more of his meetings with Fiqri Dinë, the Litas and others. But he is still sublimely unconscious of his own folly and complete

---

122 Bolanachi Oxford Dry Gin was originally distilled in Alexandria and is still produced in Egypt.

123 William Graham Tustin (1923-2001) was a year younger than Hibbert and fresh to the Balkans. He was a visiting British officer from an SOE mission in Yugoslavia.

lack of any policy other than a self-centred one. He is only with the Partisans now because he is persuaded that there lies his road to a Lt-Colonelcy or a DSO. We have always gone for the main chance. Now the main chance lies with the Partisans. The personal ambitions of BLOs have counted for a great deal in Albania. I suspect that the process has greatly helped my captaincy.

I talk a fair amount with Graham Tustin – a nice moderately intellectual type but do not find him very stimulating. Definitely provincial student category but a good conversational foil. He is fortunately recovering as is Fernando but Amerigo and Fulvio (and my horse) are still sick. It is lucky that nature is strongly on the side of our sick, as God knows there is nothing else to help them. And I am too busy to encourage their morale very much. War keeps us all terribly busy turning out miles of ruins, heaps of scrap-metal and millions of crammed waste-paper baskets. It is indifferent to problems of individuals. We are happy here as long as we live only for the present moment and keep the future firmly locked in dreams. In that way we and the world get on very well together. I find myself unwilling to return to England to meet the inevitable discord between myself and the world, unwilling to lose the simplicity of this life, unwilling to experiment with simplicity in England where society deals harshly with individualists and anarchists. This war provides a fine monastic life yet I feel that monasteries are only for those that have failed in the world. I have not failed yet; but I am afraid of failure – failure with Ann, failure to live freely, failure to create and control something in the world, failure to understand and manoeuvre amongst the complications of human change. I suppose all of our generation is afraid of itself. Most of us volunteered for our jobs to find out more about ourselves. Having done that in the war, we shall have to do it again in peacetime, which will probably be more complicated.

11th September

The usual morning routine. A telegram from Richard says that Sherif and Zybair Lita have been liquidated. That is the end of Michael Lis's winter efforts. News of Partisan successes comes in all day and is rounded off in the evening by a despatch from

Richard. 4th Brigade has mopped up Mirditë. 3rd Brigade continues to raid Tirana and our favoured 1st Brigade has occupied Krujë, causing many German casualties, and now blocks the German escape route to Scutari. It seems that Kupi and the Partisans clashed directly in Krujë. But the Kupi story has yet to reach its climax.

I write a bitter message for Bari asking for more planes and Richard sends me a signal for transmission demanding that the case for more sorties should be submitted to the 'highest authorities'. Ten planes are useless for liberating northern Albania.

An XXX message, so we stand by but nothing comes to Bizë and we grow stiff and damp in the heavy ground mists, all to no effect (incidentally we didn't know the recognition signals).

12th September

First I have to send all the news to Richard, and there is plenty. Bari promises to send in some LRDG parties shortly, although there is little enough work for them here.[124] Last night Radio Bari announced what it called 'the best Albanian news for weeks', to the effect that Cen Elezi, Xhelal Ndreu and Dan Kaloshi are now with the Partisans. If true, this would be a tribute to Partisan success; but can anything to do with those three really be the best news for weeks?

All our invalids are better today. Tustin plans to move tomorrow but finds that his horse (a) has a damaged leg and (b) is in foal. Some smart peasant has fooled him successfully.

A long political sitrep. comes in containing much incredible material about the government and Kupi, and then an eye-opener from McLean saying that Kupi has fought the Germans and allied himself with the Partisans. Either Kupi or the Partisans are lying. I doubt if the Partisans are. The Kupi drama is beginning to take a risky turn.

Some Mozart enlivens the evening. And Radio Bari surpasses itself by broadcasting in full my last communiqué on 3rd Brigade. Hulusi will be delighted.

---

124 The LRDG was the Long Range Desert Group, a British Army unit that specialised in reconnaissance and raiding, set up in 1940 in Egypt under General Wavell.

13th September

Graham Tustin rides away to Macedonia in the morning. I found it hard work entertaining him. He was too sensitive a soul for our camp – too easily offended and shocked and not forceful or strong-willed.

The radio is quiet today so that there is little work for us. A tantalising XXX comes through and is cancelled. So I lie down to read Margaret Irwin's *Gay Galliard*, an entertaining novel but not very convincing. It has a royal setting but is very ordinary underneath.

It begins to grow cold, the hard Albanian winter is creeping up on us again. It is hard to believe it as we sit here and gorge ourselves on peaches, but up here in the mountains autumn has already begun. It is high time for either the Germans or us to get out.

14th September

Tony Simcox has been made a Major. He deserves it. But I am sorry for Richard who sees the rest of us promoted but not himself. Richard will be back tomorrow.

Bari sends us something about Enver Hoxha not allocating planes to us, as though he and not the British officers ran our section. I send a sharp reply. Bari gets into ridiculous positions but it is difficult to get under Bari's skin. More reading and again no planes. I am getting bored of being chained up here with Bari doing nothing for us. But it can't last much longer. I shall see what I can concoct with Richard when he gets back.

15th September

The weather is turning very unpleasant with cold and threats of rain. I decide not to idle away any more time and try to improve my Italian by reading. That passes the day. In the evening a courier comes from Mehmet Shehu: the 4th Brigade is moving to Shëngjergj tonight. It seems that a big attack on Tirana is planned. The courier says that Muharrem Bajraktari has fought the Partisans and the 5th Brigade found British arms in Selim Nokë's house. So the last of our winter's work comes crashing down in ruins. Tony Simcox will be sad as he was M.B.'s chief sponsor and a good one too. Most of Tony's good work with M.B. was outbidden by Richard's contacts with the Dibra area chiefs and McLean's support of Kupi. But M.B. was always a doubtful starter. It was alright to play with him in the winter on the hypothesis that the Partisans could not help us in Northern Albania but once the spring came and he and other nationalists still did not take up arms, their game was up. The BLOs who have overlooked that consideration have followed a dangerous path. Have we in Stables mission yet escaped the consequences?

16th September

The weather turns definitely cold, with sudden short sighs of warmth when the sun manages to break through the thick cloud. I keep going on Italian and on *World Press Reviews* until Richard suddenly arrives in the afternoon – by car, and very proud of it too. He has been doing very little round Tirana. But he has come to the conclusion that Bari favours [Alan] Palmer and [Victor] Smith and that it is therefore better to work in collaboration with them. Our little world remains as chaotic as ever. It has one new member, Captain Oliver, who is said to be a bright spark. If so, I look forward to meeting him. If not, Albania could be better without him. We do plenty of message writing and coding.

17th September

It is difficult to remember what we do these days. We code and chatter about Albania and eat and read. And so the days pass while we wait for Bari to send some reasonable answers to our pleas on behalf of the Partisans. They have so far failed to establish the status of this Mission with Enver Hoxha, with considerable inconvenience to us. Hoxha is suspicious of our winter record: an initiative from Bari might have cleared the position up. Now we are using the radio link set up by Partisan 1st Corps H.Q. to try to arrive at a good working relationship with him. But this does not contribute to the task of squeezing planes out of Bari. Bari does not seem able to deal with the 'crisis' in Albania.

We are now trying to persuade Bari to make use of Dibra airfield. If we succeed we shall be able to go out and have some influence on Bari's thinking and also over our own fate. Meanwhile we must wait for Bari's reaction.

Radio Bari makes a good broadcast about the Partisans. The news of the 'Air Army' deployed in the Netherlands makes a strong impression here.

18th September

By 9am Richard and I are looking out over Albania from the mountain behind the camp. A climb changes our attitude to these Albanian mountains: they grow more friendly when we attack them for fun. Back in camp we find that we have at last stung Bari to bad temper over the question of supplies. That adds a bit of interest to things.

World Press Reviews still keep me amused. In this country my outlook on politics and world affairs has been changing, or perhaps taking shape for the first time in my life. I think Britain needs shaking up. I am probably too liberal to be happy with Labour Party rule. Britain will have to give a strong democratic lead if she is to keep a leading place in the world and that probably requires a left-wing government. Britain has lost material resources and is weaker than America or Russia, but European countries will follow a British lead if our policy reflects a desire to see democratic, social and economic liberty and security established everywhere.

19th September

Richard and I again tackle a mountain, this time the biggest of the Bizë group. We feel very English and proud of it, indulging in such unnecessary sport. At least our climb gives us an excuse for a bath, regardless of the freezing cold water and the wind. Some eau-de cologne from Tirana adds to our ever-growing re-discovery of civilization. We are slowly getting into practice for Italy and today, to our delight, Bari tells us that we are free to evacuate to Italy when we please. I hope that Richard will take Bari at its word.

The dropping ground at Bizë.

A chaotic drop by three planes. Two bodies arrive out of the blue, Lt. Winn and Sgt. Boulton. Winn unhappily breaks his leg, but takes it very well. We have no doctor but give rough first-aid. He passes a hard night: he has a tough time ahead.

20th September

Up with the frost to inspect the material which has come – no weapons, but clothing, explosives and medical kit. Then we carry Lt. Winn up to our camp. Looking after him is going to be a great problem. We feel very sorry for him; what we can do for him is very limited. He is an 8th Hussar and a bit of a know-all. He and we are going to need much patience to get along together.

I set off with Napoli to recce the Dibra landing-ground. A long, hard march and not very interesting. We reach Zerqan by dark, hungry and tired. We are promptly eaten by a variety of bugs. How this poverty-stricken Albanian hospitality does sicken after nine months as a BLO.

21st September

An early march from Zerqan to Dibra. Our horses are tired and so too are we. Dibra is in a mess and the occupying Partisans are all very vague about the situation. Fortunately we find Harry, Major Karmel's interpreter, returning to us from Macedonia. We find a restaurant full of flies and manage to buy a bottle of crude wine. So we fortify ourselves for the weary task of recce-ing the airfield. The recce leaves me a bit puzzled as I know so little about the needs of airplanes. But I think it will do here and Graham Tustin evidently thought so (for Lysanders).

Two German fighters attacked Partisan positions here this morning – to no effect. And in the evening there is a flap as all 18th Brigade Partisans are leaving at short notice for Peshkopijë.[125] We find the Macedonian command and they assure us the flap is unfounded. So we sleep in the open free from insects. I don't like Dibra.

---

125 The 18th Brigade was based on Esat Ndreu's çeta, augmented by recruits from Partisan-held Dibra.

22nd September

Our morning passes in an effort to catch Dibra shopkeepers unawares with their doors open. We have some successes and even more defeats. It is a dull business and we are happy to leave Dibra. Richard's horse is sick, so I join the infantry. We toil up to Zerqan where we find the umpteenth wonder of the world, an Albanian house without bugs and flies – Myslim Shehu's.

I hear that Muharrem Bajraktari has definitely thrown his hand in completely with the Germans and MarkaGjoni. A pity – a tragedy of ambition. He has probably dug his own grave.

23rd September

Major Karmel's 'Harry' still trails along with us looking like a rugged American pioneer in a deerstalker cap. We march arduously up and down and after eight and a half exhausting hours reach Bizë. We see the 3rd Brigade moving off to Kossovo and at Bizë we hear of much more movement. The Partisans are off to clear Kossovo, Gani Kryeziu included. I see no way out but to stand aside but new blood in the shape of Major Oliver and Lt. Winn thinks otherwise. I fancy they have still to be disillusioned about Albania.

The position of this mission between Bari and Enver Hoxha has become intolerable. We must get out and report. Smith is going south to Partisan H.Q. We must try to catch him on the way.

24th September

We prepare to move. The sooner we reach Bari the better. Richard writes a strong telegram of protest asking why he has not been appointed to liaise with Partisan 1st Corps H.Q. I fancy that only personal presence in Bari will produce a satisfactory answer or, at any rate, an answer. I am afraid Richard's winter contacts will tell against him.

We cypher and argue with Oliver and Winn and pack up our camp. We can take only seven Italians so we have the unhappy task of casting lots, finishing with the exclusion of Berti and Carlo. I am very sorry for Berti having to stay on in Albania while the rest of us joyfully escape.

25th September

By six o'clock we are marching – a well-ordered little column. Our routine is to march early, stopping in the middle of the morning for Elvidge's skeds, then continuing until the evening, when we try to camp outdoors. The two-meal-a-day system is very effective: it saves time and an early start without breakfast allows some good marching in the cool part of the day.

We move through Gurakuq down to Labinot. There we find Liri Gega waiting for Victor Smith. She is puzzled to see us but soon agrees with us when we explain why we are leaving for Italy. A good dinner softens her. She does not yet know if the Shkumbini [river] can be crossed tonight.[126]

We are soaked as we sleep. We move into a barn full of hay and there we are bitten by harvester bugs. Everything is soaking wet.

Liri Gega flanked by Enver
Xoxha (right) and Tito's envoy,
Miladin Popović.[127]

---

126 Liri Gega (- d.1956) was a prominent Partisan who reached the highest position in the organisation attained by a woman. She saw active service with Mehmet Shehu in the final battle for Tirana. She was a member of the first postwar Politburo. Liri later married Dali Ndreu, wartime military commander of the Partisan Army. In 1956, both were executed on Enver Hoxha's orders as supporters of the 'Titoist' tendency. They were caught escaping to Yugoslavia and shot. This was in spite of intercession by Moscow on Liri's behalf, she being pregnant at the time and the mother of two small children.

127 Miladin Popović (1910-45) was a member of Tito's Partisan forces and a leading member of the Yugoslav Communist Party regional committee in Kosova where he was active with Dušan Mugoša (1914-73) in organising the Partisan forces in Kosova. He and Mugoša were involved in the creation of the Albanian Partisan movement in 1941 and throughout the war maintained relationships between the Albanian and Yugoslav Partisans. Popović was killed in 1945 in Priština by Albanian anti-communist nationalists.

26th September

We could not cross the river last night as the Germans were on both crossing points. It rains and we huddle dolefully in a house crowded with Partisans and wounded *çeta* girls. Victor [Smith] appears with Sergeant Ersbury of the USAAF (an excellent man!) and we try some impromptu feasting. Victor is moving south urgently to take over the H.Q. Mission. He has earned it.

Liri and Victor move on ahead. We follow through driving rain and creep across the bridge, allegedly near German posts, without any incidents. Already we have lost two mules and are likely to lose more unless Richard allows us to lighten the loads by jettisoning some of the contents (which include twelve parachutes).

27th September

We waste the morning; Richard postpones reveille. The 7th and 15th Brigades are here moving into north Albania tonight. Richard and I go to meet the 7th Brigade staff but miss it due to bad Partisan organisation. We find only two officers of the new Yugoslav Mission in Albania. These are pleasant, friendly men, very much conscious of belonging to a superior culture and very much on their dignity as emissaries. They smell of eau-de-cologne and are strangely ignorant about events for officers of an official mission. I wonder what policies lie behind their laughing friendliness.

At last we march on, through the length of Polis-i-Madhë and reach a sheep fold on top of the mountains. There we eat and sleep and freeze. All our clothes and bedding are still wet. But we must keep marching. We cannot afford to stop yet.

One more mule fails us. Elvidge and Nazareno and I flog and pull and push and carry it over the last hour of the journey. The mules are overloaded. As far as I am concerned, they are not necessary. I can carry on my own shoulders all that I wish to take out of this land. Elvidge feels the same. We both await developments in the mule comedy with interest.

Mules and horses ready for the march.

28th September

The rest of us rise early which obliges Richard to do likewise. This time we march downhill, a very broken column. In the afternoon I persuade Richard to abandon the mule which broke down yesterday. Only thus can we keep a respectable marching speed. In Gjinar we manage to borrow some horses, although the 17th Brigade has mobilized nearly all the animals in this area. Harry is excellent at chatting people up: he gets us nearly everything we need. Amerigo begins to go sick. How much is truly illness and how much faint-heartedness we cannot tell. But he pushes on with us up to Selce through the rain which has started up again. There the people give us an excellent reception. We have quite a party. Fernando, Napoli and Harry are all drunk in their own ways. Very merry and very good for sound sleep.

Today we hear heavy firing all day. There is a rumour of an allied landing – a commando raid we think.

29th September

Heavy rain keeps us from our early start. We shave and decode to pass the time while the clouds sail round the mountains. A very unsatisfactory signal from Bari making the position of this mission even more obscure. It is difficult to make out what the British line is now supposed to be here.

When the rain begins to clear we march towards Gramsh – a switchback road. It rains again and heavily. We reach Gramsh to find it quite ruined. So we push on through more rain and mud to stumble up to a ramshackle and flea-filled house on the outskirts of Gramsh. There we make ourselves comfortable in the usual ways and sleep in a welter of wetness and bugs. Not very pleasant.

30th September

Again heavy rain stops us from starting early and when we do move, rain chases us along our road. We reach the level ground of the Tomorricë valley and stop before long at Sotirë. These southern people are much more gentle than the northern ones to whom we are accustomed. They make us very welcome. They are all 100% Partisan enthusiasts and they show some understanding of and interest in activities other than robbing and fighting one another. Perhaps Albania's future hope lies with the southerners. They seem to have an interest in liberal progress. Whether Britain helps them or not their leaders are on the way to achieving power.

This march has been revealing the characters of some of our followers. Most of our Italians are fair-weather boys but they won't suffer much as Richard sees to it that some standard of comfort is maintained.

The day ends with the usual raki party, an alfresco dinner and then sleep in stuffiness.

1st October

From Sotirë we march through rain once again – as dull a journey as ever and just as bad for our tempers. We reach Dobrenj and there are feasted in comfort. The country grows more and more friendly and more pro-Partisan. The sun peeps through and we march on. This time we reach David and stay with a wealthy but none too generous host by the name of Qasim. The evening mixture as usual – raki and bugs.

2nd October

Still soaked, we march up and out of the Tomorricë valley. We freeze as we wait for lunch and finally we reach Visakë. The fleas and bugs are overwhelming here, so we move outside to a hay barn and there we are eaten just the same. This march is becoming more and more a physical ordeal. We exist only to grow wet or dry, hungry or replete etc. Poor stuff for a diary.

3rd October

Today we are in reach of Odrican and today the clouds fall on us. The hills melt into mud and water. But we push on. Richard hesitates about reaching H.Q. without warning them etc. Elvidge and I are relieved when the esprit de muck-in prevails.

We arrive covered in mud and dripping water. Victor is presiding and we have just missed Lt. Col. Palmer – a pity. Talk and food and a good sleep in a luxury house. Victor proposes that I should stay on with him as I.O. to the H.Q. Mission. It would be a good job. If I can go to Italy first I think I may accept. We shall see.

4th October

The situation here is interesting. The Partisans claim to have brought Gani Kryeziu to their side. By force or by cunning? Tony Simcox is under their restraint. He has probably been following a McLean-type line. Alan is coming out, exhausted and bitter. McLean is coming out, presumably with a considerable loss of credit. Bari has promised a policy statement which will please all BLOs with the Partisans. It looks as though our work may end in a sort of success after all. It seems that McLean has at his H.Q. a most astonishing collection of Albanian collaborationists. This seems undignified and compromising at this stage of the war.

We visit the Partisan General Staff. Spiro Moisiu (a General) strikes me as a thoroughgoing fool and very unpleasant. Colonel Badri Spahiu is intelligent but somewhat doctrinaire. Frederick

A group of British and Partisan Officers: Major General Dali Ndreu (centre), Major General Mehmet Shehu (second left), Colonel Hysny Kapo (far right), Lieutenant Colonel Beqir Balluku (far left), and Majors Thornton and Oliver. Tirana, 1 December 1944.

Nosi seems a bit stupid and vain.[128] We call on the chief – Colonel-General Enver Hoxha. He exudes cleverness and charm, speaking excellent French. When he turns his charm on, his manner becomes distinguished, with a flavour of much culture in the background.[129] He deals very cleverly with Richard, thanking him profusely for his pro-Partisan work and making no mention of our sinful winter. Enver Hoxha has made a good contribution to Partisan-Allied relations this morning. The staff was a little more argumentative and touched on a few raw spots. All passes off peacefully and we turn to leave Albania with Partisan blessings.

---

128 Frederick, or Fred, Nosi was the nephew of Lef Nosi and a leading Balli Kombëtar member who had served as interpreter for Brigadier Davies at Bizë. Lef Nosi was a prominent patriot and leader of the Balli Kombëtar. He took part in the German-backed national assembly set up in 1943. Margaret Hasluck is said to have had an affair with Lef Nosi after her husband's death. She certainly had a very close relationship with him and his execution by the incoming communist regime in February 1945 is said to have hastened her death in 1948.

129 Enver Hoxha was described by Peter Kemp as 'a tall flabby creature in his early thirties with a sulky, podgy face and a soft woman's voice' and 'a fanatical Communist, cruel, humourless and deeply suspicious of the British'. (Kemp, *No Colours or Crest, op. cit.* p. 95)

Captain Tom Stefan of the U.S. Army comes to lunch and Captain Marcus Lyon arrives too.[130] Tom is of Albanian origin and seems to have grasped the situation here well.[131] The State department seems to take a clearer part in OSS work than the British Foreign Office does in SOE work. The results of its more direct interest seem to be good. Stefan is very well briefed and well focused on his job. Perhaps we need to take a few leaves out of the American book.

Marcus is as agreeably dreamy as ever and just as full of entertaining small talk. He just wants to get out. I promise to come back and take over his job if nothing attractive (e.g. in China) is on offer outside. Tomorrow we march for Italy.

5th October

We march early from Odriçan down through rain and mud and sunshine to ruined Këlcyrë. Sgt. Ersbury of the USAAF is with us and George, an American-Albanian interpreter. George is more

---

130 Like Hibbert, Captain (later Major) Marcus Lyon (1919-2007) had parachuted into Albania in December 1943. Evacuated in June 1944, he had parachuted back in July. In his final weeks he was acting senior SOE liaison officer with Enver Hoxha's Partisans. After the German withdrawal, Lyon was the only British officer to accompany Hoxha when the Partisans marched into Tirana on 17 November 1944.

131 Many émigré Albanians such as Tom Stefan, son of an Albanian family settled in the USA, were recruited as liaison officers into the Office of Strategic Services (OSS), the US wartime intelligence service. The OSS had set up an Albanian desk headed by Harry Fultz, who from 1922 to 1933 had run the Technical School of Tirana, attended by several future Partisans. Some have criticised this OSS policy, claiming that these officers would necessarily favour groups with which they had social or familial affinities (see Rhodri Jeffreys-Jones and David Stafford (eds.), *American-British-Canadian Intelligence Relations, 1939-2000* (Abingdon: Routledge, 2013), p. 32. Stefan's value lay in his social connections and his command of Albanian. In particular, Stefan spoke the Tosk dialect which he shared with Enver Hoxha. This seems to have given Stefan privileged access to the Partisans, allowing him to act as an effective go-between. For instance, he passed on recommendations that the Allies focus on supplying arms to the Partisans rather than to their nationalist rivals. Through Stefan's intermediacy 'Hoxha was able to cultivate a Western alliance that excluded his rivals.' (Eric Grynaviski, *America's Middlemen: Power at the Edge of Empire* (Cambridge: Cambridge University Press, 2018), p. 163. There were far fewer OSS agents in Albania than BLOs at any given time.

of an Albanian than an American and turns out to be a damned
fool. At Këlcyrë we enter an area of complete devastation. It
starts to rain. On through lovely Grykë e Këlcyrës, past the once
vainglorious and now pathetic memorial to the dead of the Lupi
di Toscana division and wearily on through shattered Tepelenë.[132]
A very tiring day. We sleep in a ruined house with a gale outside.
We are going hard for that coast.

6th October

We climb heavily to Harry's village, Lekëdush, which was completely
burned by the Germans in June. The people are very hospitable in
spite of having lost everything. An Italian captain is travelling with
us to contact the Italian government on General Puccini's behalf
to organize help and succour for the Italians in Albania. He is very
footsore which fortunately cuts down his talkativeness.

Lekëdush village destroyed by the Germans in June 1944.

---

132 The Italian infantry division, Lupi di Toscana (Wolves of Tuscany), took
part in the original Italian invasion of Albania in 1939 but were routed by
the Greek 15th Infantry Division near Këlcyrë in January 1941.

Our Italians are troublesome as ever when conditions are hard. We abandon one more mule. Finally we drop down into Kuç. No British mission here and no lorry to carry us to the sea. So we camp in poverty in a ruined house, eat our rice and sleep. We try to contact the Commandos who are at Borsh [on the Adriatic coast]. We obtain a vague promise of a truck. If it does not come we shall be stuck. There is nothing here for men or mules. The Germans have shown their terrorist hand here.

Harry with a small child in Lekëdush. October 1944.

7th October

We breakfast crudely and then sit on our baggage hoping for a truck to turn up. It is a magnificently hot day, but even our sunbathing spirit is soon broken and we load our mules and take to the road. At once two Artillery quads appear from nowhere and we all pile in and jolt slowly down to the coast – a strange sensation after so many months of walking these precipitous roads on foot. Our Italians are delighted by it all and so are we. On the coast we rush straight into the sea to bathe. The Adriatic is very blue, very warm and delightfully smooth. This beach is the supplies base for the Royal Artillery battery in front of Sarandë.[133] A charming Captain Raymond turns up and treats us most carefully and generously

133 Two days later, on 9 October, the British Commandos together with local Partisans captured Sarandë.

as if we were shipwrecked mariners – or half-starved refugees or even exhausted heroes. We sit around on the beach waiting to thumb a ride to Italy. Here at Borsh earlier evacuations must have been very tricky with the Germans and Balli Kombëtar on the coast road and the headlands nearby. Now evacuation is fun. There are two full Commandos holding the Borsh beachhead.

On the beach at Borsh waiting to leave for Italy, 7 October 1944.

After dark an L.C.I. comes in and we all sweat hard to unload it.[134] There is nothing romantic about this load for the Commandos – only a few cases of shells and plenty of corrugated iron sheeting to protect them from rain. When everybody is happily soaking wet, we jump aboard and cruise round to Sugar [Sarandë] Beach, the forward Commando base which the Germans have been bombarding for the last hour. There we pick up Commando wounded and sick and at last, shortly before midnight, we leave Albania, sailing through a calm and phosphorescent sea to Italy.

We find some rations and break into them and sleep. We all agree now – 'Thank God we're out'. We have had plenty of fun but after ten months the fun wears thin. Anything new will be welcome.

---

134 The L.C.I. was the Landing Craft Infantry, an amphibious ship designed to transport large numbers of men and equipment and deliver them directly onto beaches.

BARI

October-November 1944

8th October

We see the watercolour seaside of Brindisi in a brilliant blue morning light and when we berth we are most efficiently greeted by Captain Bissett, a 'conducting officer'. We quickly say farewell to our Italians, visit port security, eat a semi-civilised breakfast and are whisked away to Castellana camp. The Italian countryside with its lovely sky, its buildings full of character and its neat simplicity is very pleasing. At Castellana camp we begin to meet administration difficulties: over kit, accommodation, service records and pay. We do not feel very welcome.

A bath at Monopoli is the great event of the day and then we return to the mess to pull a line. Everyone is very kind and friendly. As a result Richard and I drink and talk too much. It is fun for us because it is novel. But everyone around us seems demoralised. We have been living in a society of enthusiasts; here we relapse into a society of unbelievers. Life here is more static than the one we've left. So we knock back the drinks.

9th October

With Elvidge in tow we cruise into Bari on the duty truck and into the office. There we talk aimlessly with Major Elliot and pertinently with Lt. Col. Alan Palmer.[135] Alan leaves for England at once. It seems that policy is veering in favour of the Partisans; but it is the Partisans themselves who are determining the course of things, not the office here. It is a bit too early to sum up the office yet.

We lunch with Elliot and Alan at the Officers' Club which is impressively civilized to us. Afterwards we take Elvidge along to the Imperiale Hotel, smuggle him in as an officer and feast him at tea, at cocktail time and at dinner. We find Michael Lis and yarn with him for hours. Again we drink too much but not so much that Richard cannot find his bed or that Elvidge and I cannot grope our way into the flat which we have found for the night.

---

135 Lt. Col. C Alan Palmer had taken over command of the British missions in Albania from Brigadier Davies after the latter was shot and captured. Consequently Palmer had five further missions to Albania.

10th October

At the Imperiale we are becoming regulars at the bar. But we tear ourselves away, meet odd people at the office and finally drive off to Castellana to collect our kit with Bill Squires who looks after us well.[136] Back to Bari and around town. We occupy the FANY flat that we have found: once we are in it will be hard for anyone to get us out. We take great care to decorate our room with draped parachutes etc. in order to impress Antoinette, the admin. officer of the FANY mess. She hides behind schoolboy spectacles but she is a good sort, a games player/scholar type, and she will not throw us out.

We dine at the Officers' Club with Bill Squires but get involved in a pro- and anti-Partisan argument with Frank White.

11th October

No one in the office seems very interested in what we have to say. Time does not seem to matter here. When we do get Watrous' ear we talk so long we forget lunch which certainly does not trouble Richard or me. Our evening looks a little blank but we find the FANY flat below ours occupied and take Pat and Hannah out to dinner. Afterwards we housewarm our flat.

12th October-4th November

We live in Bari and write our report. Our impressions of Bari are mostly unfavourable. We are only too anxious to talk about our experiences: our lives have consisted of nothing else for a year. But no one is very interested to hear them. People seem a bit afraid of us, as if we were mad or 'bolshy' or just too, too enthusiastic. Slowly we are disillusioned. We have been fighting a war that does not exist. We have learned to believe in principles which are not officially admitted. We know that the Partisans have been fighting to build a state. Here we are only allowed to think of the destruction of Germany and the spread of British influence. It is very disheartening. We find ourselves thinking on

---

136 Captain Bill Squires of the Royal Tank Regiment had the responsibility of organising sea sorties to Albania's coast.

a different plane from everyone else we meet. The facts which we know are different from their facts. Our ideas are bound to be contradictory.

Bari suffers from the same faults as Cairo. All the staff officers should be packed away in a camp in the country and female staff reduced to a minimum. The towns should be open to leave personnel only – this in the elementary interests of military efficiency.

Our conducting officer Bissett (a Captain of 5 years standing!) is useless. We have disgraceful trouble in trying to obtain kit and accommodation. Finally Richard and I fix ourselves up in a FANY flat, drape it with parachutes and open it up in night club style. Soon we spend as much time organising our social life as we ever took organising our mission. A great and luxurious dinner is the highlight of our entertaining. Everyone agrees that it is wonderful, goes away to sleep and forgets tomorrow that anything unusual has happened. Bari society is like that. We plunge in drunkenly (literally) merely for the joy of changing our way of life. Our life is inconsequentially full of much ado about nothing for the first time in a year.

We visit endless people, entertain and are entertained in turn, talk shop, talk nonsense, drink hard and stop talking, eat hard and stop drinking, take girls out and stop thinking that anything matters at all. Theatres, dinners, dances and nights on the tiles follow one another until they begin to pall. It is all too easy here – you don't have to work or fight to live. Antoinette, Pat, June, Nancy – all easy come, easy go. And when we can borrow a jeep or a truck, easier than anything else in the world. Only a young innocent, fresh from England promises to be interesting. She and I have some fun together until she goes into hospital. But most of the FANYs fresh from England are terribly naïve and dull.

In the firm, we soon find that personalities and personal relationships play a much greater part than brains or ability. Strong men are disliked and put aside for fear of their power of shattering the established order of mediocrity. Eliot Watrous is a weakling in every sense, preserved in his powerful position only by his 'usefulness' to men higher up. We learn to hate his guts.[137] Lord Harcourt, the Commander, is a mature and pleasant officer, too full of breeding to have any fire or force left in him. Nowhere is there really anyone who really knows or cares what he is doing – except for the G3s for Policy and Intelligence. John Eyre is a true intellectual, not over-brilliant but very clever and stimulating.[138] John Naar is a bogus intellectual of the dilettante variety with no reserves of originality but plenty of understanding and very skilled in the art of selling his goods. John Eyre is so sincere that that he offends his fellow officers by not noticing them or being interested in them. He does not start to be charming until one knows him well. John Naar is charming from the start but his character is not a house of many mansions always fresh and interesting to explore. Both these Johns are confirmed left-wingers and convinced pro-Partisans like ourselves, even if not well informed about the way things happen in Albania – convinced of the absolute necessity that Britain should support the popular fronts and left wings of Europe if she is to maintain her place in the world. This we believe on grounds of practical necessity as well as theoretical belief.

All the staff officers have their secretaries who complicate business by their fantastic network of personal relationships. Phyllis Rasmussen and Sheila Stone are the only two whom we are friendly with as they are the only two who are human and normal in their attitude to this hungry majority of men.

---

137 Eliot Watrous, at this time only twenty-three years old, was Head of SOE's Albanian Section in Cairo. He had replaced Major Philip Leake. He had sole responsibility for transmitting messages and information back to London but was not a Foreign Office man as such. His family background was in insurance and, commissioned into the Royal Artillery, he had spent two years in Malta before joining SOE in Cairo.

138 John Eyre (b. 1918) was certainly left-wing if not a communist (as he was described by Peter Kemp). Unlike James Klugman in SOE's Yugoslav section, he was certainly not an agent of Moscow and no evidence has been produced that any member of the Albanian team was a Soviet agent in spite of subsequent suspicions and accusations circulated by pro-Kupi BLOs. Hibbert suggests that the ultimate influence on policy of left-wingers and pro-Partisan BLOs was very limited and some modern historians have also taken this view. See Roderick Bailey, 'SOE in Albania: The conspiracy theory reassessed', in Mark Seaman (ed.), *Special Operations Executive: a New Instrument of War* (Abingdon: Routledge 2006), pp.179-92.

We live on the best of terms with other BLOs even with those who have been on the other side of the political fence in Albania. We are all united by a common dislike of the firm – above all of Eliot Watrous. No BLO is foolish enough to think that he has the power to change the face of history, to dictate the future of Albania. We are all too conscious of the blind force of events which is shaping Europe to a far more tremendous pattern than any individual can conceive. We hope only to adjust British policy to this flow of events: but Eliot has a power complex as so many men connected with the Foreign Office have. He fancies himself building the post-war world and playing a kingmaker's role. He has hardly a clue as to the true facts of Albania's situation. Instead of learning from the facts what he should do, he thinks he can create facts of his own. What a fool! And the world is ruled by fools like him.

Our department depends for its policy on the Foreign Office and the F.O. is in the hands of a hopelessly misinformed, outmoded, unprogressive, unenlightened and unimaginative conservative clique. That becomes hopelessly obvious as soon as we mention Russia for they still think in terms of musical comedy and melodrama of the Red bogey. They cannot understand that communism is the product of economic necessity, not of imperialist and nationalist bloody mindedness.

People like Eliot have an eye to their own careers and are not prepared to stand up to the F.O. to hammer into its thick head the plain hard facts about occupied Europe which contradict everything the F.O. holds dear. And BLOs such as Lt. Col. Palmer, Victor Smith, Alan Hare and others make the mistake of staying on in the firm in the hope of influencing policy for good instead of resigning from the business and leaving it to find dishonest instruments for its dishonest policy. Billy McLean and Julian Amery were fundamentally dishonest in the field. But here Billy is thought charmingly naughty and will probably be rapped over the knuckles with a bar to his D.S.O. Not a single decoration has gone in our section to the men who deserve them: but then no credit goes to the Partisans who have deserved everything. Happily the Partisans will be able to get what they want without reference to Bari.

Slowly our zeal for our work diminishes and our desire for our own private lives grows strong. We try to find new jobs for ourselves via England. Richard obtains permission to go to England but with no definite job. I obtain the certainty of a return to regimental life but no leave in England. Tony Simcox comes out of the field. Michael Lis is in Bari. We grow to like Brian Ensor. We meet old friends and make new ones until we can leave shits like Eliot out of our lives altogether. So our old circle is joined up again. Soon, with old and new friends, we can forget all about the office and its staff. All the tension of our work is gone.[139] Our disillusionment is complete. We achieve a Tolstoyan faith in the unimportance of things and events and in the supreme importance of individual lives. We write our huge report and with it bury our past and our responsibilities. But we don't forget the past. We only recognize our smallness in it and turn away to pursue our own lives.

I have learned much from Albania about men and women and society and politics and history. It has contributed something to my character and mind and faculties. That something is all that I carry away with me. I take up the threads of my former life again. I write and receive letters. I start to find my own amusements once more. I feel I have been somewhere near to history in the making. I now become once more one of the millions of men who feel the results of history and never glimpse its shifts and their causes. Once more, in fact, an individual man.

22nd November

Letter to Ann

At present I am suffering from unemployment. Only for a few days I think. I shall be descending to the humble rank of a regimental lieutenant on the Italian front. I imagine the life to be so much more simple and straightforward than anything which I have known in the past year. As you say, I have grown older but I hate to admit it.

---

139 Hibbert changed this in the first transcription to 'living and sharing Albania's fate is gone'.

23 December

Letter to his parents

As you see I shall spend Christmas in new circumstances. Our Christmas promises to be as festive as possible, though probably not as gay as last year which was very picturesque. There were plenty of us of all nationalities crowded in a ramshackle house in the mountains, drinking local firewater and eating barbaric meals of wild pig, chicken, fruit and goats milk cheese. Our specialities were some precious Italian chianti, beer and cognac. You can guess that we had a wild and fantastic party by fire- and candle-light with songs and speeches in every language available and with Moslems making huge efforts to help a Christian feast on its way with much firing of weapons and shouting and public speech-making. This Christmas will be very sober by comparison

Letter from Eliot Watrous,
HQ Force 399

to Lt. R.A. Hibbert
4th Queen's Own Hussars

12 January 1945

My Dear Reg

Many thanks for your letter which I have just received. I am glad to know that the situation you now find yourself is satisfactory and I trust that your duties do not cause you to wallow in the mud overmuch.

I have just returned from three weeks inside the country in which you spent a year. I was able to meet most of the persons whom I had heard of and written about during the last year and a half. A most enjoyable and interesting visit, which will not be forgotten.

I am not entirely able to agree with your remarks on British Foreign Policy, but unlike you I am more of a tool in the hands of those who decide than you were. Our problem has, in the main, been one of trying to reconcile a long term with a short term. Possibly we have failed but it rather depends in which way you look.

I would like to thank you very much indeed for the excellent report that you and Richard wrote. I have at last had time to read it and can assure you that benefit has been reaped from it. It represents a picture, a most essential picture to put forward when wishing to view the Left as opposed to the Right and it helps a person like myself and those high above me who are interested in ALBANIAN affairs and wish to obtain a clear picture from both sides of the fighting and non-fighting fronts.

Have BRITAIN and AMERICA the privilege of imposing governments on the Publicans and Sinners of EUROPE? Your remark re the Publican is pertinent and the policy which you would pursue may eventually be the one which your Government will adopt.

I did little to help you on your way but am glad that the little I was able to do caused you a measure of happiness

Best wishes from myself and the Section,
Yours ever

REG HIBBERT'S POST-WAR CAREER

In Bari in the winter of 1944, Hibbert rejoined the 4th Hussars and took part in the Italian Campaign. At the end of the war he took the crash course in Russian run by Professor Elizabeth Hill at Cambridge and joined the Foreign Service in 1946. His very first assignment was as a junior member of the British negotiating team at the Paris Peace Conference in October 1946. Immediately after, in November, he joined Ernest Bevin's team in New York for the Big Four Conference, attending the negotiations at Bevin's side to provide additional interpretation. In his own words, 'My surprise excursion into the lofty circle of the foreign ministers was very much eased by Mr Bevin's avuncular manner, "Just come along with me my boy. You'll be alright".'

His subsequent career frequently mirrored his Albanian experience since it always appeared, or so it seemed to his family, that political change was happening or about to happen as soon as he arrived.

Hibbert's first posting to Romania in 1947 saw the final installation of the communist regime. In Bucharest he witnessed the aristocracy and middle classes selling their possessions laid out on tablecloths in the streets. On his return to London, still suffering the after effects of hepatitis, he married Ann Pugh in February 1949, having finally proposed to her by telegram. Two years later, and with a small child, the family travelled by train to Vienna, which at the time was still occupied by the Allied Powers, Britain, France, the United States and the Soviet Union. His second child was born in the military hospital in the British sector.

Reg Hibbert and his daughter Jane,
Vienna 1952.

Vienna was followed by two years in London. Hibbert's Russian meant he joined the team receiving the Soviet Premier Bulganin and Communist Party First Secretary Nikita Khrushchev, when they visited London in 1955. He was always proud of the Soviet camera 'B & K' presented him with. Hibbert's slightly uncertain reputation in the Foreign Office thanks to Lord St. Oswald's accusations meant that he spent very few of the next twenty years in London while his postings appeared unlikely to end in a prize ambassadorship. In 1956 he found himself running the British Legation in Guatemala City just as Guatemala attempted to annexe British Honduras. His next post was Ankara as First Secretary when the Baghdad Pact, the post-war military alliance of Iran, Iraq, Pakistan, Turkey and Great Britain, became the Central Treaty Organisation, CENTO, after the Iraqi monarchy was overthrown. A brief and rather dull couple of years in Brussels as Commercial Attaché, however, was followed by a posting that called on all his Albanian experience.

In 1964 Hibbert was sent to the Mongolian People's Republic (at the time referred to as Outer Mongolia but now Mongolia) to open the first British diplomatic mission in Ulaanbaatar (Ulan Bator). The Spartan conditions of running the only Western diplomatic mission from a Soviet-era hotel bedroom and the long journeys by Land Rover across the empty miles of Mongolia's vast steppe to visit remote state farms with their sheep, goats and sturdy horses appealed to the love of wilderness and taste for challenge first aroused in Hibbert by his time in Albania. In 1966 he followed this up with a research sabbatical at Leeds University.

The Mongolian experience which Hibbert had loved was followed by another Asian posting. In 1968 he was sent to Singapore as Political Advisor to the Commander in Chief Far East. This was a critical post because in 1967 Britain had declared that it would withdraw its forces from all the island's bases by the mid-1970s. Hibbert's role was to provide political liaison between the armed forces, the British government and the government of Singapore to ensure a smooth withdrawal. This became particularly challenging when the British government accelerated the process to a completion date of 1971. As Sir Alan

Campbell, his diplomatic colleague, said, 'As the linchpin in the commissioner-general's office, Hibbert played a central part in steering a way through the difficulties'.

After four years in Singapore he returned to Europe as minister in the Bonn Embassy. Germany was still two separate states at the time. Here he was immersed in European politics for the first time since the 1950s and once again he worked with Nicholas, by now Sir Nicholas, Henderson who was his Ambassador and had been his colleague and friend in Vienna.

In 1975, however, Hibbert's political skills were rewarded by a long period in London working under a Labour government, first as Assistant Under-Secretary for Europe at the Foreign Office and then in 1976 as Political Director for Europe where, according to Campbell, he improved methods of cooperation and usually 'succeeded in his advocacy of the British point of view'. Hibbert had great pleasure in travelling around the capitals of Europe and revisiting the Balkans while operating at the highest political level. David Owen was Foreign Secretary at the time and, to many people's astonishment given Hibbert's non-Establishment background, Owen appeared to appreciate Hibbert's combative style and in 1979 appointed him as Ambassador to France. Hibbert himself had always hoped for Ambassador to the USSR and had never dreamed of such a posting. In Paris his lifelong command of French and his love of culture came into play and by all accounts his ambassadorship was a success.

Unfortunately for Hibbert his service in Mongolia and the Far East were deemed hardship posts, which meant earlier retirement than he would have liked. In 1983, he took up his last role as director of the Ditchley international conference centre, which was followed a few years later by retirement. Retirement, of course, meant he could follow his passions. He spent the years until his death in October 2002 absorbed in his interest in the countries he had come to love, Albania, Mongolia and France while tending his garden and woodland overlooking the Dovey Valley in West Wales. Ann survived him by eleven years and died in 2013.

ACKNOWLEDGEMENTS

While the idea of publishing these diaries has been at the back of several people's minds for a long time, not least that of my father, Reg Hibbert, himself, it is only recently that two have made it possible. First and foremost, I am deeply grateful to Professor James Pettifer and to Bob Churcher not only for approaching me with the idea of publication but also for their guidance and support throughout the process. My thanks also go to Miranda Vickers for her kindness and advice with the historical background.

One of the great pleasures of editing these diaries has been reaching out to strangers in the hope that that they might help me with information and images. Each time I was met with nothing but generosity, kindness and interest. Chance put me in touch with the family of former SOE officer Captain Donald MacDonald who worked with the Partisans in Macedonia and was a lifelong friend of Reg. I must thank Coll, Lachlan and Cassidy MacDonald, for showing such a keen interest and for sharing Donald MacDonald's archives and photos with me, providing an extra dimension to events in July 1944.

I would like to thank Mr Erion Kaloshi for responding to my approach out of the blue and allowing me to include a rare and important photograph of the Kaloshi family and *bajraktars* of the Dibra region.

In my search for images of Mount Korab where Stables Mission spent so much of 1944, I encountered Zoltán Fehér, Head of the Department of Zoology at the Hungarian Natural History Museum, and his colleagues who have made several field trips to the area to find specimens. My thanks go to him, Gellért Puskás, Tibor Kovács, László Dányi and Dávid Murányi for sharing their wonderful collections of photos of Mount Korab. They too used mules and horses to access the wilder spots for their research and their images visualised for me the descriptions of the beautiful and forbidding landscape in the diaries.

I am also very grateful to Sophie Bridges at the Churchill Archives Centre, Churchill College Cambridge, who has been so patient and helpful throughout the process of sifting and choosing images.

Finally I am immensely grateful to James Ferguson of Signal Books who guided me expertly through the whole process with kindly forbearance and good humour.

My family and friends have shown huge enthusiasm and encouragement for this project and I thank them all. My ultimate gratitude, however, goes to my late mother, Ann, a constant in my father's life since 1942, who patiently created the first typescript over months on her manual typewriter, working with the cramped pages of the little diaries or taking dictation from my father reading them aloud.

Credits

Most of the images are from Reg Hibbert's own collection unless otherwise stated. The photo of Liri Gega, Enver Hoxha and Miladin Popović is in the public domain. The image of British and Partisan Officers. Tirana, December 1944 was supplied by Associated Press. I am grateful to the Churchill Archives Centre for the following images: Richard Riddell, Peter Kemp and Alan Hare (AMEJ 10/17/1), Baba Faja Martaneshi and Brig. 'Trotsky' Davies (AMEJ 10/20/3), Villager with loaves of bread (AMEJ 10/19/2), Abas Kupi (AMEJ 10/17/1), Muharrem Bajraktari, (AMEJ 8/1/8), Major 'Billy' McLean and Enver Hoxha at Labinot. July1943, (AMEJ 8/1/8), Views of the Korab massif (AMEJ 10/24), Abas Kupi and Lt. Colonel Neil 'Billy' McLean. July 1944 (AMEJ 8/1/8), The First Partisan Brigade standard bearer (AMEJ 10/18), Mehmet Shehu and the First Partisan Brigade (AMEJ 10/20/2),

Jane Nicolov

FURTHER READING

SOE Memoirs

Amery Julian, *Sons of the Eagle: A Study in Guerrilla War* (London: Macmillan & Co., 1948)

Davies Brigadier 'Trotsky', *Illyrian Venture: The Story of the British Military Mission to Enemy-Occupied Albania 1943-1944* (London: The Bodley Head, 1952)

Kemp Peter, *No Colours or Crest* (London: Cassell and Co., 1958)

Smiley David, *Albanian Assignment* (London: Chatto & Windus, 1984)

SOE Studies

Bailey Roderick, *The Wildest Province: SOE in the Land of the Eagle* (London & New York: Vintage, 2011)

Foot M. R. D., *SOE: An Outline History of the Special Operations Executive 1940-1946* (London: The Bodley Head, 1999)

Hibbert Reginald, 'Albania, Macedonia and the British Military Missions, 1943 and 1944', in James Pettifer (ed.), T*he New Macedonian Question* (London: Palgrave Macmillan, 1999)

Seaman Mark (ed.), *Special Operations Executive: A New Instrument of War* (London: Routledge, 2006)

History of Albania, Kosova and Macedonia

Durham M. Edith, *High Albania* (Illustrated edition) (Teddington: The Echo Library, 2009)

Elsie Robert, *Historical Dictionary of Albania* (Lanham, Toronto, Plymouth: The Scarecrow Press, 2010)

Fischer Bernd Jürgen, *Albania at War*, 1939-1945 (London: Hurst and Co., 1999)

Hibbert Reginald, *Albania's National Liberation Struggle: The Bitter Victory* (London: Pinter Publishers, 1991)

Lucas Peter, *The OSS in World War II Albania: Covert Operations and Collaboration with Communist Partisans* (Jefferson, North Carolina, and London: McFarland & Co., 2007)

Malcolm Noel, *Kosovo: A Short History* (London: Macmillan, 1998)

Pearson Owen, *Albania in the Twentieth Century, A History: Volume I: Albania and King Zog, Independence, Republic and Monarchy 1908-1939* (London: Centre for Albanian Studies and I. B. Tauris, 2004)

Pettifer James (ed.), *Albania and the Balkans: Essays in Honour of Sir Reginald Hibbert* (Port Isaac and Pristina: Elbow Publishing, 2003)

Vickers Miranda, *The Albanians: A Modern History* (London: I. B. Tauris, 1995)

Balkan History

Crampton R. J., *The Balkans Since the Second World War* (Abingdon: Routledge, 2013)

Glenny Misha, *The Balkans 1804-2012: Nationalism, War and the Great Powers* (London: Granta, 2012)

Sugar Peter F., *Southeastern Europe under Ottoman Rule, 1354-1804* (Seattle: University of Washington Press, 1996)

Fiction

Kadare Ismail, David Bellos (ed.), Arsha Pipa (trans.), *Chronicle in Stone* (Edinburgh: Canongate Books, 2018)

Kadare Ismail, John Hodgson (trans.), *The Fall of the Stone City* (Edinburgh: Canongate Books, 2013)

Kadare Ismail, Derek Coltman (trans.), *The General of the Dead Army* (London: Vintage Books, 2008)

Kadare Ismail, Tedi Papavrami and David Bellos (trans.), *The Successor* (Edinburgh: Canongate Books, 2006)

INDEX